The
ILLUSTRATED HISTORY OF
WORLD WAR II

Owen Booth
and
John Walton

INDEX

This edition published 1998 for Index
Henson Way
Kettering
Northants NN16 8PX

ISBN 1-897884-40-0

Editorial and design by
Brown Packaging Books Ltd
Bradley's Close
74–77 White Lion Street
London N1 9PF

Printed in Singapore

Project Editor: Brian Burns
Editor: Brenda Ralph-Lewis
Design: wda
Picture Research: Adrian Bentley

Contents

Introduction

The Second World War remains the largest military conflict in history. Lasting for over six years, it involved soldiers and civilians from across five continents and resulted in the deaths of nearly fifty million people. It saw the rise and fall of empires and the breaking up of entire nations, the creation of new superpowers, the invention of awesome atomic weapons and attempted genocide on a scale never witnessed before or since.

It was a war fought on land, at sea and in the air, from western Europe to the steppes of Russia, from the deserts of North Africa to the jungles of South-East Asia, and across the Atlantic, Pacific and Indian oceans. It was a war fought to defend democracy, in which the territorial ambitions of Nazi Germany, Fascist Italy and Imperial Japan were opposed by a grand and unlikely alliance between the USA, Soviet Russia and the British Empire. It was a war that witnessed countless moments of incredible bravery and sacrifice alongside those of unspeakable cruelty and terror.

Most of all it was a war fought by millions of ordinary people, as entire nations were mobilised in a global life-or-death struggle. While enlisted men in huge mechanised armies endured terrible conditions at the front, people at home poured into the factories or risked their lives at sea transporting vital supplies to support the war effort. At the same time, the introduction of massive aerial bombing campaigns against towns and cities on both sides put civilians in the front line in a way that no war had ever done before. And in numerous occupied nations, resistance movements made up of people from all walks of life endured the appalling consequences of their refusal to surrender to the enemy.

For six years the world was engulfed by a single conflict. This book seeks to tell the story of those years.

OPPOSITE: US SOLDIERS USING FLAME-THROWERS AND
DYNAMITE TO BRING THE JAPANESE OUT OF THEIR COCONUT
LOG PILLBOXES, BOUGAINEVILLE ISLAND, DURING THE
BATTLE OF THE PACIFIC, 1943.

CHAPTER 1

The Gathering Storm

Immediately after taking power Hitler set about rebuilding Germany's war machine with the aim of overturning the German defeat in the First World War. Hitler was determined that Germany would not be on the losing side a second time.

SURRENDER AT MUNICH

The storm clouds of war seemed to be gathering over Europe when the British Prime Minister, Neville Chamberlain, returned from Munich on 30 September 1938, after completing tense diplomatic negotiations with the dictator of Nazi Germany, Adolf Hitler.

Chamberlain's quest had been peace, but the British public were so fearful of failure that there had been a run on the gas masks already pouring off the production lines. Fear of gas attack, inspired by its use in the First World War of 1914–18, was a potent one, but then so was fear of German air raids.

RIGHT: HITLER TAKES CENTRE STAGE AT ONE OF THE NAZI PARTY'S FAMOUS NUREMBERG RALLIES. HELD EVERY YEAR, THE RALLIES WERE THE FOCAL POINT OF THE NAZI POLITICAL CALENDAR. THE PARTY FAITHFUL AND THOUSANDS OF ORDINARY GERMANS WOULD FLOCK TO NUREMBERG EACH YEAR TO HEAR THEIR FÜHRER'S SPECTACULAR AND MESMERISING SET PIECE SPEECHES.

An air raid warning system was prepared in case German bombers attempted to attack British cities, and plans were laid for the evacuation of children from the major towns to the safety of the countryside. Half a million men and women, in a mood of defiance and trepidation, volunteered to serve in the ARP – Air Raid Precautions. The catchphrase of the time was 'the bombers will always get through', and both civilians and the military believed it. So did former prime minister Stanley Baldwin, whom Chamberlain had replaced in 1937.

Chamberlain had not hidden the grim nature of the crisis from the public. Before he left for Munich, he broadcast on BBC radio, and told listeners: 'How horrible, how fantastic, how incredible it is that we should be digging trenches and trying on gas masks here because of a quarrel in a faraway country between people of whom we know nothing.'

The people 'of whom we know nothing' were the Czechs, whose republic had been creaed only 20 years before, after the end of the First World War in 1918, and the Germans, the enemy defeated the same year by Britain, France and their allies. The quarrel concerned the Sudetenland, which was part of Czechoslovakia, but was claimed by Hitler on the grounds that its mainly German-speaking population was, he said, being persecuted.

On his return, Chamberlain emerged slowly from his plane to tell reporters waiting at Heston aerodrome that his negotiations with Hitler had been successful. Britain and Germany, he said, had agreed 'never to go to war with one another again'. This, the Prime Minister claimed, was 'peace for our time' and 'peace with honour', not only for Britain but for the whole of Europe.

Overnight, it seemed, tension drained away. The relief was overwhelming, the reaction ecstatic. Chamberlain's face-saving deal with Hitler had saved Europe from a second war within a generation.

But not everyone was convinced. Some MPs denounced the Munich agreement as 'a sell-out to Hitler'. The French Prime Minister, Edouard Daladier, who had been with Chamberlain at Munich, surveyed the wildly cheering crowds that greeted his return to Paris and remarked: 'Bloody fools!' These sceptics already realised the truth behind the Munich Agreement.

For those who wanted to see it, the evidence was already there. At Munich, Hitler's approach had not been conciliatory, but threatening. He had warned Britain and France that another war was inevitable unless they could convince the government of Czechoslovakia to cede the Sudetenland to his Third Reich. This, he said, was his 'last territorial claim in Europe'. It meant that three million Sudeten Czechs would find themselves in German territory, but, in return, Hitler undertook to guarantee the independence of what was left of Czechoslovakia, and, he promised, there would be no war.

The Czechs were stunned. They had not been consulted about the carving up of their young country and they were in a mood to fight. Morale was high in their army, which was one million strong. Their soldiers were well equipped with modern weapons from their own sophisticated arms factory at Brno, and they believed they could count on aid from Britain and France if the Nazis attacked.

How wrong they were. In 1938, Britain and France preferred to appease Hitler and give in to his demands, and the Czech President, Eduard Benes, had no option but to follow suit. As events were soon to prove, Czechoslovakia, the first nation to be gobbled up by the Nazis, would not be the last.

'How horrible, how fantastic, how incredible it is that we should be digging trenches and trying on gas masks here because of a quarrel in a faraway country between people of whom we know nothing.'
Neville Chamberlain in a broadcast to the British people, 1938

For the moment, though, Neville Chamberlain was riding a high tide of popularity. Even the ruling monarch, King George VI, approved of the policy of appeasement, and despite the warning note sounded by MPs who opposed it, Parliament gave the prime minister a rapturous response. At the time, giving in to Hitler appeared the sensible thing to do in order to avoid a Europe-wide conflict for which Britain was not prepared, and which she could not afford and did not yet possess the will to fight. The long, dreadful shadow cast by the First World War strongly influenced the British people, whose memories of mass carnage were still vivid. That alone made another war unthinkable, and both the British public and the British press stood full square behind Chamberlain. *The Times* newspaper, which led the applause for the prime minister, even went so far as to assert that the dismemberment of Czechoslovakia had in some way been a service to humanity.

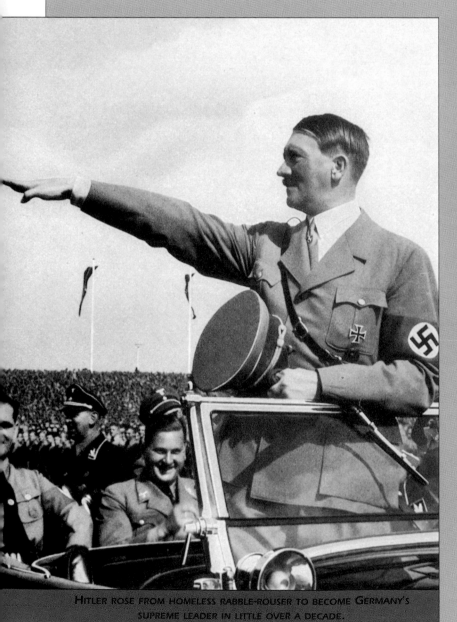

HITLER ROSE FROM HOMELESS RABBLE-ROUSER TO BECOME GERMANY'S SUPREME LEADER IN LITTLE OVER A DECADE.

HITLER

The fact that a man like Adolf Hitler succeeded in becoming Chancellor of Germany is still an example of one of the most astonishing rises to power ever to take place. Hitler was born in 1889 at Braunau in Austria to lower middle-class parents. At school, he was described as an arrogant and lazy child who found conventional discipline impossible to accept, so it was ironic that after spending years living in hostels and doing occasional work as a labourer Hitler was to find life in the German Army during the First World War his most important and formative experience. Hitler relished the war. He received two Iron Crosses for bravery and when Germany was finally beaten by the Allies in 1918, he made it his life's work to overturn his adopted country's defeat.

To this end, he became a politician and combined his profound nationalism, contempt for democracy and violent hatred of Jews, communists and socialists into a coherent political platform. The retributive terms of the Treaty of Versailles after Germany's defeat in the First World War and the harsh economic crises of the 1920s and 1930s left many Germans penniless or unemployed, and with little faith that their new democratic government could solve the nation's problems.

As Germany's politics became increasingly violent, Hitler's Nazi Party seemed to many people to be the only organisation capable of challenging the large and powerful Communist Party. This social and political upheaval provided Hitler, who would in other circumstances have languished on the lunatic fringe of politics, with a ready audience for his ideology and his policies. After the Nazi Party became Germany's larger single party at the polls, Hitler was reluctantly appointed Chancellor by the aged President Paul von Hindenburg on 30 January 1933. Hindenburg, however, died in 1934 and after that Hitler ruthlessly exploited any opportunity to crush opposition to his dictatorship inside Germany, and to extend German power in Europe.

The critics, however, were not silenced. Winston Churchill, a strong and long-standing opponent of appeasement, long labelled 'a warmonger' for his robust views, told the House of Commons that the Munich agreement was a 'total and unmitigated defeat'. His statement was greeted with jeers, but Churchill was not alone. In France, Prime Minister Daladier was now convinced that war was inevitable, and had no illusions that the decision to let Czechoslovakia fall prey to Nazi ambitions was in any way a noble one. The cheers that greeted Daladier on his return from Munich to Paris surprised him: he had fully expected to be booed.

Having secured, in effect, the submission of Britain and France, Adolf Hitler wasted no time. In less than a week, on 5 October 1938, President Eduard Benes had resigned and German troops had marched into the Sudetenland. Less than six months later, on 15 March 1939, Hitler cynically broke his word and invaded the rest of Czechoslovakia. By April, the country had ceased to exist, having been broken up and absorbed into Hitler's empire. Britain and France did nothing, and because of their unwillingness to fight, Hitler had gained territory, resources and treasure without firing a single shot.

The central, cardinal mistake in Neville Chamberlain's approach was now fully apparent. He had assumed that Hitler was a man of honour and that the Nazis could be trusted

ABOVE: GERMAN SOLDIERS EXECUTE CZECH CIVILIANS AT BRNO IN MORAIVIA, 1942. OVER 300,000 CZECHS DIED DURING THE GERMAN OCCUPATION. BUT EVEN THIS HORRIFIC FIGURE PALES BESIDE THE HORRORS THE GERMANS WERE TO COMMIT ONCE THEY INVADED POLAND AND THE SOVIET UNION, WHERE MILLIONS OF INNOCENTS WERE SLAUGHTERED.

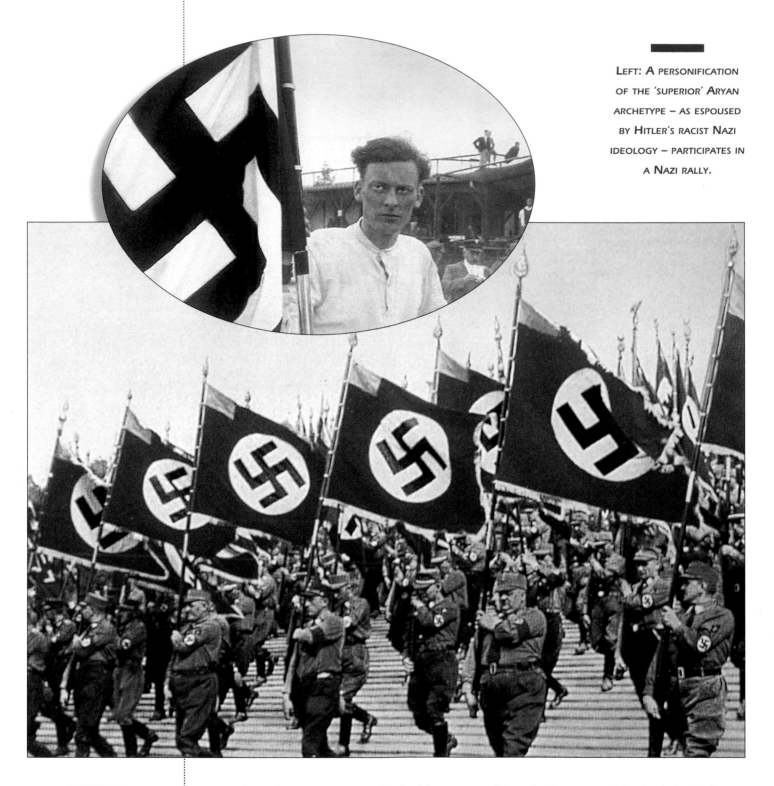

LEFT: A PERSONIFICATION
OF THE 'SUPERIOR' ARYAN
ARCHETYPE – AS ESPOUSED
BY HITLER'S RACIST NAZI
IDEOLOGY – PARTICIPATES IN
A NAZI RALLY.

THE NAZI PARTY RALLIES:
AN OPPORTUNITY FOR SET
PIECE DISPLAYS AND
ANNOUNCING IMPORTANT
PIECES OF NAZI
LEGISLATION, INCLUDING THE
NOTORIOUS 'NUREMBERG
LAWS' OF 1935.

to stick to their agreements. He had been proved hopelessly wrong. Nor had the Sudeten-land been Hitler's 'last territorial claim', as he had asserted. Only a few days after the Munich conference, it became clear that Hitler had his eyes on Poland, where the 'Polish corridor', a narrow strip of land designed to give the Poles access to the sea, separated East Prussia from the rest of Germany. The corridor had been granted to Poland, at Germany's expense, at the end of the First World War. Now, Hitler wanted it back.

With the German occupation of Czechoslovakia now complete and another small country, Poland, under threat, even Neville Chamberlain had no choice but to accept that appeasement had failed. On 31 March 1939, Britain and France pledged to aid Poland if the Nazis attacked, but their credibility was lacking. Having got away with so many broken promises after Munich, Hitler had no reason to believe that Britain and France would take their pledges any more seriously than he took his.

THE GERMAN ROAD TO WAR

In 1939, Hitler's attention turned towards Poland and the conquest of eastern Europe. Meanwhile, Britain and France belatedly redoubled their preparations to fight a war that they could now no longer avoid. Gradually, civilian populations in both countries became aware that the fragile peace had only months left to run.

Soon, husbands would leave their families behind for the unfamiliar life of soldiering, while their wives would be left to cope on their own as best they could until they, too, were fully absorbed into the war effort. Words like 'blackout', 'ration book' and ' blitz' would soon become common in Britain, while the French would have to cope with the full onslaught of the Nazi war machine as it geared up for war on their borders.

Ever since Hitler had come to power in Germany in 1933, a second world war in Europe had seemed possible. Hitler and his Nazi ideology glamourised war, depicting it as the supreme test of a nation's vitality. He was determined to create a nation of warriors who would make Germany the foremost military power in Europe, and enable him to rip up the peace treaties signed after the First World War. He refused to be bound by the Treaty of Versailles of 1919, the main terms of which included the surrender of all German colonies as League of Nations mandates, the payment of reparations, the demilitarisation and 15-year occupation of the Rhineland, a ban on the union of Germany and Austria, and a clause accepting Germany's guilt in causing the war. The German Army was limited to 100,000 men, and was denied tanks, heavy artillery, aircraft or airships. The navy was limited to vessels of under 10,000 tons, and was not allowed to have any submarines or an air arm. Hitler wanted the humiliating treaty destroyed and a new German empire put in its place. Whether this was achieved by peaceful means or by force of arms was, to him, irrelevant.

The German people soon began to feel the effects of Hitler's desire to rebuild the army. Conscription was introduced in 1935. Young men were expected to spend a year in the army, followed by time spent working in the national labour corps. The task of finishing the education of German youth was no longer the responsibility of schools but of the army. Nazi ideals were drummed into Germany's young men in the hope that they would produce the political soldier who would know both how to use his weapons and understand why he was destined to fight for t he Fatherland.

Meanwhile, in defiance of the terms of the Treaty of Versailles, Germany was rearming in secret. Hitler soon put his army to use. In 1936, again in defiance of Versailles, he sent German soldiers back into the Rhineland. When Britain and

BELOW: A NAZI PROPAGANDA POSTER ENCOURAGES THE YOUNG MEN OF GERMANY TO BECOME SOLDIERS FOR THE FATHERLAND.

France failed to react, Hitler did not hesitate to strike again. Two years later, in 1938, the German Army marched into Austria and incorporated the whole country into the Nazi Reich, so accomplishing the Anschluss, the banned Austrian–German union.

Britain and France watched these developments with growing unease. But while Hitler seized the initiative, rebuilt his army, navy and air force and prepared his people for war, Britain and France did little to stop him. Pacifism had gained much ground in Britain after the carnage of the First World War, which saw the slaughter of 908,371 soldiers from Britain and the British Commonwealth and Empire. France lost 1,357,800 men. Britain and France were further hampered in their efforts to rein in the Nazis because the USA did not appear keen to join them. The USA had fought with them against the Germans in the last months of the First World War, but now inclined to a policy of isolationism and neutrality, and had no desire to become actively involved again with events in Europe.

THE ANNEXATION OF AUSTRIA

THE ALLIES ON THE BRINK

In total contrast to Nazi Germany, the British Government, led from 1937 by the Conservative Prime Minister, Neville Chamberlain, regarded rearmament as an unnecessary expense. Rearming would raise taxes and endanger the government's chances at the coming general election. Meanwhile, the Labour opposition decried the actions of Nazi Germany, and also those of Fascist Italy, especially their involvement in the civil war in Spain (1936–9), in which they aided the Nationalist General Francisco Franco. Unfortunately, however, Labour was so divided over how best to mount an effective challenge to Hitler that they could not offer a coherent, alternative policy.

Many of those high up the British Government and the Conservative Party in fact found much to admire about the Nazis. They approved of the way Hitler had revived the German economy, which had been shattered by the First World War. They welcomed the national pride he seemed to have instilled in his people. Many, too, were more inclined to take sides with Hitler than with communist Russia and its leader, the dictator Josef Stalin. Stalin seemed a much more important target than Hitler, who was, after all, constantly pledging himself to a crusade against the 'red menace' in the East. If resisting Hitler, whether in Spain, Austria or Czechoslovakia, meant getting into bed with the communist Russians then, as far as the British Establishment was concerned, resistance was not an option.

This fear and distrust of the Soviet Union was to undermine the Allies' only real chance of creating a popular alliance of states that would be able to contain Nazi Germany. The complaisant attitude of the British Establishment towards the Nazis was reinforced by the fact that Britain was still more concerned with maintaining her global empire than with events on the Continent. And, with the economic effects of the First World War and the Great Depression of the 1930s still being felt, Britain simply could not afford to fight another war.

Stalin seemed a much more important target than Hitler...If resisting Hitler, whether in Spain, Austria or Czechoslovakia, meant getting into bed with the communist Russians then, as far as the British Establishment was concerned, resistance was not an option

If the British were anxious to avoid war, the French had even more reason to fear another plunge into that abyss, as it was clear that any future conflict would be fought, like the First World War, on French soil. People, politicians and the French Army all hoped and believed that the Maginot Line, a series of defensive fortifications along the Franco–German border, would prevent a Nazi invasion should one be attempted. Rather than strive to contain Germany as she began stretching out to claim greater and greater

RIGHT: IN TANDEM WITH TALKS BETWEEN BRITAIN, FRANCE AND THE SOVIET UNION, AND GERMANY AND THE SOVIET UNION, GERMAN FOREIGN MINISTER, JOACHIM VON RIBBENTROP, IS CAREFUL TO NURTURE CLOSE RELATIONS BETWEEN GERMANY AND JAPAN.

BRITISH CHILDREN PREPARE FOR THE HORRORS OF WAR: GAS MASK DRILL 1939.

ARP – AIR RAID PRECAUTIONS

During the Munich crisis, the fear of war, in the shape of squadrons of German bombers, gripped both the British people and authorities alike. It was during Munich that Air Raid Precautions – ARP – were taken seriously for the first time. Lessons learned from the First World War produced the popular – and accurate – wisdom that in the next war, civilians would find themselves in the front line and under attack from the air. So, it was no surprise that panic almost ran riot as the official forecasts of civilian casualties from the first German raids were calculated at nearly two million killed and injured. Overnight, this appalling statistic inspired half a million people to volunteer for the ARP. Impromptu air raid trenches were dug in public parks and gardens and 38 million gas masks were issued. Trying on the terrifying-looking equipment made the fear of war real and the chance of death seem closer. As a result, people rushed to make wills and the rate of marriages increased fivefold.

If the British were anxious to avoid war, the French had even more reason to fear another plunge into that abyss, as it was clear that any future conflict would be fought, like the First World War, on French soil

LEFT: BRITISH HOLIDAY MAKERS RELAX BY THE COAST DURING WHAT WOULD PROVE TO BE THE LAST PEACETIME SUMMER FOR SIX YEARS. THE SUMMER OF 1939 WAS PARTICULARLY HOT AND SUNNY GIVING MANY THE OPPORTUNITY TO CAST ASIDE WORRIES ABOUT EVENTS IN FAR AWAY 'COUNTRIES OF WHICH WE KNOW NOTHING'.

The astute and
cunning Stalin was
quick to realise that...
if he could not gain
friends with whom to
combat the Germans,
he had little choice but
to come to terms with
Hitler himself

chunks of Europe, the French chose a cautious policy, hoping and believing that the 400,000 troops manning the Maginot Line would deter the Germans from striking.

As Spring 1939 blossomed across Europe, German troops moved into what remained of Czechoslovakia while the British and French began desperately casting about for an ally who could help them stop Hitler's relentless forward march. As luck would have it, the Soviet Union, the ideological arch-enemy of Nazi Germany, was keen to relaunch the First World War alliance of Britain, Russia and France.

The Soviets were as concerned as the Allies by Germany's growing strength, so the Soviet Foreign Minister Maxim Litvinov proposed a straightforward military pact with Britain and France, who, though keen to gain allies against Germany, were unsure at first how to respond. The countries that Britain and France were hoping to preserve from Nazi domination, Poland and Romania, both feared Soviet Russia. To bring in Stalin to help guarantee their independence would have unsettled the people of Poland and Romania as much as it reassured them. But Britain and France could not do the job on their own and, therefore, entered into talks with the communists, but they were, in reality, playing for time.

THE WAR IN SPAIN

Before the Second World War finally broke out on 3 September 1939, Europe had already had a glimpse of terrifying things to come. On 19 July 1936, civil war erupted in Spain. The left-wing Republican government was attacked and eventually overthrown by the Nationalist Spanish Army led by General Franco, but not before the German Air Force, the Luftwaffe, fighting on the Nationalist side, had been given the chance to practise its bombing techniques on civilians.

On 26 April 1937, the undefended Basque city of Guernica was bombed by the German Condor Legion on market day. Eighteen planes spent over an hour raining bombs down on helpless civilians. The town was turned into a ghastly panorama of smoking ruins. Although the Nationalists denied the raid had taken place and asserted that Guernica had been destroyed from the ground by the Republicans, world opinion was not inclined to believe them. Guernica became a martyr to Nationalist tyranny, and the cynicism displayed by Italy and Germany in using Spain as a testing ground for their armed forces served

THE NOTORIOUS CONDOR LEGION, WHICH CYNICALLY RAINED BOMBS ON UNPROTECTED SPANISH CIVILIANS.

only to increase civilian fears about another war in Europe. While Italy and Germany intervened in Spain, Britain and France once again stood back and did nothing, so encouraging Hitler and Mussolini, the Italian Fascist dictator, to believe that their future plans for conquest and rearmament would meet little resistance.

The astute and cunning Stalin was quick to realise that the Allies were unable to set aside their longstanding reservations about the Soviet Union and decided that, if he could not gain friends with whom to combat the Germans, he had little choice but to come to terms with Hitler himself.

While Stalin continued talking to the Allies, he entered into secret negotiations with the Nazis. The talks quickly bore fruit. Germany, eager to attack Poland, needed to be sure that the Soviets would not come to the aid of the Poles. Stalin, for his part, was keen to share in the destruction of Poland and to use the opportunity it presented to consolidate the Soviet position in the Baltic. The two dictators quickly entered into a secret pact, signed on 22 August 1939, to carve up eastern Europe between them. They would split Poland down the middle, and then Russia would be free to extend its influence in Latvia, Estonia, Lithuania and Finland. Once Poland was destroyed, Hitler would be free to wage war against France without fear of Soviet intervention.

Before the ink on the Nazi–Soviet agreement was dry, Hitler, confident that the Allies would once again shy away from war, ordered his generals to prepare for the conquest of Poland. The agreement was announced to the unsuspecting world on 23 August 1939. International opinion was stunned. Britain and France were, after all, still negotiating a treaty with the Soviets. Honour still counted for something at that time, and honour had been cynically contravened. At a single stroke, it appeared, the whole political world had been turned upside down.

Hitler began his preparations for the invasion of Poland with his customary deviousness. Several prisoners from Nazi concentration camps were murdered. Their bodies were dressed in Polish Army uniforms and dumped close to the radio transmitter near Gleiwitz on the German–Polish border. The Nazis used the bodies as evidence of a Polish attack and ordered revenge. The world was once again at war.

CHAPTER 2

The Rape of Poland

A GERMAN MOTORISED COLUMN RIPS THROUGH POLAND
IN 1939. IT WAS TO TAKE HITLER'S SOLDIERS JUST ONE
MONTH TO BRING POLAND TO HER KNEES. OVER THE NEXT SIX
YEARS POLAND SUFFERED ONE OF THE MOST BRUTAL
OCCUPATIONS IN HUMAN HISTORY.

BLITZKRIEG

Without a declaration of war, German planes and artillery opened fire on Polish positions before dawn on 1 September 1939. The Wehrmacht, the German Army, was about to realise Hitler's dream of recapturing the once-German port of Danzig and the Polish corridor, both of which had been lost to Germany in 1919.

Everything was perfectly set for the Germans. With Stalin's signature on the Nazi–Soviet pact, Hitler could be sure that the Soviet Union would not intervene and if everything went according to plan, new German military techniques would destroy the Polish Army before help could arrive from Britain and France.

But inside Germany, Hitler's initiative in starting this war was not greeted with the enthusiastic crowds that had gathered to cheer Kaiser Wilhelm II when he joined hostilities 25 years earlier. The Germans had no choice but to follow their Führer Hitler into war, but they did so with feelings of foreboding and unease. Those who later remembered the German soldiers setting off for the front in 1939 described them as looking like gloom personified.

As the first artillery barrages opened up, the Luftwaffe began destroying the Polish Air Force on the ground. Poland was now to experience the devastating effects of an entirely new form of warfare: blitzkrieg, or 'lightning war', based on fast-moving armour and maximum firepower brutally applied.

The German airborne assault was carried out with pinpoint accuracy. Fighting with the fascists in the Spanish Civil War had given the Luftwaffe the chance to perfect a deadly

THE SS, HITLER'S DARK KNIGHTS, CHOSEN FOR THEIR 'RACIAL PURITY', THEIR FANATICAL OBEDIENCE AND THEIR WILLINGNESS TO COMMIT ACTS OF OBSCENE BRUTALITY.

THE SS

From its early role as an élite personal bodyguard of the Führer, the SS or Schutzstafeln (protection squads) grew to control the German police force, where it was given the task of destroying the internal enemies of the Reich. However, once war broke out, the SS, under their leader Heinrich Himmler, soon extended their role to take on the responsibility for the annihilation of all enemies of the National Socialist movement found in the newly occupied areas of Europe.

Himmler saw the men under his control as the cutting edge of the Nazi movement – racially pure, physically fit and utterly ruthless. Having already bloodied themselves on the rounding up of political prisoners inside Germany, the SS had few qualms about putting Nazi ideology into practice elsewhere. To secure the future of the German race, Himmler's men killed without compunction. Jews, communists, Christians, homosexuals and anyone else who resisted the establishment of Germany's New Order were on their hit lists.

Those who were not killed outright by the Einsatzgruppen or action squads of the SS were frequently worked to death. As Himmler said: 'Whether or not 10,000 Russian women collapse from exhaustion while digging a tank ditch interests me only in so far as the tank ditch is completed for Germany.'

new technique: dive-bombing. It was used in Poland for the first time and on a very large scale.

In this context, the Junker Ju-87 Stukas proved themselves as weapons of terror. Their pilots began a steep dive as they approached their targets, and released their bombs just as they pulled up and soared skywards. The spectacle was terrifying to behold and to hear. The planes would plunge from the sky at breakneck speed, making a fearful whining sound known as the 'trombones of Jericho' before releasing bombs that fell on soldiers and civilians alike. This new technique proved three times more accurate than conventional, higher-level bombing.

The Poles had no means of resistance, and their antiquated air force was destroyed within days. Now, the Stukas – short for 'sturzkampfflugzeug' – turned their attention to bombarding

railways, roads, bridges and, of course, civilian targets. It was hoped that the panic and death they caused would further confuse Polish attempts to organise resistance to the German onslaught.

With the Stukas acting as their advance strike force, the Wehrmacht's armoured columns thrust into Poland from the north, south and west. Although only about one-sixth of the German Army was made up of motorised and armoured 'panzer' divisions, it was these modern, mobile and well-armoured forces that made all the difference. When the

ABOVE: GENERAL HEINZ GUDERIAN, THE BRILLIANT GERMAN PANZER COMMANDER WHOSE THEORIES ON ARMOURED WARFARE PAVED THE WAY FOR THE NAZI SUCCESS IN POLAND.

LEFT: CIVILIANS ERECT MAKESHIFT DEFENCES IN THE POLISH CAPITAL. THE DEFENCE OF THE POLISH CAPITAL WAS SPIRITED BUT ULTIMATELY DOOMED. THE POLES SIMPLY HAD NO REPLY TO THE DAZZLING NEW TACTICS OR THE FEROCIOUS MACHINES OF WAR UNDER HITLER'S CONTROL.

tanks, supported by mobile artillery, motorised infantry and Stukas launched themselves across the Polish frontier, they hurled themselves at weak points in the Polish defences and, once victorious, quickly drove deeper and deeper into Polish territory, using their speed and firepower to crush and encircle opponents while the regular army followed behind, making good the advance.

The Polish forces were quickly thrown into disarray. Their strategy for defending the 3500-mile border with Germany proved a dreadful mistake. Instead of retreating to solid defensive positions behind the Vistula, Narew and San rivers, the Polish commander, Marshal Edward Smigly-Rydz, spread his forces thinly at the frontier, where the German blitzkrieg soon crashed straight through them and began to race headlong towards the Polish capital, Warsaw.

BRITAIN AND FRANCE DECLARE WAR

The British and French were badly shaken by the onslaught against Poland. Chamberlain was keen to attempt another negotiated settlement similar to that of Munich. But the House of Commons would not stand for it. Chamberlain was backed into a corner and had little option but to declare war. The French were even less keen than the British, but, as Chamberlain soon realised, his government would fall unless he acted, so he put pressure on his reluctant ally to honour their joint commitments.

At 9 a.m. on Sunday, 3 September 1939, the British Government delivered an ultimatum: unless an undertaking was received from the German Government within two hours that their troops now waging war in Poland would be withdrawn, Great Britain would be forced to enter into a state of war with Germany.

When no such undertaking was received, Chamberlain was obliged to make good his warning, and announced, in a radio broadcast to the British people, that Britain was once again at war. The ageing statesman, heartbroken at the failure of his hopes for enduring peace, spoke to the British people about the nature of the foe they faced: 'It is evil things we shall be fighting against, brute force, bad faith, injustice, oppression and persecution.'

As he spoke, Chamberlain had little idea how right his words would prove to be.

Meanwhile, in Washington, the President of the USA, Franklin Delano Roosevelt, declared America's neutrality. France, however, declared war on the same day as Britain.

THE POLISH CAMPAIGN

German attacks 15–27 September
Polish Bzura pocket
Russian attacks 17–27 September

THE RAPE OF POLAND

Even as the blitzkrieg's first advances pushed aside Polish resistance, another Nazi innovation was beginning to make its presence felt, not on the battlefield, but in the areas of Poland that had already fallen into Nazi hands. For the three SS regiments that followed behind the regular German Army, the war was not to be fought against the active

'It is evil things we shall be fighting against, brute force, bad faith, injustice, oppression and persecution'
Neville Chamberlain, in a broadcast to the British people, 3 September 1939

LEFT: GERMAN SOLDIERS EXECUTE POLISH CIVILIANS WITHOUT TRIAL, DECEMBER 1939. SCENES LIKE THIS WERE TO BECOME ALL TO FAMILIAR DURING THE GERMAN OCCUPATION OF POLAND.

THE JU-87 STUKA

The Stuka dive-bomber was one of the most successful and feared warplanes in the early days of the war. It was a light two-man bomber powered by a 1200hp engine and was used to devastating effect in both the Polish campaign and later during the Battle of France. The Stuka was designed to carry out bombing raids with pin-point accuracy, destroying enemy positions as a prelude to the main German advance. Its accuracy was such that its bombs routinely fell within 30 metres of its targets. This was in part due to its ability to dive in a near vertical position. The Stuka's airbrakes enabled the plane to slow down during its dive to give the pilot sufficient time to aim carefully. The Stuka could carry one 1100lb bomb or one 550lb and four 110lb bombs. It was also armed with three 3.7mm machine-guns and had a top speed of 292mph. The notoriety of the Stuka was so great that it became the most prestigious plane to fly with the Luftwaffe, at least until Allied pilots discovered its great weakness: the Stuka was vulnerable as it commenced its dive. That was the moment when the dive-bomber could be shot down.

THE STUKA: GERMANY'S FLYING ARTILLERY.

members of the Polish armed forces. Instead, their targets were civilians: men, women and children, as well as prisoners of war. It soon became clear that the Geneva Convention, an international agreement first outlined in 1864, which gave prisoners of war the right to medical treatment and other benefits, was not going to be applied to the Poles, whom the Nazis' racist ideology classed as subhuman.

As the SS entered captured Polish towns and villages, the full extent of their malignant brutality quickly became apparent. Anyone suspected of being an enemy of the German Reich was summarily executed. Among these 'enemies' were Jews, intellectuals, homosexuals, teachers, lawyers, priests and Polish patriots. The murders were frequently preceded by humiliation and torture so horrific that many members of the Wehrmacht were shocked. Some took the dangerous step of complaining to their Führer. Hitler listened to their protests, but quickly overruled them, giving the SS, not the army, his backing and sanction.

COLLAPSE

By the time the Allies declared war on 3 September, German forces had already sealed off the Polish corridor. The Polish Army, which lacked the modern weapons that might have enabled it to compete on equal terms with the Germans, quickly found itself encircled. In contrast to the Wehrmacht, Poland's forces were made up almost entirely of infantry and cavalry divisions. For mobility, they were dependent on the railway network, but that had already been destroyed by the Stukas. As communications broke down between the armies in the field and their commanders, the Poles had little choice but to stay put and wait for the German onslaught. Inevitably unsupported, cavalry divisions

> Anyone suspected of being an enemy of the German Reich was summarily executed... The murders were frequently preceded by humiliation and torture so horrific that many members of the Wehrmacht were shocked. Some took the dangerous step of complaining to their Führer

GENERAL SIKORSKI AND THE POLISH GOVERNMENT-IN-EXILE

As the Polish republic collapsed, key members of the government attempted to escape into Romania to form what would be the first of many European governments-in-exile. Unfortunately, they were interned by the Romanians and it fell to former prime minister General Sikorski to head the new exiled government. The formation of a new Polish government in France was essential if the Polish nation was to survive the war. After all, both Hitler and Stalin had already begun to display their ruthless determination to ensure that the independent Poland created after the First World War would never re-emerge.

Sikorski and about 90,000 Polish troops under his command fought during the battle of France in 1940. The remnants of this force were ferried across the Channel to England, which Sikorski was forced to accept as his new home. The Polish leader was now in the familiar position of exiled leaders: he was entirely dependent upon the British for aid. But as long as he continued to put troops in the field against the Germans, it could never truly be claimed that Polish resistance had been totally extinguished.

POLISH RESISTANCE DID NOT DIE WITH THE OCCUPATION OF THEIR HOMELAND.

RIGHT: MODERN WARFARE
SPARED NEITHER SOLDIER
NOR CIVILIAN. TENS OF
THOUSANDS OF POLISH
CIVILIANS DIED DURING THE
POLISH CAMPAIGN.
MILLIONS WERE TO DIE
DURING THE NAZI
OCCUPATION.

proved no match for Panzers. Nevertheless, Polish resistance was both valiant and fierce.

A counter-attack was launched on 9 September. The Polish Army around the River Bzura attacked the German 8th Army and succeeded in destroying one of its divisions. The action slowed the German advance on Warsaw, but the respite was short-lived. Within five days, the Polish Army was once again in retreat as the Germans now focused their attention on the Polish capital.

As bombs fell on the beautiful city, the Allies, despite their pledges, were entirely unequal to the task of aiding the beleaguered Poles. Instead, they began dropping leaflets urging the

ABOVE: THE POLES WERE
NOT READY FOR THE HIGHLY
MOBILE WARFARE THE
GERMANS UNLEASHED IN
SEPTEMBER 1939. THE
DAYS OF TRENCH WARFARE
WERE OVER.

IN THE KATYN FOREST, ONE OF STALIN'S MANY VICTIMS IS EXHUMED.

THE KATYN FOREST MASSACRE

Of the many atrocities committed in Poland during the war, the Katyn Forest Massacre, perpetrated by the Russians, remains one of the most notorious. After Stalin's successful defeat of Poland, nearly 200,000 prisoners of war fell into his hands. In order to proceed with incorporating his half of Poland into the Soviet Union, Stalin, like his German counterparts, was keen to destroy the Polish élite from which the main resistance to Soviet rule was likely to come. The Soviet dictator had his secret police, the NKVD, select 15,000 captured officers who were then sent to three special camps – Kozielsk, Ostaszkow and Starobielsk. After May 1940, they were never heard of again. Attempts to locate them by Polish leaders seeking to recreate the Polish Army met with no results until, in 1943, the Germans uncovered a mass grave in the Katyn forest containing 4400 bodies. Although the Russians denied responsibility at the time, they later admitted in 1989 that the massacre had been conducted by the NKVD. The remaining 10,000 officers have never been found.

Germans to overthrow the Nazis. The mentality behind this was a cautious one: the British were wary of delivering anything more substantial in case it 'provoked' the Germans.

French efforts on the Western Front proved equally dismal. On 9 September, French forces advanced into the Saar, in western Germany. The Poles were relying on their allies in the West to make the Germans fight a war on two fronts, and thereby reduce the pressure on their own country. But the Germans failed to take the bait and withdrew as the French advanced towards the West Wall, or Siegfried Line. This was Germany's answer to the Maginot Line, but a less elaborate one. Confronted by the German fortifications, the French paused, then retreated. Meanwhile, bombs continued to rain on Poland, but even worse was to come.

With the Polish Army all but defeated, Stalin stepped in to seal their fate. On 17 September, Soviet troops stormed into Poland after the new Soviet Foreign Minister, Vyacheslav Molotov, declared that the Polish state no longer existed. Within days, the Soviets had linked up with their Nazi allies. Polish resistance had by now shrunk to the area around Warsaw. The *New York Times* was blunt in its assessment of the Soviet Union: 'Germany having seized the prey, Soviet Russia will seize that part of the carcass that Germany cannot use. It will play the noble role of hyena to the German lion.'

The German bombing of Warsaw began the same day as the Polish counter-attack. Warsaw, defended by over 100,000 troops, was able to hold out for 17 days, but indiscriminate bombing, fires and lack of food took their toll on the inhabitants. On 26 September, Warsaw surrendered. By the beginning of October, all organised resistance had ceased.

Twenty-five thousand Poles had been killed by German bombers in barely a month. Sixty thousand troops had died fighting the Germans, who had now captured over half a million Polish soldiers. But in a gesture of defiance, General Wladyslaw Sikorski set up a

'Germany having seized the prey, Soviet Russia will seize that part of the carcass that Germany cannot use. It will play the noble role of hyena to the German lion'
The New York Times, September 1939

Polish government-in-exile in France on 30 September. Sikorski was able to keep the flame of Polish resistance burning as 90,000 Polish troops began their escape to the West. These were to be joined by Polish sailors who managed to sneak two submarines and three destroyers through the German naval blockade. The Poles, who included a number of airmen, were gradually absorbed into the Allied war effort, to fight most prominently in the aerial Battle of Britain in 1940 and in Italy after 1943.

THE NAZI–SOVIET OCCUPATION OF POLAND

With the fighting over, the Germans and Russians divided Poland between them. The Nazis took the west of the country, which contained the bulk of the Polish population and industry, while the Soviets took the rural east. The two zones of occupation were divided by the River Bug.

Although the Nazis and Soviets remained ideological opponents of the most virulent kind, both set about the occupation with the same aim: the complete destruction of the Polish state and Polish culture. The German zone, containing over 20 million people, was divided into two new provinces: the Wartheland and the General Government. Over the next six years, German-occupied Poland was to become a living laboratory in which the Nazis tested their racial theories with utter ruthlessness and disposed of their 'enemies' in death camps.

BELOW: GERMAN TROOPS ENTER GDANSK, 1939. WHILE HIS BLITZKRIEG STILL RAGED IN THE REST OF THE COUNTRY, HITLER HIMSELF ENTERED DANZIG ON 19 SEPTEMBER AND RECEIVED A WARM WELCOME FROM THE CITY'S LARGELY ETHNIC GERMAN INHABITANTS. WITH THE OCCUPATION OF THE FREE CITY OF DANZIG HITLER HAD RIPPED UP YET ANOTHER CLAUSE OF THE VERSAILLES TREATY.

BELOW: BEHIND THE
SCENES, THERE IS CLOSE
CO-OPERATION BETWEEN
GERMANY AND THE SOVIET
UNION IN THE BUILD-UP
TO WAR.

ABOVE: SS TROOPS MOP UP
THE LAST POCKETS OF
POLISH RESISTANCE
IN DANZIG.

The Wartheland was to be completely Germanised and was formally absorbed into the Third Reich, while the General Government was reduced to the status of a massive labour colony. The untold human cost of this decision was felt immediately, but grew in severity as the months passed. Well over two million Polish Jews were now in German hands. Nazi theorists wasted no time going to work on a solution for what they euphemistically termed the 'Jewish problem'.

LEFT: CAPTURED POLISH WEAPONS IN WARSAW SQUARE, AFTER THE FALL OF THE CITY, 1 OCTOBER 1939.

SS Chief Reinhard Heydrich took up the task with relish. Genocide was the only logical outcome of the fanatical Nazi hatred of the Jews and Heydrich set about organising its initial phases with chilling efficiency. From October, all Jews between the ages of 14 and 60 were expected to perform forced labour for the Nazis. Their property rights were restricted, they were removed from the countryside and they were herded into ghettos in Polish cities.

Life in the ghettos was harsh and squalid. Thousands were confined in a cramped area, and were refused sufficient food. There was little or no sanitation. These horrific conditions quickly took their toll on the old, the sick and the young, thousands of whom died. In these early stages, this campaign against the Jews was being carried out slowly. Within two years, though, it had accelerated, claiming the lives of millions.

To further the Germanisation of the Wartheland, those Poles considered 'racially unfit' to belong in the Reich were dumped in the General Government, their property having been confiscated. One and a half million people, including 300,000 Jews, were taken from their homes and put into cattle trucks. The Germans treated them worse than animals, offering them neither food nor sanitation. Many died before they reached their destination. Their homes, possessions and businesses were taken over by ethnic Germans, who were encouraged to leave the Baltic states for the Wartheland. Polish children

considered to be of the appropriate racial stock were taken from their parents and shipped to Germany, to be raised as Nazis. The Polish language and culture were now fiercely suppressed. All occupants of the Wartheland were designated German.

Life in the General Government was even more appalling. With Hans Frank's appointment as governor, the persecution of the Poles was stepped up. Frank made clear his intention to treat the Poles as slaves. Libraries and universities were closed and mass deportations began as thousands of Poles were taken to Germany, where they would be forced to spend the duration of the war toiling for the German war machine.

The Soviets undertook the pacification of their portion of Poland with no less gusto. Stalin, like Hitler, had no intention of tolerating an independent Polish state and quickly set about absorbing Soviet-occupied Poland into the Soviet Union He was quick, too, to eliminate any potential 'enemies' of the working class, his principal target being the Polish officer corps.

LEFT: THE PEOPLE OF POLAND ARE ALERTED BY PUBLIC NOTICE TO THE INTRODUCTION OF LAWS TO RESTRICT MOVEMENT AS PART OF THE IMPLEMENTATION OF THE NAZI POLICE STATE.

It is estimated that Stalin had 15,000 of these officers executed. In April 1943, when the tide of war had washed the Soviets out of Poland and washed the Germans in, Nazi soldiers discovered 4400 bodies buried in the Katyn forest near Smolensk. Their hands were tied behind their backs with wire and there were bullet holes in the backs of their heads. The remaining 10,000 officers were missing. They were never found. In total, the Soviets deported one million Polish citizens to labour camps in Siberia and Central Asia before the Germans broke their pact with Stalin and attacked Russia, through Poland, in 1941.

With Poland absorbed, Hitler made the Allies a cursory peace offer. He attempted to 'reason with them'. Their declaration of war on 3 September had, in fact, taken the Nazis by surprise and there was a certain amount of trepidation at the thought of facing the mighty French Army. But success in Poland bred a growing confidence and Hitler felt able to speak to the Allies as a victor.

'Why should this war in the West be fought for the restoration of Poland?' Hitler asked. 'The Poland of the Versailles Treaty will never rise again.'

Hitler proposed a conference for the purpose of discussing the situation in the East. But the Allies had learned a hard and humiliating lesson. Hitler's offer was rejected out of hand by both Chamberlain and the French Prime Minister, Daladier.

Characteristically, Hitler had already been making other plans. He reasoned that if the Allies were to reject his peace offer, France and Britain would both have to be knocked out of the war. Hitler's thirst for conquest and his ambitions soared as he now turned his attention towards an invasion of France.

CHAPTER 3

The Phoney War

ALL QUIET ON THE WESTERN FRONT. BRITISH TROOPS IN FRANCE RELAX WHILE THEIR COMRADES COMPLETE THE 100-YARD DASH. MEANWHILE, HITLER'S GENERALS WERE DRAWING PLANS FOR A CRUSHING INVASION OF FRANCE DESIGNED TO KNOCK THE ALLIES OUT OF THE WAR FOR GOOD.

THE BORE WAR

As the smoke of blitzkrieg slowly cleared from the plains of Poland and the horrors of the Nazi–Soviet occupation began to make themselves felt, the war in the West entered a new phase – the so-called 'Phoney War'.

As the Nazi tanks rolled into Poland, tens of thousands of British children had been evacuated from the major cities and from those areas considered to be under most threat from German air attack. Yet, by the beginning of 1940, as the expected German bombers failed to arrive, nearly half had returned to their homes. For the British there had, as yet, been little real change from peacetime routine. Food rationing and the blackout had been introduced but, as the war effort had yet to come into full effect,

unemployment was still high at over one million and no British forces were engaged in open warfare on land.

On 4 September, as the Germans sealed off the Polish corridor, the first men of the British Expeditionary Force began their journey to France under the command of Lord Gort, former Chief of the Imperial General Staff, and Britain's highest-ranking soldier. As in the First World War, these soldiers, like their fathers before them, were to come under the command of the French, but with the terrible losses of 1914–18 in mind, no offensive action by these troops, or by the French Army itself, was planned.

RIGHT: BRITISH TROOPS' DAILY ROUTINE IN FRANCE. ALTHOUGH BRITAIN AND FRANCE HAD BOTH DECLARED WAR ON GERMANY DURING THE PHONEY WAR, SOLDIERS HAD YET TO SNAP OUT OF THE ATTITUDES OF PEACE TIME. YEARS LATER ONE BRITISH SOLDIER SAID IT WAS SIMPLY CONSIDERED 'BAD FORM' TO WANT TO SHOOT ONE'S RIFLE AT THE ENEMY.

BELOW: OBSERVING A LOW-FLYING AIRCRAFT FROM BEHIND AN **AA** GUN EMPLACEMENT AND PROTECTIVE SANDBAGS.

LEFT: WORK MOVES AHEAD TO CONSTRUCT AIR RAID DEFENCES IN LONDON'S FASHIONABLE KENSINGTON GARDENS. PUBLIC PARKS AND GARDENS THROUGH-OUT THE CAPITAL WERE DUG UP DURING THE WAR TO PROVIDE TRENCHES THAT COULD BE USED AS AIR RAID SHELTERS AS WELL AS AA GUN EMPLACEMENTS. SOME WERE EVEN DUG OVER TO PROVIDE ALLOTMENTS TO BOOST THE NATION'S FOOD SUPPLIES.

This period of apparent inactivity on the Allied side, in marked contrast to the fierce energy displayed by the Germans, was soon nicknamed 'the Phoney War' by watching American newspapermen. Other wits labelled it the 'bore war' or 'sitzkrieg' – the sitting war. Prime Minister Chamberlain hoped the conflict could be won without the gigantic land battles that had scarred Europe 20 years earlier, and placed more faith than was reasonable in the chance that a British naval blockade of Germany would bring Hitler to his senses.

RATIONING

Food rationing was introduced into the UK on 8 January 1940, although petrol had been rationed from the outset five months before. The general public had to register with the govenrment for ration books. They were also required to register with a local shopkeeper, whom they would use exclusively until the end of the war. The first foods to be rationed were bacon and butter, both at 4 oz. per week. Sugar was another of the first foods to be rationed. Ironically, rationing allowed the British public to eat more healthily than either before the War or after it, as people's diets were carefully controlled by the state. Clothes rationing was introduced on 1 June 1940, and everyone was given 66 ration coupons a year. A pair of trousers 'cost' eight coupons, a skirt seven, a pair of socks three and pants, four. During the height of rationing in 1942, people were each allowed meat to the value of 1s 2d. a week. This scarcity of meat encouraged some to keep pigs or poultry – the chickens were also used to produce eggs over and above the ration – while others turned to their allotments and grew their own food. Some items were never rationed in wartime, including bread, fish, potatoes, vegetables and, last but not least, offal.

Ration books for food and clothing, 1942–3.

ABOVE: 'READY FOR THE NEW WAR LOAN ISSUE'. POST OFFICE EMPLOYEES PROUDLY PRESENT THE NEW NATIONAL SAVINGS CERTIFICATES.

The French Army, under the command of General Gamelin, seemed content to sit behind the defensive buttress of the Maginot Line and wait for the German invasion. Aggressive operations against the Germans, including the dropping of mines in the River Rhine, as suggested by Winston Churchill, now First Lord of the Admiralty, were rejected by the French for the apparently odd reason that they were likely to provoke a German response.

As Hitler and Stalin destroyed Poland, the world waited in vain for an Allied response. The little fighting that did take place during this period of the war occurred at sea, where German raiders and U-boat submarines hunted Allied shipping bringing vital war supplies back from the USA.

With Poland on its knees by the beginning of October, Hitler was keen for his armies to deliver a crushing blow to the British and French in the west. The Führer's generals were, however, horrified. They were concerned that the German Army was not properly prepared for operations against the Allies, but their protests were ignored. If they could not deny him, though, the climate could. As bad weather closed in with the approach of winter, Hitler was forced to concede that an attack in the west would have to wait until the spring of 1940.

In the meantime, both sides sat facing each other in tense silence and inactivity along the Franco–German border. Neutral Belgium and the Netherlands were eager to avoid a confrontation and ignored Allied offers of military co-operation in case the Germans responded by launching an invasion. While their guns remained idle, Allied soldiers occupied themselves with cards and visits to cafés. Little effective training took place, but the fear remained that inaction might soon explode into the furnace-heat of battle.

THE WINTER WAR

While the weather on the Western Front prevented Hitler from proceeding with the war, Stalin felt himself under no such constraint. On 30 November 1939, Soviet troops poured across the 600-mile Russo–Finnish frontier and the Red Air Force began the unannounced bombing of the Finnish capital, Helsinki. Air raid sirens managed to give only one minute's warning before the bombs came raining down. Dozens lost their lives amid flames, rubble and wreckage. As the bewildered population looked up at the sky, they saw leaflets fluttering down and unfamiliar bombers. Incongruously, they declared: 'Soviet Russia will not harm the Finnish people.'

Stalin had been eager to capitalise on his gains in Poland by strengthening his position in the Baltic and around Leningrad, by creating a buffer against Germany. However, unlike the Baltic states of Latvia, Lithuania and Estonia, Fin-land refused to allow the Russians to establish defensive bases on their territory. They were not impressed by threats from Russians whose tsars, now long gone, had ruled Finland from 1809 until the revolution of 1917. The Finns had, in fact, driven the Russians out of their country and they were not about to relinquish the independence they had so recently won. But Stalin was not to be denied. Word was sent to Marshal Kiril Meretskov, commander of the Leningrade military district, to invade Finland. The neutral country, with its tiny population, was about to be absorbed into the Soviet Union or, at least, that was the plan.

The Red Army was confident of victory. With over one million men, 1500 tanks and 3000 planes to draw upon, the Red Army expected a swift, decisive victory; so swift, in fact, that Stalin's troops were not equipped with winter uniforms. Winter, they had

BELOW LEFT: THE FINNISH COMMANDER MARSHAL MANNERHEIM LED HIS TINY ARMY IN AN INCREDIBLE CAMPAIGN OF RESISTANCE AGAINST THE MIGHT OF THE RED ARMY, WHOM HE STAVED OFF FOR THREE MONTHS BEFORE SHEER EXHAUSTION RENDERED HIS MEN INCAPABLE OF FIGHTING ANY FURTHER.

BELOW: A FINNISH SNIPER, ONE OF THE BIELAJA SMERT OR 'WHITE DEATH', FULLY EQUIPPED WITH A TELESCOPIC SIGHT, WAITS IN THE SNOW-COVERED FORESTS FOR STRAY SOVIETS.

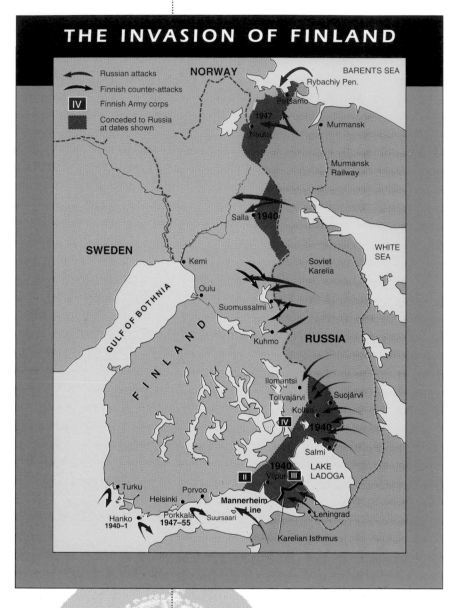

THE INVASION OF FINLAND

Russian attacks
Finnish counter-attacks
IV Finnish Army corps
Conceded to Russia at dates shown

reckoned, would arrive long after the Finns had been crushed.

The Finns, by comparison, never managed to put more than 175,000 men in the field. They had little by way of artillery, tanks or anti-tank weapons or an air force. Yet, despite all these seeming disadvantages, the Red Army was going to be rudely awakened by the Finnish. The Finnish commander, Marshal Mannerheim, succeeded in immediately halting the initial Soviet advance. Finnish defensive positions were well prepared and Mannerheim's soldiers were resolved to resist the invader. The freezing winter conditions made the going very tough for the Soviet tanks, infantry and air force. Finnish soldiers were trained in winter warfare, and were appropriately dressed in layers of warm clothing. Although under-equipped in weapons, the Finns soon learned to improvise tactics and that made the Russians easy prey.

Finnish troops attacked the Soviet tanks at night, approaching them swiftly and silently on skis, and camouflaged in the snowy conditions by their white clothing. Their familiarity with the territory in which they were operating and their easy mobility startled the Russians, who often found tanks set alight by 'Molotov cocktails' before they were even aware they were under attack. The Molotov cocktail was a primitive but deadly weapon made from a glass bottle filled with petrol, and a piece of rag at the neck that served as a fuse. Light the rag, throw the bottle and an extraordinarily effective weapon was created – so much so that the cocktails could incinerate crews inside their tanks before they had any chance of escaping.

In addition to using the cocktails to disable Russian tanks, the Finns also crept up on them and wedged logs into the tank tracks. This wrecked the gearing and rendered them useless and unable to move. Disguise was also employed with some success. Some Finns dressed as Soviet communication troops and calmly directed entire supply columns into Finnish-held territory.

When backed by fighters capable of such skill and imagination, it was no surprise that Marshal Mannerheim's defensive positions – eponymously named the Mannerheim Line – were able to hold despite the huge enemy onslaught.

Stalin's attack on Finland was greeted by outrage in the rest of the world. The Soviet Union was summarily expelled from the League of Nations, the forerunner of the United Nations, which had been formed after the First World War. In addition, hundreds of volunteers from countries as diverse as Britain, Hungary, Italy, France and Sweden flocked to the Finnish cause. The Swedes were technically neutral and remained so throughout the war, but in 1939 they sent two full battalions to aid their Scandinavian neighbour. In addition, the Allies responded more vigorously to the invasion of Finland than they had to the invasion of Poland three months earlier. Firm in the conviction that Finland must not be 'allowed to disappear from the map', Neville Chamberlain and Edouard Daladier committed their countries to sending 100,000 troops to the tiny country's aid. The Allies' motives, however, were not entirely altruistic. Any troops they sent to Finland would have to pass through Sweden, which supplied the German war machine with 70 per cent of its iron ore imports. It would be very beneficial to the Allies if their troops just happened to occupy these ore fields, so denying them to the Germans and gaining a valuable resource for themselves as they made their way through Sweden to fight the Red Army.

This tempting idea never materialised. By the time the decision to aid the Finns was made, on 5 February 1940, the Allies' plans had been overtaken by events. Although they destroyed four Soviet divisions in December 1939, the Finns were slowly being ground down by the sheer number of Soviet troops.

The Soviets suffered enormous losses, but their army did not lose heart and their commanders quickly learned from their mistakes. However, not every commander was given a second chance by Stalin. General Vinogradov was not one of the lucky ones. He was executed after the Soviet 63rd and 144th divisions were lost to the Finns at Suomussalmi. Despite these successes, it was becoming apparent to Mannerheim and the Finnish President, Risto Ryti, that the Finnish Army was slowly bleeding to death. It could not go on. In January 1940, secret peace negotiations with Stalin began.

All branches of the Soviet armed forces, Timoshenko decided, were to attack the Finns in concert. General Stern promised Stalin that Soviet troops would cross the Mannerheim Line over a bridge of corpses. They did, but not quite in the way Stern had intended

VIDKUN QUISLING

Vidkun Quisling was born in Norway in 1887. His name became a synonym for 'traitor' after he attempted a pro-German coup d'état on 9 April 1940, the day the Germans invaded. Quisling had already forged strong links with the Nazis before the war and his National Union Party had received German funding. Indeed, Quisling could claim some of the responsibility for the Nazi conquest of Norway as he encouraged the Führer to consider the invasion of Scandinavia at a time when Hitler had no plans to move German troops north. Quisling's announcement that he had formed a pro-German government proved to be another spur to Norwegian resistance. Ultimately, his regime proved a political failure. Quisling remained in power for less than a week. Despite the problems and the embarrassment he caused the Germans, they continued to use him as their puppet, retaining him in positions of influence. On 1 February 1942, the Germans appointed Quisling Minister-President.

After the war, Quisling was executed for collaborating with the Germans on 24 October 1945.

QUISLING, ONE OF THE WAR'S MOST NOTORIOUS TRAITORS.

However, as the peace talks proceeded, the fighting went on, and in February the Red Army prepared for a decisive offensive. The military preparations fell to Stalin's old associate, Marshal Timoshenko. All branches of the Soviet armed forces, Timoshenko decided, were to attack the Finns in concert. General Stern promised Stalin that Soviet troops would cross the Mannerheim Line over a bridge of corpses. They did, but not quite in the way Stern had intended.

True to Stern's word, the Mannerheim Line was breached on 11 February. But the bridge of corpses comprised more Russians than Finns. Even so, Marshal Mannerheim's troops were exhausted and peace was signed a month later. Under Stalin's terms, Finland had to cede Hango and the Karelian isthmus to the Soviet Union and as a result lost 10 per cent of its territory. However, it did at least keep its independence. The Russians paid for their victory with the lives of 200,000 soldiers. The Finns lost 25,000 men killed.

On 12 March 1940, President Ryti concluded the peace agreement in sombre mood, muttering that the hand that signed such a document deserved to wither. By dramatic coincidence, Ryti suffered a stroke shortly afterwards that paralysed the whole of his right side.

A second campaign had finished before the British and French had been able to act, but this was not going to happen a third time.

THE WAR MOVES NORTH

King Haakon VII of Norway was woken in the early hours of 9 April 1940 to be told that his country's neutrality had been violated and that Norway was now at war. The startled king could only ask: 'With whom?'

The question was not as peculiar as it sounded. Norway had been jealously guarding her neutrality, but her strategic importance on the eastern side of the North Sea could not be overlooked either by the Allies or by the Germans. The Norwegian port of Narvik was the only all-weather port through which Swedish iron ore could reach Germany, and the ore trade was vital to the German armaments industry. Understandably, the Allies were eager for this trade to cease. As for the Norwegians, they were aware of British plans to mine their territorial waters and force German ore ships out into the open sea where the Royal Navy could deal with them. It was obvious that any British action was bound to provoke a violent German response, but faced with a choice between the devil and the deep blue sea, the Norwegians could only watch, wait and hope.

After the conquest of Poland, Hitler had ignored Scandinavia as he focused all his energies on plans to attack France. However, Grand Admiral Erich Raeder, chief of the Kriegsmarine, the German Navy, had other ideas. He believed that not only would an invasion of Norway secure the sea lanes for importing Swedish iron ore, it would

ABOVE: LETTERS HOME –
A WELL DUG IN GERMAN
SOLDIER IN NORWAY TAKES
TIME OUT TO WRITE BACK
TO THE FATHERLAND.

LEFT: THE GERMAN POCKET
BATTLESHIP THE ADMIRAL
GRAF SPEE GOES DOWN OFF
URUGUAY AFTER BEING
TRAPPED BY THE ROYAL
NAVY, WHO HAD CHASED IT
FOR SEVERAL DAYS DESPITE
BEING OUTGUNNED.

also serve to give Germany naval bases in the Atlantic from which U-boats could attack the Allied supply routes to America.

Then, on 13 December 1939, the Royal Navy dealt the Germans a great humiliation with their destruction of the pocket battleship *Admiral Graf Spee* outside Montevideo, Uruguay. Later, on 16 February 1940, the Royal Navy liberated 300 British sailors held prisoner in Josing fjord on board the prison ship *Altmark*, which, ironically, had once served as *Graf Spee*'s supply ship. An enraged Hitler suddenly became more interested in Raeder's plans.

The Allies also had their eyes on Norway. First Lord of the Admiralty, Winston Churchill, was increasingly concerned that the Germans would move north after the defeat of Finland. Churchill pressed for action, but despite the public pressure on both Chamberlain and the new French Prime Minister, Paul Reynaud, who had replaced Daladier in March 1940, little was actually done. Britain and France seemed unable to agree on any joint plan of action, but eventually decided that the mining of Norwegian waters would go ahead on 8 April. British minelayers accordingly set sail on 6 April. On 5 April, in what was to become a masterpiece of bad timing, Neville Chamberlain declared to the House of Commons that Hitler had 'missed the bus'.

The Norwegian Government, preoccupied with the presence of the Royal Navy, never even saw the Germans coming. Surprise was total. On 9 April, the world's first parachute force was used in combat and speedily captured Norway's major airports at the capital, Oslo, and at Stavanger. Troops were put ashore at Narvik, Trondheim, Bergen, Kristiansand and Oslo.

Denmark, too, was invaded at the same time to secure the land routes into Norway. The Danish Government, stunned by the speed of the German invasion, capitulated at 6 a.m. on the same day.

Norway resolved to fight the invader, but the nation's defences were poor. There were no tanks, no anti-aircraft weapons and, for the sake of economy, the Norwegian Navy, which was in proud possession of two of the world's oldest battleships, had not left port since 1918. To make matters even

THE INVASION OF NORWAY

GERMAN
→ Seaborne landings and attacks
▽ Paratroop landings

ALLIES
→ Norwegian landings and attacks
⇠ Withdrawls

9 April 1940
German forces land simultaneously at Oslo, Kristiansand, Stavanger, Bergen, Trondheim and Narvik

NORWEGIAN SEA

Glowworm sunk X

SWEDEN

Königsberg sunk X

Altmark boarded X

Karlsruhe sunk

9 April 1940
German forces occupy Denmark

Harstad · Bjerkvik · Narvik · Bodo · Mo-i-rana · Mosjöen · Namsos · Steinkjer · Hegra · Trondheim · Molde · Dragset · Andalsnes · Tynset · Alesund · Dombas · Kvam · Rendal · NORWAY · Lillehammer · Elverum · Honefoss · Bergen · Kongsberg · OSLO · Stavanger · Arendal · *Blücher* sunk · *Lützow* damaged · SKAGERRAK · Aalborg · DENMARK · COPENHAGEN

EVACUATION

As the German Army began its march into Poland on Friday, 1 September 1939, millions of British children and their teachers together with expectant mothers left Britain's metropolitan centres and headed for the safety of the countryside, where the German bombers were thought less likely to strike. Over the first weekend, more than 700,000 children were evacuated from London alone, prompting a *Times'* leader writer to explain that London looked as if it had been visited by the Pied Piper of Hamelin. The British evacuated more of its children than any other country during the War, a total of well over three million. The exodus was organised by local government bodies and schools.

With their address labels hanging round their necks and clutching their few belongings and gas masks, children were often taken to school by their parents, who then wished them farewell as they made their way from there to the local station in a single group. The experience of individual evacuees and those who billeted them differed widely. Many children from the cities had never before seen the countryside and found it idyllic. Others, however, found themselves the unwelcome guests of those who had been forced to take them in. Some carers of these city children were astounded at the condition of many poor evacuees, some of whom were covered in lice and raggedly dressed. Some did not even know how to use a knife and fork and had precious little toilet training. These revelations were to have their effect in forcing the British to realise that something had to be done to

A WELCOME INVASION: BRITAIN'S CITY KIDS ARRIVE IN THE SAFETY OF THE COUNTRY.

improve the lot of these waifs. This, in turn, had its effect on the creation of the Welfare State in Britain after the war.

As the Phoney War continued, the vast majority of evacuated children, who were greatly missed by their parents, drifted back to the cities, only to depart again when the Blitz began in September 1940.

Those children who were left in the cities had little to do. Most schools were closed, badly affecting their education and leading in some cases to increased juvenile delinquency

worse, the defence minister was a former pacifist, and the commander of the army, General Kristian Laake, was incompetent.

By contrast, King Haakon, originally a Danish prince who had been elected to the throne of Norway in 1905, was an inspirational monarch who, from the first, exemplified Norwegian resistance to the Germans. Despite setbacks, therefore, the Norwegian defence in 1940 was resolute. The German cruiser *Blucher* entered Oslo fjord only to find itself falling victim to a devastating attack from an onshore battery of 19th-century cannon. Though antiquated, the firepower was effective. The cruiser was crippled and over 1000 Germans died as aviation fuel and ammunition caught fire and exploded. This setback for the Nazis gave King Haakon and his government time to escape from the capital and move north to continue the fight.

This, however, left a power vacuum in Oslo, and an eccentric Nazi sympathiser, Vidkun Quisling, whose name later became a synonym for 'traitor', stepped into it to form a collaborationist regime. This simply enraged the Norwegians and spurred them on to further resistance.

The Allies, acting quickly on this occasion, immediately offered to aid the beleaguered Norwegians. British and French forces reached Norway on 14 April, five days after the

The Norwegian Navy, which was in proud possession of two of the world's oldest battleships, had not left port since 1918. To make matters even worse, the defence minister was a former pacifist

'You have sat too long here for any good that you have been doing …Depart I say, and let us have done with you. In the name of God, go!'
Conservative MP Leo Amery to Neville Chamberlain, in the House of Commons, May 1940

ABOVE: LONDONERS FLOCK TO WATCH PARLIAMENT ASSEMBLE. THE NATION'S FUTURE HUNG IN THE BALANCE WHILE PARLIAMENT DEBATED THE DIRECTION OF THE WAR.

LEFT: COMETH THE HOUR, COMETH THE MAN. AFTER THE STORMY DEBATES IN THE HOUSE OF COMMONS, WINSTON CHURCHILL EMERGED AS BRITAIN'S NEW PRIME MINISTER.

Germans, but in stark contrast to their enemies, their effort was poorly planned, ill-equipped and badly executed. If liaison between the British and the French was bad enough, then between the Allies and the Norwegians it was little short of abysmal.

Allied troops were given little air cover and few anti-aircraft weapons. They were not properly trained for the Arctic conditions and confusion reigned among their commanders over objectives. Supplies were sent to the wrong places and were badly damaged in transit. The Labour opposition leader, Clement Attlee, was furious with the British Government's conduct of the war, and expressed his view bluntly: 'In a life and death struggle, we cannot afford to leave our destinies in the hands of failures.' A House of Common debate on the situation ensued. It was scheduled for 7–9 May 1940, and when he entered the House, Chamberlain was greeted with raucous cries of: 'Who missed the bus?'

Winston Churchill, nevertheless, tenaciously defended the government's record, but the broadsides delivered by one of their own MPs, Leo Amery, proved too much. In a direct address to Chamberlain he quoted Oliver Cromwell, using the same words the Lord Protector had addressed to the Rump Parliament in 1653: 'You have sat too long here for any good that you have been doing,' said Amery. 'Depart I say, and let us have done with you. In the name of God, go!'

When a vote of confidence was taken at the close of the debate, the government's majority was so critically reduced that Chamberlain was forced to consider resignation. The coup de grâce was delivered when the Labour Party made clear its refusal to serve under Chamberlain in a National Coalition Government. With that, Chamberlain had no choice but to go. Winston Churchill, 64 years old, and a man untainted by pre-war appeasement, was chosen as Britain's new prime minister. Meanwhile, the first German units began to push for the Ardennes, in Belgium, to begin the invasion of France and western Europe.

This, however, was ultimately to seal the Norwegians' fate. Resistance to the invaders continued for two months, denying the Germans the relatively easy victory they had won in Poland. But the Allies' help was crucial. When the Nazi invasion of western Europe reached its height during June 1940, and Britain was under threat, the Allied forces were withdrawn from Norway on 8 and 9 June. This enabled the Germans to complete their conquest and Norway, too, fell under the heel of the Nazi jackboot.

King Haakon and his government sailed away with the Allies and, like the Polish General Sikorski, set up a government-in-exile in London, where he remained until the end of the war.

CARELESS TALK MAY COST HIS LIFE
DON'T TALK ABOUT AERODROMES or AIRCRAFT FACTORIES

ABOVE: A BRITISH PROPAGANDA POSTER UNDERLINES THE CRUCIAL ROLE PLAYED BY THE ROYAL AIR FORCE IN THE DEFENCE OF BRITAIN. WITHOUT THOSE WHOM CHURCHILL LABELLED THE 'FEW' BRITAIN WOULD HAVE BEEN UNABLE TO PREVENT A NAZI INVASION.

CHAPTER 4

The Fall of France

ACHTUNG PANZER! A GERMAN PANZER DIVISION UNDER
THE COMMAND OF GENERAL ERWIN ROMMEL PLOUGHS
THROUGH THE FRENCH COUNTRYSIDE AS THE WAR IN
THE WEST FINALLY GETS UNDER WAY.

OPERATION YELLOW

On 10 May 1940, the Phoney War came to an abrupt end as Hitler's armies moved into France and the neutral Low Countries – Belgium, the Netherlands and Luxembourg. The war in the west was finally under way. The speed of the German invasion and the skill with which it was executed took the Allies and the neutrals by surprise. German paratroopers captured key bridges in the Netherlands, where they were aided in part by Dutch Nazis disguised as military police. Meanwhile, 78 paratroopers landed gliders on what was described as the world's greatest fortress, Eben Emael, on the Albert Canal in Belgium. Next day, the Germans captured the fortress and the key defensive positions it commanded with the aid of

RIGHT: GERMANY'S ELITE PARATROOPERS. THESE MEN HAVE JUST PULLED OFF THE IMPRESSIVE STUNT OF CAPTURING THE 'WORLD'S STRONGEST FORTRESS', EBEN EMEAL IN BELGIUM, IN JUST 24 HOURS.

BELOW: THE 51ST HIGHLAND DIVISION SURRENDERS AT VALERY-EN-CAUX. ROMMEL (LEFT) STANDS NEXT TO MAJOR GENERAL VICTOR FORTUNE.

explosive charges. They lost only six men in the process.

Hitler had mobilised 136 divisions, over 2000 tanks and more than 4000 planes against the Allies in the hope of conquering France in a single knockout blow before wheeling his armies around to the east and attacking Russia. There, Hitler aimed to defeat Stalin, his ally, which would leave Germany free to colonise eastern Europe and, at the same time, deal worldwide communism a mortal blow.

As the Nazis began their assault on France and the Low Countries, the neutrals immediately asked the Allies for assistance. Accordingly, the cream of the British and French armies now moved north to take up defensive positions along the Dyle Line in Belgium. Unfortunately, their movements were just as Hitler had predicted and before the Allied armies could move forward to take up their new positions, Nazi paratroopers were already overwhelming the Belgian defenders. The Germans gave the Allies no time to set up firm defences in either the Netherlands or Belgium. The day before he launched the attack, codenamed Operation Yellow or 'Fall Gelb', Hitler told his generals: 'Gentlemen, you are about to witness the most famous victory in history.' Although the risks he was taking were enormous, Hitler was not far wrong.

The German paratroopers fighting to secure the bridges and communications in the Netherlands and Belgium were only part of one of the three German Army groups now advancing on the Allies. Hitler had divided his 136 divisions into three main groups. Army Group B under General von Bock moved into Belgium. Army Group C under General Ritter von Leeb advanced against the Maginot Line on the Franco–German border, with the intention of keeping the 400,000 men garrisoned there tied down. Both these attacks had been anticipated by the Allies, but what they failed to predict was the route taken by Army Group A, which, under General von Runstedt, possessed the greater part of Germany's armoured divisions.

Following a plan put to him by General von Manstein, the outstanding German strategist of the war, Hitler sent Army Group A with its seven panzer divisions through the Belgian Ardennes. This, of course, exposed the great weakness of the much-vaunted Maginot Line, which ended at the Franco–Belgian frontier. When the Line was built in 1935–6, it had not been thought right to place this massively strong defence line along the border of a friendly country, but the omission was a fatal one. Some reassurance had been drawn from the notion that the Germans could not penetrate the heavily wooded terrain of the Ardennes at the western end of the Maginot Line. Certainly, the Allies never imagined that the German tanks could get through. Therefore, the French had felt it unnecessary to place top-class soldiers close to the Ardennes. In fact, the French forces in

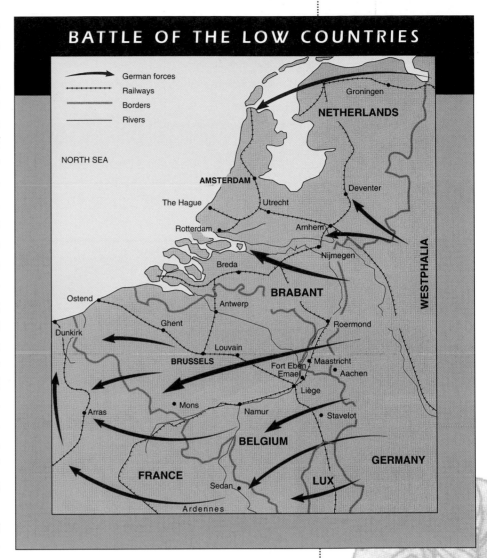

BATTLE OF THE LOW COUNTRIES

German forces
Railways
Borders
Rivers

NORTH SEA

NETHERLANDS
Groningen
AMSTERDAM
Deventer
The Hague
Utrecht
Rotterdam
Arnhem
Nijmegen
Breda
BRABANT
WESTPHALIA
Ostend
Antwerp
Ghent
Roermond
Dunkirk
Louvain
BRUSSELS
Fort Eben Emael
Maastricht
Aachen
Liège
Mons
Namur
Stavelot
BELGIUM
Arras
GERMANY
FRANCE
Sedan
LUX
Ardennes

the area, General Corap's 9th Army and General Huntziger's 2nd Army, were not of the highest quality.

The Germans, however, confounded all expectations, circumventing the Maginot Line, pushing through the Ardennes and emerging in good order on 12 May. Even then, the French were not unduly concerned. But what they failed to realise was that the forces now massing on the opposite bank of the River Meuse comprised the main force of the German attack. According to military textbooks of the First World War, which were still regarded as relevant 20 years later, the Germans would take several days to cross the Meuse. In the event, the received military wisdom got it wrong again. General Erwin von Rommel, commanding the 7th Panzer Division at Dinant and General Hans Guderian, a tank expert, commanding the 2nd and 10th Panzer Divisions at Sedan, were across the river in a single day. By 13 May, both generals, aided by the German terror dive-bombers and tanks, had crossed the Meuse with frightening speed, using captured footbridges, pontoons and rubber boats.

Just as they managed to establish a panzer bridgehead on the western banks of the Meuse with unprecedented speed, so the Germans were eager to break out into the countryside of north-eastern France and force their way towards the Channel coast. When he

heard the news that the Germans had crossed the Meuse and taken Sedan, the French General Alphonse Georges, Commander of the North-East Front, burst into tears.

Within days of their attack, the Germans had managed to tear a hole in the Allied lines that the Allies would never manage to plug. On the same day, the Dutch port of Rotterdam was bombed by the Luftwaffe and over 800 civilians were killed. Just one day later, on 14 May, the Dutch Army, which had not fought a war since 1830, surrendered. The Dutch Queen, Wilhelmina, fled to England.

Winston Churchill, who had become British prime minister on 10 May, the same day as the German invasion of western Europe, flew to Paris to discuss the rapidly deteriorating situation with his French allies. Churchill was appalled by both the scene and the news that greeted him. At the Quai d'Orsay, officials of the French foreign ministry were burning government papers in huge bonfires. It was a dark portent of the impending French defeat and the country's future.

As the Allied front began to collapse, Churchill asked the French Commander-in-Chief, General Gamelin, which troops he was going to use to shore up the widening gap in the Allied line. Gamelin dumbfounded Churchill by saying he had no troops to spare. Without a mobile reserve to stop it, the German advance could now proceed virtually at will.

Realising the situation was desperate, French Prime Minister Reynaud sought a replacement for his Commander-in-Chief. Banking on the reassurance of past successes, Reynaud sent for two heroes of the First World War: General Maxime Weygand, aged 73, was to replace Gamelin, and Marshal Philippe Petain, 84, was to serve as Reynaud's deputy.

Meanwhile, the Germans continued their race for the Channel, following the line of the River Somme, where they had succeeded in opening up a 'panzer corridor' between the Allied armies fighting in Belgium and northern France, and those positioned further south towards Paris. As German armour fought its way to the sea, the Allies mistakenly assumed they were heading for the French capital. This had been Hitler's intention all along and he was correct when he observed that the Allies had 'failed to appreciate the basic idea of our operations'.

On 20 May, the Germans reached Abbeville and by 21 May had established themselves on the Channel coast. The Allied armies, including the British Expeditionary Force, had been separated from their supplies and communications and were effectively cut in two. The obvious course of action would have been to counter-attack in force, separating the

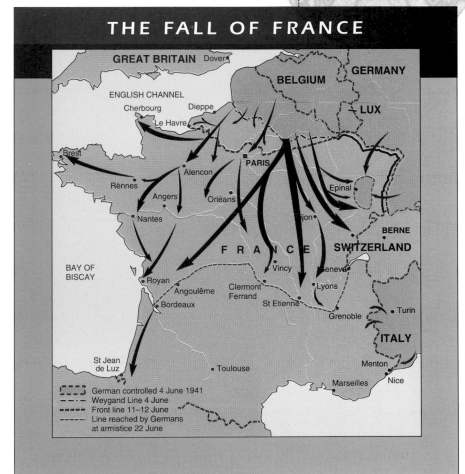

THE FALL OF FRANCE

German controlled 4 June 1941
Weygand Line 4 June
Front line 11–12 June
Line reached by Germans at armistice 22 June

German tanks at the head of the 'panzer corridor' from the infantry and supplies following behind them. But neither the French nor the British were capable of such a move. The speed of the German blitzkrieg was something no Allied general had contemplated before the war. In order to mount an effective counter-attack, the Allies needed time – something that Hitler was certainly not prepared to give them.

DUNKIRK: THE SCENES ON THE BEACHES

As May 1940 drew to its close and the speed of the German advance caused increasing British fear for the safety of its army in France, steps were taken to evacuate the rear echelons of the British Expeditionary Force. As the situation darkened, British and French frontline troops retreating to the Dunkirk perimeter found that, fortunately, the local countryside was ideal for fighting a rearguard action. But it was here that the breakdown of the Franco–British alliance became clear. While the French were hoping to defend Dunkirk, the British were retreating back to their island home and did not intend to leave anything behind that could help the enemy. Consequently, in one incident, British troops took 28lb sledgehammers to their brand-new lorries, trucks and Bren gun carriers, but when the French refused to do the same, the two sides almost came to blows.

The shallow beaches at Dunkirk, which afforded precious little draught, made the evacuation extraordinarily difficult for Royal Navy vessels and also for the civilian volunteers, who between them brought nearly 900 'little ships' across the Channel. Before their rescue, troops were forced to stand out in the water while small craft, many owned by British or Belgian fishermen, took them on board and ferried them to the larger ships further offshore. Most men were prepared to queue in an orderly fashion, but some officers managed to maintain discipline only at gunpoint.

Conditions on the beaches were appalling. Much of Dunkirk was on fire and the smell of burning machinery and corpses hung oppressively over the shoreline. The RAF, which lost over 170 planes in the process, did its best to provide air cover for the stranded soldiers, but due to limited resources, the British and French troops were left unprotected for periods of half an hour or even 90 minutes. That was when they were exposed, helpless, to the ministrations of the Luftwaffe. During this time, German planes were able to bomb the beaches and the shallows at will.

Nor was the ordeal of the British 'Tommies' finished once they had managed to board a rescue ship. German aircraft, torpedo boats and U-boats operating in the Channel claimed many lives. Nevertheless, 338,226 exhausted men returned safely to Britain.

The evacuation lasted 10 tense, perilous days, and once back home, the Tommies were greeted by volunteers and the Salvation Army offering tea, cigarettes and pork pies.

TOP: BRITISH TRUCKS AND ARMOUR LIE DESTROYED AFTER THE BEF'S WITHDRAWAL FROM FRANCE, JUNE 1940. ABOVE: BATTERED TOMMIES DISEMBARK IN SOUTHERN ENGLAND AFTER THEIR SAFE RETURN FROM THE HORRORS OF THE BEACHES AND THE LUFTWAFFE'S PURSUIT ACROSS THE CHANNEL.

With the evacuation complete, Prime Minister Churchill, speaking to the House of Commons, made clear to the Germans and whoever else was listening, that Britain's resolve to fight on was absolute. Dunkirk, as Churchill reminded the House, may have been a defeat, but he said: 'We shall fight in France, we shall fight on the seas and oceans, we shall fight with growing confidence and growing strength in the air, we shall defend our island whatever the cost may be. We shall fight on the beaches, we shall fight on the landing grounds, we shall fight in the fields and in the streets, we shall fight in the hills. We shall never surrender!'

DUNKIRK

On 19 May 1940, the British Commander, Lord Gort, finally realised that the British Expeditionary Force was now surrounded. He issued orders to start preparations to evacuate British forces from France should this become necessary. The situation was grave in the extreme. If the British Expeditionary Force was destroyed or captured, Britain would be without an army with which to defend itself from a German invasion, if and when it came. The Belgian Army to the north was absorbing the full fury of the German attack. Should the Belgians fail, nothing would stand in the way of the German forces and Dunkirk, France's fourth-largest port and the British Expeditionary Force's only means of exit. Of the alternatives, Boulogne was captured by the 7th Panzers on 21 May and the British garrison at Calais was isolated on 22–3 May.

LEFT: THE FACE OF DEFEAT. A FRENCH PRISONER IS LED AWAY BY HIS GERMAN CAPTORS. THE SPEED OF THE GERMAN VICTORY IN FRANCE BELIES THE COURAGE DISPLAYED BY THE FRENCH IN RESISTING THE INVADER.

The British were somewhat secretive about telling their ally that preparations were afoot for a British evacuation from the Continent. The French had been counting on sup-

FREE FRENCH SOLDIERS TRAIN IN SOUTHERN ENGLAND FOR THEIR HOMELAND'S EVENTUAL LIBERATION FROM THE NAZIS.

DE GAULLE AND THE FREE FRENCH

As the French Government collapsed and Marshal Petain took it upon himself to make peace with the Germans, Brigadier-General Charles de Gaulle escaped to Britain. On 18 June, he began the task of organising French resistance to the Nazis. Speaking on BBC radio from London, he rejected outright the verdict of the battlefield, declaring: 'This war has not been decided by the battle of France. This is a world war.'

De Gaulle's defiance of the Germans was spirited but seemed to have little hope of bearing fruit as the whole of the French Empire at first rejected his call against the collaborationist Petain. Later, while French territories in north Africa – Algeria, Tunisia, Morocco – remained loyal to Vichy, further-flung territories, such as Cameroon in west Africa, switched allegiance to de Gaulle and the Free French. Above all, de Gaulle had sown the seeds of the Free French movement, which the British recognised as the legitimate government of France 10 days after de Gaulle's broadcast, on 28 June.

Over the ensuing years, with both British and American help, de Gaulle was able to keep an organised French fighting force in the field, and eventually led them in triumph through liberated Paris in 1944.

ABOVE: BRITISH TROOPS
SNATCH A FEW MOMENTS
REST AS THEY RETREAT
THROUGH FRANCE IN THE
SUMMER OF 1940. UNLIKE
THEIR FATHERS 20 YEARS
EARLIER, THESE TOMMIES
WERE GIVEN NO CHANCE TO
DIG IN AND FIGHT.

port from Lord Gort to mount a counter-attack, but although he was officially under French command, Gort had other priorities. He used the troops earmarked for operations with the French to give support to the rapidly disintegrating Belgian Army. Gort's decision probably saved the British Expeditionary Force, but he earned no plaudits from the French. But even with Gort's aid, the Belgians were no longer capable of mounting effective resistance. After struggling valiantly for 18 days and losing over 6000 men killed, King Leopold III decided enough was enough: Belgium surrendered on 28 May. The French were furious and Reynaud quickly labelled Leopold a traitor. The king was hardly that, since, unlike Haakon of Norway and Wilhelmina of the Netherlands, he had decided to stay with his people and bear the pain of German occupation with them. Reynaud's accusation was unjust but, though Churchill knew this, he did little to challenge it.

Two days before Leopold's surrender, the Royal Navy began ferrying British troops from Dunkirk back to England. The disastrous defeat suffered by the Allies in France was softened only by the success of the Royal Navy, and the hundreds of civilian vessels – the 'little ships' – which volunteered their help in carrying the British troops home. From there, with the help of the vast and unconquered British Empire, they could carry on the fight against Nazism. But this deliverance was made possible only by the bravery of the Belgian Army in the days before its collapse and by the fierce resistance offered the Germans by the French 1st Army at Lille. The vigour of the RAF also counted for a great deal

NEWS CHRONICLE, Wednesday, June 5, 1940.

News Chronicle

No. 29,355   ONE PENNY   WEDNESDAY, JUNE 5, 1940   RADIO, PAGE 7

"We shall defend our island whatever the cost may be. We shall fight on the beaches, we shall fight on the landing grounds, in the fields, in the streets and in the hills. We shall never surrender."—Mr. Churchill

335,000 MEN EVACUATED

Men of the B.E.F. assembled with French troops on the beach at Dunkirk, ready to be taken off by the Navy.
MORE PICTURES OF THE EVACUATION ARE ON THE BACK PAGE.

Dunkirk at Last Abandoned : The Withdrawal Complete

LAST night the French Admiralty and the British War Office announced that Dunkirk has now been abandoned by the Allies after the most remarkable withdrawal in military history.

In the House of Commons during the afternoon Mr. Churchill (whose speech is fully reported on this page and Page Three) declared that no fewer than 335,000 British and French troops had been evacuated from the port.

B.E.F. losses were : 30,000 killed, wounded and missing ; 1,000 guns and all transport and armoured vehicles lost.

LATE NEWS

Nazis Bomb Havre Again

PARIS. — German planes bombed Havre district for second night in succession. Raid lasted hour.—B.U.P.

U.S. Minister's Warning

NEW YORK.— If England and France are conquered, America will be next objective," said Mr. Wallace, U.S. Secretary of Agriculture, in a broadcast. He called for economic as well as military preparedness.—Reuter.

Italy is Still Prepared
—Says Rome

Reynaud Tells Italy, Door Open

Telephone communication between Italy and France has been cut, it was announced in Rome last night, says B.U.P.

PREMIER PREDICTS ANOTHER BLOW AT THE ALLIES SOON

By E. CLEPHAN PALMER
The Parliamentary Correspondent

THE full gravity of the military position was brought before the House of Commons last night by the Prime Minister in a speech of matchless oratory, uncompromising candour and indomitable courage.

Call-Up Speed-Up This Month

BELOW: GERMAN SOLDIERS ENTER THE FIERCELY BURNING TOWN OF ROUEN.

ABOVE: THE BRITISH TABLOID PAPER THE NEWS CHRONICLE LENDS ITS HAND TO ONE THE MOST SENSATIONAL PIECES OF POLITICAL 'SPIN' IN HISTORY. AIDED BY CHURCHILL'S TRULY INSPIRATIONAL CALL TO ARMS UNDER THE MAST HEAD, THE PAPER BEGINS TURNING THE BRITISH EXPEDITIONARY FORCE'S ABSOLUTE DEFEAT IN FRANCE INTO THE 'MIRACLE' OF THE DUNKIRK EVACUATION.

and so did the daring of the Royal Navy, the tenacious fighting spirit of the British Expeditionary Force and, most ironically, a serious miscalculation on the part of Adolf Hitler.

With the British Expeditionary Force surrounded, the Belgians on the verge of capitulation and the French Army in total disarray, the Germans had their opponents at their mercy, with a string of successes behind them hardly ever matched in the history of warfare. Yet, at this juncture on 26 May, Hitler ordered his panzer divisions to halt. They remained halted for two days, but even then did not resume their assaults for another eight days. This was to prove a fatal mistake and one that may have ultimately cost Hitler the war, but the reasoning behind it seemed rational enough at the time.

Hitler knew he needed to preserve the majority of his armour for the coming assault on Paris, and the Chief of the Luftwaffe, the flamboyant Hermann Göring, vainly assured his Führer that his air force could prevent any evacuation by the British. At this time, of course, the Luftwaffe had not yet encountered an air force anywhere near its equal. What

The French were furious and Reynaud quickly labelled Leopold a traitor. The king was hardly that, since, unlike Haakon of Norway and Wilhelmina of the Netherlands, he had decided to stay with his people and bear the pain of German occupation with them

neither Hitler nor Göring realised, therefore, was that the RAF was going to be the first such force to give as good as – if not better than – it got. The RAF possessed a fighting spirit the Germans had not yet encountered.

Operation Dynamo, the code name given to the evacuation of Dunkirk, was carried out under the direction of Vice-Admiral Ramsay. It was a truly perilous mission. The Royal Navy was forced to engage ships in extremely shallow waters while under ferocious attack from the Luftwaffe, but then the stakes could not have been higher. Estimates varied concerning how many men the Royal Navy could successfully retrieve and return to England, but the figure, officials believed, would not rise above 50,000. It was a gross underestimation. Miraculously, or so it appeared, between 26 May and 3 June 1940, a total of 338,226 British and French troops were taken safely across the Channel. Of these, over 100,000 were French, but all of them returned to France more or less at once, where they continued with ever-increasing vigour to challenge the German advance, even though this was by now a hopeless task.

THE FALL OF FRANCE

The German tanks began to roll forward once more on 5 June. The new Allied front, named the Weygand Line after its French creator, was hastily put into place and although the military strategy behind Weygand's final roll of the dice was sound, he did not have the resources to put it into proper effect.

The Belgians, the Dutch and, to a large extent, the British were all out of the fighting, and the French Army itself had lost one-third of its strength. Despite desperate French pleas, Churchill, after grim warnings from the head of the RAF, Air Marshal Sir

RIGHT: THE 6TH AND 7TH RIFLE REGIMENTS AND THE 7TH MOTOR CYCLE REGIMENT OF ROMMEL'S 7TH PANZER DIVISION ADVANCE ACROSS THE FIELDS OF FRANCE. THEIR COMMANDER WAS TO NOTE WITH SURPRISE THAT AS THE FRENCH NEARED EVER CLOSER TO DEFEAT THEIR RESISTANCE CONTINUED TO STIFFEN.

Hugh Dowding, was not willing to commit any more RAF aircraft to the fight against the Germans in case the defence of Britain was compromised. In days, Hitler's forces were crossing the Seine and rapidly approaching Paris. The French, unable to halt or even slow down the German advance, declared Paris an open city in the hope of saving it from the fighting and consequent destruction.

RIGHT: ON THE ROAD.
REFUGEES SALVAGE WHAT
FEW BELONGINGS THEY CAN
AS THEY TAKE TO THE
ROAD, NORTHERN FRANCE,
JUNE 1940.

BELOW: MARSHAL PETAIN
(LEFT) SHAKES HANDS WITH
HITLER (RIGHT) AND
INITIATES A FOUR-YEAR
PERIOD OF COLLABORATION
WITH NAZI GERMANY.

Under the strain of the German victories and the French collapse, which now seemed inevitable, the alliance betwen Britain and France was falling apart. As the German forces approached the French capital, leading figures in the French Government began to accept the idea that France would have to sign a separate peace treaty with Germany, even though this was contrary to their alliance with the British. Churchill hoped to combat

French defeatism by attempting to draw the USA into the fighting on the Allied side. He hoped this would keep the French in the war, but American President Roosevelt would not play ball: the USA, he told Churchill, was going to remain neutral. On 16 June, Churchill even suggested a Franco–British Union that would effectively make the two countries into one, with common citizenship. The French would have none of that. They had been traditional enemies with Britain for seven centuries before coming together for mutual defence against Germany with the Entente Cordiale of 1904. Some residual enmity remained and, in 1940, the French were not about to sink their identity into that of an ex-foe who was, in their view, proposing to leave them to their fate.

Meanwhile, German soldiers had already marched into Paris in triumph, on 14 June, watched by numbed crowds in which many were shedding bitter tears of grief and humiliation. But, dreadful as this was, it was only the culmination of a fearful week for the French. On 10 June, the French Government had fled Paris, and on the same day, Hitler's ally Benito Mussolini brought Italy into the war on the Nazi side. Mussolini had repeatedly told Hitler that Italy would be unable to embark on a major European conflict until 1943, but Mussolini was afraid that unless he entered the fray now, he would never realise his dream of setting up a new Roman Empire and turning the whole Mediterranean into an 'Italian lake'. Mussolini was also convinced that Hitler was well on the way to winning the war; and the winning side was the place to be.

ABOVE: HITLER STANDS IN THE RAILWAY CARRIAGE IN THE COMPIÈGNE FOREST, WHERE GERMANY SIGNED THE ARMISTICE THAT ENDED THE FIRST WORLD WAR. HERE, IN HITLER'S PRESENCE, THE GERMAN GENERAL KIETEL READ THE HUMILIATING CONDITIONS OF THE FRENCH SURRENDER IN 1940 TO THE GATHERED DELEGATES OF THE FRENCH GOVERNMENT.

ABOVE: A NAZI PROPAGAN-
DA POSTER THAT READS: 'YOU
HAVE THE KEY TO THE CAMPS.
FRENCH WORKERS YOU CAN
FREE THE PRISONERS BY
WORKING IN GERMANY.' IF
THE FRENCH DIDN'T WORK
FOR THE NAZIS, THEIR COM-
RADES HELD CAPTIVE IN
GERMANY WOULD NEVER
BE RETURNED.

RIGHT: HITLER VISITED THE
FRENCH CAPITAL THE DAY
AFTER THE ARMISTICE
AGREEMENT WAS SIGNED.
HE LEFT THE CITY SAYING
'I AM GRATEFUL TO FATE TO
HAVE SEEN THIS TOWN
WHOSE AURA HAS ALWAYS
PREOCCUPIED ME.'

Next day, with the Norwegian surrender on 11 June, Norway became the seventh
country to capitulate to the Nazis. But the eighth would soon follow.

With most of his cabinet unwilling to continue the fight, Reynaud resigned and, on 17
June, Philippe Petain opened peace negotiations with the Germans. By 22 June, the peace
terms had been agreed and France was, for the moment, out of the fight. The aged Petain

WAR'S FIRST CASUALTY

AMERICA FIRST COMMITTEE

141 West Jackson Boulevard
CHICAGO

THE AMERICA FIRST COMMITTEE WAS SET UP AFTER THE FALL OF FRANCE WITH THE EXPRESS PURPOSE OF KEEPING THE US NEUTRAL.

THE USA AND THE FALL OF FRANCE

Both the American public and politicians alike had been little more than spectators in the European war since its outbreak and the defeat of France by the Nazis. Although it aroused American sympathy, it did little to persuade them to enter the war on the Allied side. The USA had had little desire to repeat the experience of the First World War. President Roosevelt closely identified himself with the Allied cause but his hands were tied by the Neutrality Acts passed by an isolationist Congress and pacifist public in 1936 and he could do little to help the British and French democracies as they struggled first to contain Hitler and then to avoid destruction on the battlefield. Despite his desire to see the Allies defeat Hitler, Roosevelt was a consummate politician who realised there was no desire on the part of the American people to involve themselves in another European war. This lack of action on the part of the USA led to the rather acid comment by Chamberlain that 'It is always best and safest to count on nothing from the Americans but words.' The Fall of France, however, led to a change of attitude. Churchill pleaded with Roosevelt to declare war on the Germans days before the French surrender. The president refused but he did agree to send 500,000 rifles, 80,000 machine-guns, 130,000,000 rounds of ammunition, 900 75mm field guns and 1,000,000 shells to the British. It was a brave act. These resources constituted a large part of the supplies the USA had reserved for her own defence and as France fell under the rule of the Nazis, Britain's future as an independent power was by no means secure. As Hitler began his preparations for the invasion of Britain many Americans expressed grave concern that they could soon find the weapons they had so recently given to Britain being used against them.

imagined that he was retrieving some honour for France, but the peace terms barely allowed France to continue as a sovereign state. She was, however, allowed to keep her overseas colonies, and acquired, in the south, a nominally French government under Petain, while the north was to remain under German occupation. Petain set up his headquarters in the spa town of Vichy, which gave his government its name, and embarked on a policy of collaboration with the Nazi conquerors in the north.

Collaboration was, however, passionately rejected by a young and till then unknown French commander, Brigadier-General Charles de Gaulle. De Gaulle had made a dramatic escape from France by jumping into a moving aircraft as it taxied for take-off bound for England. He totally refused to accept the French defeat as final. On 18 June, in a seminal radio broadcast from London, de Gaulle pledged to keep the flame of French resistance alive and invited all who could to join his Free French forces. Britain had now given sanctuary to yet another exile, and for all De Gaulle's passion and his talk of resistance, the sombre fact remained that his homeland was now prostrate before her conqueror and Britain was left to face the might and fury of Nazi Germany alone.

For all De Gaulle's passion and his talk of resistance, the sombre fact remained that his homeland was now prostrate before her conqueror and Britain was left to face the might and fury of Nazi Germany alone

CHAPTER 5

Britain Stands Alone

THE DOCKS IN LONDON'S EAST END BURN, CASTING A
HUGE PALL OF SMOKE OVER TOWER BRIDGE AND THE TOWER
OF LONDON. WITH THE BATTLE FOR FRANCE OVER, THE
BATTLE OF BRITAIN WAS SOON IN FULL SWING.

BELOW: WHAT DID YOU DO
IN THE WAR MUMMY? MRS
T. CHARLESWORTH WORKED
IN MUNITIONS, WHERE SHE
USED A LATHE TO FASHION
17-POUNDER GUN CHAM-
BERS. BRITAIN CONSCRIPTED
WOMEN INTO THE WAR
EFFORT, A STEP TAKEN BY
NEITHER GERMANY NOR
THE USA.

OPERATION SEALION

With the French out of the war, the British, together with their Empire, were left to fight the Nazis alone. This plight would last for exactly one year, and during that time, the outcome of hostilities and the future of the entire world hung on whether or not Britain's ability to resist the Nazis.

The days after the Fall of France were therefore crucial to British morale. While the growing spirit of defiance, which Winston Churchill was starting to personify, was taking hold in the minds of many civilians, there were still those in high places who had come to believe that making peace with Hitler was the only sensible option. Their number included former prime minister Neville Chamberlain, the incumbent Foreign Secretary, Lord Halifax, and David Lloyd George, who had been Liberal prime minister during the First World War. They reasoned that with France under occupation and the Americans still holding back, Britain was unlikely to fight the war to a successful conclusion. Peace, therefore, seemed the only recourse. This same attitude lingered in the minds of some of those men of the British Expeditionary Force who had barely managed to return from France after the Wehrmacht had driven them, in many cases quite literally, into the sea. After this shattering experience, some were convinced that Britain could not fight on against such a deadly and determined foe. Besides, they believed, Britain had very little with which to fight Hitler. The British Expeditionary Force had destroyed all its heavy equipment during the retreat from France. Everything, from trucks and tanks to Bren gun carriers, had been smashed or left behind. Army units

ABOVE: THE SPITFIRE, THE SPEARHEAD OF BRITAIN'S LAST-DITCH FIGHT
AGAINST NAZI INVASION.

SPITFIRE

The Supermarine Spitfire is credited by many, whether justly or not, as the plane that won the Battle of Britain, although the less glamorous Hawker Hurricane actually shot down more German aircraft. The Spitfire, however, is remembered with greater affection. Everything about this aircraft seemed romantic, from its aerodynamic shape, to the brave young men who flew it in 1940, to the self-sacrifice of the designer R.J. Mitchell, who worked himself to death to produce it. It was an incredibly agile plane for its day and its 1030hp Rolls Royce Merlin engine gave it a top speed of over 360mph, not far from the practical limit for propeller-driven aircraft during the war. Armed with eight Browning 303mm machine-guns, it was more than capable of wreaking destruction on the slow-moving German bombers that got in its way. In 1940, it made up about one-third of Fighter Command's frontline strength during the Battle of Britain, the rest being made up by the Hurricane. In all, the Spitfire ran to 16 different variants.

RIGHT: HITLER AND HIS STAFF LOOK OUT ACROSS THE CHANNEL COAST TO ENGLAND. ONCE FRANCE HAD SURRENDERED IN LATE JUNE, HITLER HOPED TO INVADE BRITAIN BY SEPTEMBER. IT WAS TO PROVE AN IMPOSSIBLE TASK.

RIGHT: HITLER AND HIS STAFF LOOK OUT ACROSS THE CHANNEL COAST TO ENGLAND. ONCE FRANCE HAD SURRENDERED IN LATE JUNE, HITLER HOPED TO INVADE BRITAIN BY SEPTEMBER. IT WAS TO PROVE AN IMPOSSIBLE TASK.

LEFT: MEN OF THE SS VERFUGUNSTRUPPE LOAD ARTILLERY ON TO AN INVASION BARGE IN PREPARATION FOR THE 'INVASION OF BRITAIN', SUMMER 1940. WITHOUT WINNING AIR SUPREMACY, THESE MEN AND THEIR SHIPS WOULD PROVE SITTING DUCKS ONCE IN THE CHANNEL. WHILE THE RAF HELD OUT, BRITAIN WAS SAFE.

presently being formed in Britain had little equipment more lethal than heavy machine-guns. Surely then, the argument went, if the Germans invaded Britain, they could cut through what remained of the British Army like a knife through butter.

Some outside observers were also convinced that Britain's chances of survival were slim. Joseph Kennedy, the American ambassador to Britain, told President Roosevelt that the country's defeat was imminent. Hitler, too, thought the British were beaten but were simply too foolish to recognise it. However, the British demonstrated their 'foolishness' when His Majesty's government ignored Hitler's peace overtures. As far as the Führer was concerned, there would be no second chance. On 16 July 1940, therefore, he ordered preparations for the invasion of Britain, code-named Operation Sealion.

OPERATION SEALION

Gloucester   St Albans   Maldon   NORTH SEA

SCHELDE ESTUARY

Oxford

LONDON

Bristol

Rochester   Ramsgate   Ostend

GREAT BRITAIN

Reigate   Folkestone   Dover   BELG.

Dunkirk

Southampton   Portsmouth   Bexhill   Calais

Brighton   Eastbourne   Boulogne

Lyme Regis

Ventnor   Isle of Wight

FRANCE

Army Group A

Airborne landings

1st Connected bridgehead

1st Objective

- - - - - - 2nd Objective

Le Havre

Cherbourg

Channel Islands   **Army Group B**

0	Miles	60
0	Kilometres	100

Although the situation was desperate, there remained one vital defence: the English Channel, which more than once in the past had saved the British from invasion. This strip of water might be narrow, but its weather patterns were unpredictable and as a barrier it was backed by two further obstacles – the Royal Air Force and the Royal Navy. There was no hope that an invasion would be successful unless Germany could smash the RAF and win control of the skies over England, then neutralise the Navy. These defences had to be broken down first, and Hitler gave the job to his deputy, the Commander-in-Chief of the Luftwaffe, Hermann Göring.

The German Army and Navy were not keen on Hitler's plans, however. The Kriegsmarine had not yet recovered from the mauling it had suffered during the invasion of Norway and the army lacked the necessary resources to mount a full-scale invasion. The vainglorious Göring, though, was confident that he could crush the British. His confidence, if overweening, seemed well founded. Until now, Göring's Luftwaffe had carried all before it, proving itself the vital spearhead for the Wehrmacht's assaults on Poland, Norway and western Europe. Now, Göring believed, the Luftwaffe could step out from the supporting cast and carve out a strategic role of its own,

THE COCKNEY HEART

IMPREGNABLE TARGET

ABOVE: THE 'COCKNEY HEART': LONDON EVENING STANDARD CARTOON.

one that no air force had ever before achieved: the destruction of an opponent without the interference of either army or navy, a triumph all their own.

This was easier said than done. Right from the start, the Luftwaffe was engaged in a race against time. As the first skirmishes of the air war began over the English Channel in mid-July, Göring had only two months to seize supremacy in the air over Britain before 15 September, the date that Hitler had set for the completion of the invasion preparations.

The Luftwaffe had to overcome serious setbacks if it were to succeed. As its previous role had confined it to supporting attacks by the army, it lacked a heavy bomber with which to inflict fatal damage on the British defences and war industry. Furthermore, the British would have the advantage of fighting over their own home territory, giving them longer flying time over the combat zone. If they were shot down and survived, British pilots could bail out and fight again another day. But Luftwaffe pilots in the same position would become prisoners of war.

However, even more fatefully, the Luftwaffe also lacked a clear overall strategy with which to deliver a knockout blow to Britain. The priorities and objectives of the German High Command shifted constantly during the

THE MESSERSCHMITT BF109 – THE SPITFIRE'S DUELLING PARTNER.

MESSERSCHMITT BF 109E

The Messerschmitt Bf 109 was the Spitfire's chief opponent during the Battle of Britain. It was, in fact, the most frequently manufactured German fighter of the war. As a fighter, the Me-109 was at least the equal of the Spitfire, but it suffered from several key limitations, including problems with wing design and a cockpit that gave pilots poor visibility. Most crucially for the dogfights that took place over southern England during the summer of 1940, the Me-109 had a poor range that severely curtailed its flying time over enemy territory. Its main role during the battle was to escort the Heinkel 111s and the Dornier bombers. For this task, it was euipped with two 7.92mm machine guns and 2x20mm cannon. The Me-109's 1100hp Daimler Benz engine gave it a top speed of 354mph.

OPPOSITE PAGE (BOTTOM): YOUNG BOY SCOUTS HELP TO STRETCH BRITAIN'S LIMITED RESOURCES AS FAR AS POSSIBLE. BRITAIN EXISTED IN A STATE OF SIEGE FOR MUCH OF THE WAR, AND BY COLLECTING WASTE PAPER FOR SALVAGE THESE SCOUTS WERE HELPING TO FREE UP SPACE IN THE ATLANTIC CONVOYS FOR ESSENTIAL WAR MATERIALS.

battle, from targeting shipping, to striking at aerodromes and factories, until finally settling on heavy bombing of civilians in London. This was a truly fatal mistake. Destroying the RAF on the ground was what the Luftwaffe really needed to do. Instead, they attempted to break civilian morale and so terrify the British into submission. But Londoners' nerve never broke. If anything, the bombing increased their will to resist.

In addition, the Luftwaffe's change-and-change-about tactics gave the British vital breathing spaces. The island nation may have appeared to the Nazis to be a sitting target – a view that was to some extent shared by the British people. However, the British were resolved to survive. As for their enemies, the built-in drawbacks of fighting a long-range battle were amplified by the Nazis' many strategic mistakes. Whatever advantage they may have had, they effectively threw away.

Nevertheless, the danger in which Britain stood in the summer of 1940 – a beautiful, clear, warm summer ideal for uninterrupted aerial combat – could hardly have been more grave.

The man given the demanding and awesome task of organising Britain's air defences was Air Chief Marshal Sir Hugh Dowding, Commander-in-Chief of RAF Fighter Command. No one was better suited to it. Dowding, who was as reserved as Göring was vain and boastful, had spent the previous four years preparing Britain's air defences for just such an eventuality. Using the latest technology, Britain had installed a chain of radar stations running along the coast from Orkney in the far north down to Cornwall in the extreme south-west. The radar stations, along with the men and women of the Observation Corps, would track enemy planes as they approached their targets. The waiting squadrons of Spitfires and Hurricanes could then be 'scrambled' to intercept the invaders. Radar also gave Dowding the ability to husband his scarce resources carefully. This advantage was to prove vital as the German attack pushed Britain's precious reserves of pilots to the very limit.

Britain was fortunate, too, in possessing the latest fighter technology in the shape of the Hawker Hurricane and the Supermarine Spitfire. The Spitfire's designer, R.J. Mitchell, had virtually sacrificed his life to prepare a fighter that could, and would, one day have to challenge the Luftwaffe in the struggle for Britain's survival. Though he was suffering from cancer, Mitchell defied doctor's orders to work on the Spitfire, which he developed from the seaplane that had won Britain the Schneider Trophy outright in 1931. Mitchell, sadly, never lived to see the Spitfire's finest hour in the Battle of Britain. He died, at the age of 42, in 1937.

It was 1939 before the Spitfires and the Hurricanes started arriving with the RAF in appreciable numbers. However, the RAF had suffered severe losses both during the Battle of France and while defending the British Expeditionary Force on the exposed beaches of Dunkirk. Winston Churchill, realising that the future of Britain depended on there being sufficient numbers of fighters to repel the Nazis, gave the job of marshalling aircraft production to Lord Beaverbrook, the maverick Canadian newspaper publisher. Under Beaverbrook's eccentric management, housewives were encouraged to part with their aluminium pots and pans to make fighter aircraft. The results were mixed, and not always crucial to the war effort, but Dowding never lacked planes and British production vastly outstripped that of the Germans. In fact, Dowding had more planes at his disposal after the Battle of Britain than before it. However, the really critical shortfall was the scarce supply of trained and experienced pilots.

BELOW: CHILDREN FILL SAND BAGS AS A DEFENCE AGAINST GERMAN AIR ATTACK. THE BLITZ WAS NO RESPECTER OF AGE.

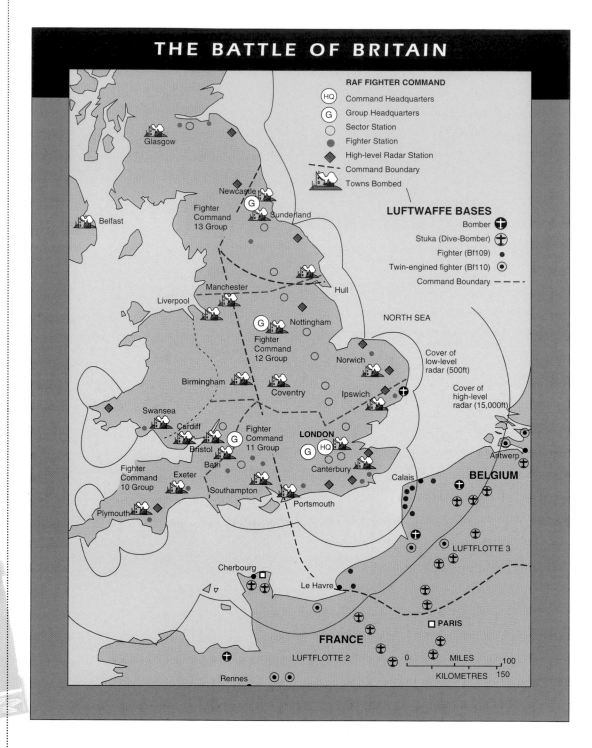

After concentrating his opening shots on British shipping in the Channel, Göring turned his attention to the destruction of Fighter Command. With an arrogance typical of the man, he intended to deliver the RAF a single, overwhelming knockout blow. The date, 13 August 1940, was code-named 'Adlertag', Eagle Day. For the next week, German fighters – the Messerschmitt Bf 109s and the slightly less manoeuvrable Me 110s, along with Dornier and Heinkel bombers – attempted to batter the RAF into submission. Although the combat proved indecisive, the RAF gave better than it got and forced Göring to change tack. Dowding, anxious to conserve RAF strength, was not allowing his fighters to attack their German counterparts head on. Instead, he instructed them to attack the more

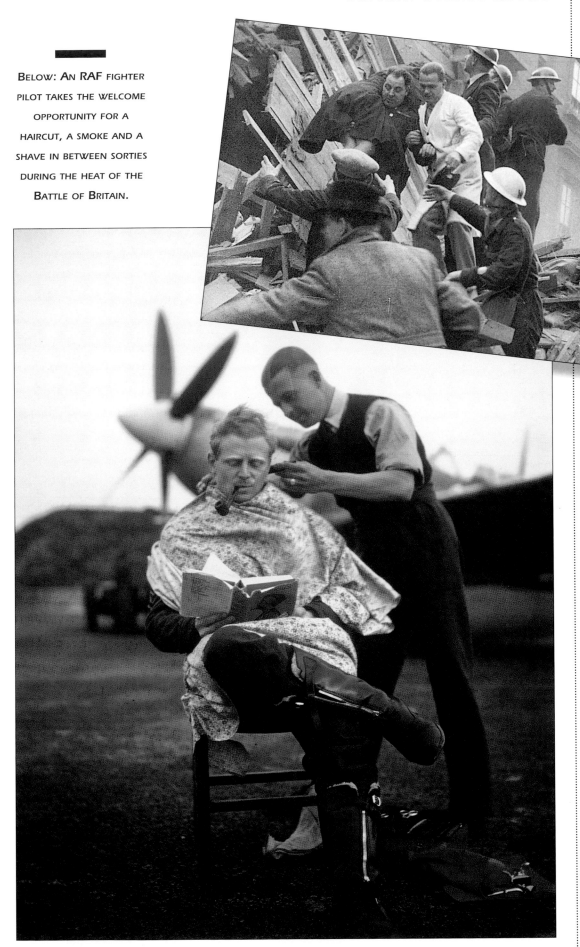

BELOW: AN RAF FIGHTER
PILOT TAKES THE WELCOME
OPPORTUNITY FOR A
HAIRCUT, A SMOKE AND A
SHAVE IN BETWEEN SORTIES
DURING THE HEAT OF THE
BATTLE OF BRITAIN.

ABOVE: RESCUE WORKERS
PULL THE INJURED FROM
THE RUBBLE OF WHAT HAD
BEEN, ONLY MINUTES
EARLIER, THEIR HOMES.
LONDON TOOK A BEATING
DURING THE BLITZ YET,
REMARKABLY, DESPITE THE
INTENSE PRESSURE OF
NIGHTLY BOMBING RAIDS,
OFFICIALLY RECORDED
INCIDENCES OF MENTAL
ILLNESS FELL – AS DID
THOSE FOR SUICIDE.

> To meet the emergency, new pilot training was cut from six months to six weeks. These young men had, in many cases, never fired guns in anger before setting out to do battle...and by the beginning of August, when the full fury of battle was approaching, only half of Dowding's pilots had actually been in combat

vulnerable German bombers. Seeing this, Göring decided to pick targets the British would definitely have to defend. He chose the RAF aerodromes.

It was between 24 August and 6 September that the Germans came closest to victory. Though Dowding's frontline strength never fell below some 600 planes during this fortnight, he was, despite all his care, losing more of them than could be replaced, and his most experienced pilots were either exhausted or dead. To meet the emergency, new pilot training was cut from six months to six weeks. These young men had, in many cases, never fired guns in anger before setting out to do battle. Some had very little experience of flying Hurricanes at all, and by the beginning of August, when the full fury of battle was approaching, only half of Dowding's pilots had actually been in combat.

The new type of warfare that characterised the aerial battle of Britain was carried out at unprecedented speeds. The Spitfire had a top speed of over 360mph and demanded pilots of the highest quality. They had to have exceptionally keen eyesight as well as lightning-quick reactions. Most successful 'kills' of enemy aircraft happened at extremely close range, often less than 100 metres, and ammunition was available only in very short bursts. The Spitfire, for instance, carried enough for a mere 14 seconds of firing. The German Bf 109, however, had even less. Both planes were frequently in the air for little over an hour at a time. After flying from bases in France, the Bf 109 had not much more than 30 minutes combat time over southern England, and pilots from both sides could expect to make

WINSTON CHURCHILL

Winston Churchill, who was 64 when he became prime minister on 10 May 1940, on the same day Nazi forces invaded western Europe, had had a long and varied political career that began when he first entered Parliament in 1900. First Lord of the Admiralty in 1911–15, he became chancellor of the exchequer for the period 1924 to 1929. Afterwards, though, he spent 10 years in the political wilderness, labelled as a warmonger for his perpetual warning against the menace of Nazi Germany. Churchill returned to the Cabinet as First Lord of the Admiralty once again at the outbreak of war in 1939. When he was appointed prime minister, coming to power when Britain faced the greatest emergency in its history, Churchill said that he felt his whole long life had been preparing him for this one great challenge. A great war leader, though less effective afterwards in peacetime, it was under Churchill's passionate, committed leadership that the British developed the will to fight on against Hitler in 1940, when any rational analysis of their plight would have counselled surrender. But Churchill was not a rational politician. He was romantic and emotional, with a devotion to democracy and the British Empire to sustain his unshakeable belief in Britain's ultimate triumph, however black and fearful the future might seem. His greatest gift, apart from the energy he displayed in prosecuting the war, was his ability to communicate this confidence and optimism in speeches that have since rivalled Shakespeare for their quotability. Churchill's stirring rhetoric, written out in the form of blank verse, touched a chord in the British people and inspired them to mammoth efforts. He helped both to define and inspire the fighting confidence they needed to survive their finest, but also their darkest, hour as the beleaguered island fought on alone against the Nazis for a whole year after the Fall of France.

CHURCHILL DISPLAYS LIONHEARTED DEFIANCE IN THE FACE OF THE NAZI THREAT.

several sorties a day. The strain was almost unbearable. Some pilots would return unhurt to base after being shot down, only to be put at once into a new plane to carry on the fight.

After a while, the Spitfire and Messerschmitt Me 109 acquired a legendary reputation as latterday knights jousting in the air much as medieval warriors had once challenged each other in the lists. The pilots, who included a large number of Poles, were heroes every one, young men who one moment sat nonchalantly in armchairs on the sun-drenched airfields, reading newspapers, playing cards, telling jokes, and the next were leaping for their cockpits and roaring off to do battle. However, the pilots on both sides never forgot their grim purpose, survival for one, victory for the other. Neither did the people who watched their 'dogfights' from fields and streets in southern England. In the extraordinarily clear and sunny summer of 1940, they knew that, as they watched the rivals wheel, manoeuvre and fire high up in the brilliant skies above, they were watching their fate being worked out.

Göring, naturally, was impatient. He was keen for the battle to reach a conclusion and though his tactics seemed to be paying off, he was not getting the results he wanted fast enough. Over-optimistic German intelligence reports had encouraged Göring to believe that the RAF was at breaking point and had far fewer planes than was actually the case. Consequently, Göring was convinced that just one more push would finish off the British, so he changed target yet again.

On 7 September, hundreds of German bombers, with their fighter escorts, headed for London, and while Fighter Command stood by to defend their vital airfields, German bombs fell almost unchallenged on the capital. The battle of London had begun.

On that bright, sunny Sunday afternoon, the Germans made a beeline for London's docks. They did not stop coming until the early hours of Monday morning. The first wave opened up with incendiary bombs, providing a beacon of burning buildings for the bombers that followed. The whole of London possessed only 92 anti-aircraft guns with which to meet the crisis, and as Fighter Command had been wrong-footed by the Germans' change of target, the city was virtually undefended. The docks around Tower

ABOVE TOP: THE DAILY MIRROR ON 16 SEPTEMBER 1940. THE FRONT-PAGE SPLASH, PROCLAIMING 'BOMB HIT QUEEN'S APARTMENT', DISPLAYS THE LEVELLING EFFECT OF THE BLITZ IN GRAPHIC FASHION.

ABOVE LEFT: BETTER SAFE THAN SORRY. A BABY FITS SNUGLY INSIDE ITS ALL-ENCOMPASSING GAS MASK.

London's East End became one terrible, all-consuming bonfire. Over 400 Londoners were killed during this, the first night of 'the Blitz'. The blaze in the docks was so fierce that one fire officer told his superior to 'send all the bloody pumps you've got – the whole bloody world's on fire'

Bridge and the residential areas of London's East End became one terrible, all-consuming bonfire. Over 400 Londoners were killed during this, the first night of 'the Blitz'. The blaze in the docks was so fierce that one fire officer told his superior to 'send all the bloody pumps you've got – the whole bloody world's on fire'. For the next 76 nights, bar one, London was bombed over and over again.

The following Sunday, 15 September, saw the climax of the Battle of Britain. That day, according to the BBC, 185 Luftwaffe aircraft were shot down over London. That day, too, Winston Churchill was watching the German attacks being plotted on maps at RAF Fighter Group 11 at Uxbridge, Middlesex, 15 miles west–north-west of London. During the fighting over London and southern England, Churchill watched with mounting tension as all the available RAF units were committed to the battle. Eventually, he knew, there would be no squadrons left in reserve. Yet, despite pushing the RAF to the very edge, the Luftwaffe again suffered the heavier losses and, more importantly, they were shocked to see that the RAF could still put formidable numbers of planes in the air. It was becoming increasingly apparent to the Germans that the RAF was not finished at all and that their intelligence reports had been crucially wrong.

Even worse, as far as the Germans were concerned, was what all this meant: Göring had failed in his attempt to gain control of the skies over England. Without that vital supremacy, there was no point in carrying on. On 17 September, therefore, Hitler postponed the invasion of Britain 'indefinitely'.

Even so, the Germans had by no means finished raiding Britain and, though the Luftwaffe could always be sure of a defiant reception by the RAF in daytime, by night their bombers were able to operate in much greater safety.

RIGHT: A DOUBLE-DECKER LONDON BUS FALLS INTO THE CRATER LEFT BY A DIRECT HIT ON THE UNDERGROUND TUBE LINE IN BALHAM, SOUTH LONDON. MANY LONDONERS WERE SHELTERING IN THE TUNNELS UNDERNEATH. THERE WERE OVER 600 CASUALTIES.

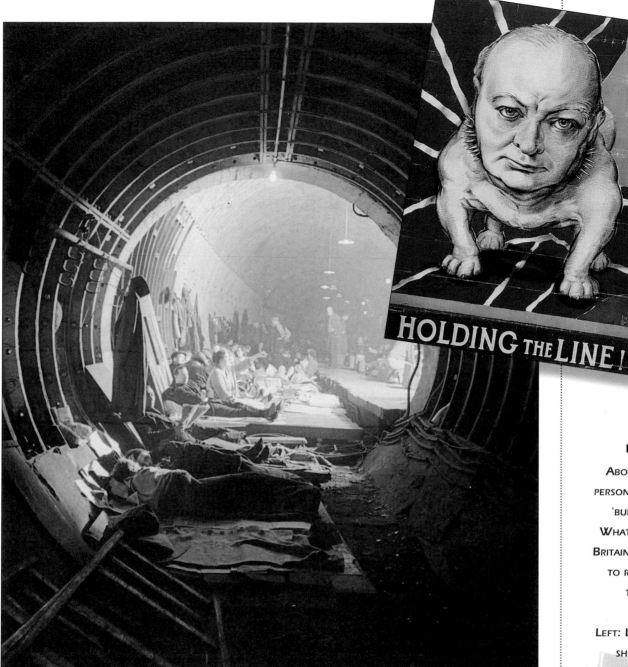

HOLDING the LINE !

ABOVE: CHURCHILL
PERSONIFIES THE BRITISH
'BULLDOG SPIRIT'.
WHATEVER THE COST,
BRITAIN WAS NOT GOING
TO ROLL OVER FOR
THE NAZIS.

LEFT: LONDONERS TAKE
SHELTER IN THE
CAPITAL'S SUBWAY SYSTEM.
THE UNDERGROUND
HAD ORIGINALLY BEEN
DESIGNATED AS 'STRICTLY
NO ADMITTANCE' DURING
AIR RAIDS. BUT, AFTER
PRESSURE FROM THE CITY'S
INHABITANTS, THE TUBE
WAS OPENED UP DURING
RAIDS DESPITE FEARS FROM
THE AUTHORITIES THAT
SOME MAY NEVER RETURN
TO THE SURFACE.

THE BLITZ

Britain had suffered bombing raids by Zeppelins during the First World War, but the experience, though terrifying and unprecedented, had been limited. The Blitz, however, brought civilians right into the front line in a way never before experienced in the whole of British history. Bombing raids on British towns and cities meant that the battlefield had now intruded into the very homes of ordinary civilians. The one place in which people had always been able to feel safe was no longer secure. But they were not entirely helpless. In their struggle against the Luftwaffe, the public could count on, or indeed join, one of the many networks of interlocking civilian organisations that had been established during the run-up to war to deal with German air attacks.

Air raid wardens – both men and women – were given the responsibility of enforcing the blackout and reporting hits in their areas, while firemen tackled the blazes as heavy rescue squads attempted to dig civilians from the rubble. First-aid posts and shelters for those made homeless by the bombs were organised, as were daredevil teams from the Royal Engineers who dealt with the removal and destruction of unexploded bombs.

The Blitz proved the sternest of tests for the British people. They were not invariably cheery and smiling, as has often been depicted. They suffered fear and depression. Their nerves could be shot to shreds. But overall, and despite often woeful preparations by certain local authorities and the inadequate resources of central government, the people proved equal to the challenge. Providing air raid shelters was often a problem, though. Over two million Anderson shelters, strong, above-ground structures designed to house a family during raids, had been distributed free of charge by the time of the first big night-time raids. In addition to Andersons and the Morrison shelters that were sunk into garden lawns, larger public shelters were erected in many streets. Some people, however, never used them and chose to remain in their own homes. In London, the underground subway was used as a deep shelter. This was never in government plans. The people just moved in and many regularly slept on the platforms in the bunks that were afterwards installed. Many, sadly, emerged next morning to find their streets or their houses a mess of rubble and smoke, with wardens picking over the ruins in the hope of finding survivors. The space beneath sturdy railway bridges also served as shelters, but there were drawbacks: the sanitation in the underground and in some of the larger public shelters was poor. It was

BELOW: A TASTE OF THINGS TO COME? GERMAN SOLDIERS MARCH IN THE CHANNEL ISLANDS, THE ONLY PIECE OF BRITISH TERRITORY TO BE OCCUPIED BY THE NAZIS DURING THE WAR. THE ISLANDS, CLOSER TO FRANCE THAN BRITAIN, REMAINED IN GERMAN HANDS UNTIL VE DAY, AFTER BEING 'DEMILITARISED' BY THE BRITISH DURING THE FALL OF FRANCE.

THE BRITISH EMPIRE

The British Empire, now long gone, was the mightiest overseas empire the world has ever known. At its zenith, at the end of the 19th century, Britain ruled over one quarter of the world's surface and one quarter of its population. It was said, with truth, that the 'sun never set' on the British Empire because its territories were so far-flung across the globe.

Though past its heyday, the Empire was still a formidable proposition during the Second World War. Despite lacking allies after the Fall of France on 22 June 1940, until the German invasion of Russia on 22 June 1941, Britain was able to draw on the support, manpower and resources of this huge empire. There was also the advantage that most Empire territories were well beyond the reach of Nazi Germany or the other 'Axis' powers, Italy and Japan. That meant that factory production in, for example, New Zealand, was completely safe from attack, and Canada, where pilots were trained, was likewise far from danger.

When Britain declared war on 3 September 1939, Canada, Australia and New Zealand followed immediately, and after some hesitation – and by only one vote – so too did South Africa. These were the self-ruling dominions of the Empire and they had also followed Britain into war in 1914. However, their attitude by 1939 had changed somewhat. The dominions were keen to maintain as much independence of action from Britain as possible. In Australia, for instance, memories of the appalling fate of thousands of ANZAC troops at Gallipoli in 1915, and the belief that they had been sacrificed for the sake of the much more valued British soldiers, were still fresh enough for caution.

India, where the British Raj had united the continent and flourished after 1757, was in a different category. This 'jewel in the crown of the empire' was Britain's largest colony and was brought into the war by the British Viceroy, the second Marquess of Linlithgow. His failure to consult the Indians, whose leaders Mahatma Gandhi and Pandit Nehru were imprisoned during the war along with their families, caused a great deal of bitterness and resentment.

Many of the pilots who fought in the Battle of Britain were Canadian, and Australian troops fought with distinction in the Middle East, Asia and the Pacific. The Indian Army bore the brunt of the fighting against the Japanese in Burma. The same applied to the Ghurkas from Nepal, even though Nepal was not part of the Empire.

The Empire gave Britain far more punch than it could possibly have had on its own, but the war placed it under an intolerable strain. Defeats at the hands of the Japanese in Singapore in 1942 and the political exigencies of the war in India allowed subject peoples to see the British as

TOP: A MEMBER OF THE BRITISH INDIAN ARMY DESERTS TO JOIN UP WITH THE JAPANESE-SPONSORED INDIAN NATIONAL ARMY. ABOVE: MEMBERS OF THE AUSTRALIAN AND NEW ZEALAND ARMY CORPS LEAVE MELBOURNE AND SET SAIL TO JOIN IN THE EMPIRE'S WAR EFFORT.

vulnerable and not so mighty as they may have formerly believed. This helped to advance already existing movements aiming at independence. The Indian Congress Party, in fact, had been working for freedom since 1880, and, perhaps appropriately, India, with Pakistan, was the first to be granted independence, on 15 August 1947. This was the first of many breakaways, although the old empire later evolved into the British Commonwealth, many of whose members are former colonies.

also, occasionally, the cause of some fear that the morals of the young were being corrupted by spending the night in close company with members of the opposite sex.

Although London was the main focus for the Blitz, many ports and centres of industry across the nation were also hit; among them were Southampton, Portsmouth, Birmingham, Derby, Sheffield, Liverpool, Manchester, Clydebank and Glasgow. However, by far the most notorious raid on a British provincial town took place on the night of 14 November 1940.

That night, over 500 German bombers made their way to the industrial centre of Coventry. Their targets were

ABOVE: THIS HOSPITAL IN LONDON WAS HIT THREE TIMES, FINALLY FORCING THE PATIENTS TO BE EVACUATED. MANY OF BRITAIN'S RED CROSS VOLUNTEERS HAD BEEN CIVILIANS ONLY MONTHS EARLIER. THEY WERE TO RECEIVE THEIR BAPTISM OF FIRE IN THE AUTUMN AND WINTER OF 1940.

RIGHT: THE MORRISON SHELTER. NAMED AFTER HOME SECRETARY HERBERT MORRISON, THIS INDOOR SHELTER WAS DESIGNED TO PROVIDE PROTECTION FROM BOMBS FOR THE WHOLE FAMILY. THE WIRE MESH ON THE SIDES WAS REINFORCED BY A STEEL PLATE ON THE TOP OF THE STRUCTURE.

the many industrial, armaments and aero-engine plants situated around the town. One German news agency boasted that the raid was the 'most severe...in the whole history of war'. Over 500 people were killed and war production was badly slowed for many months. The entire heart of medieval Coventry, including its beautiful 14th-century cathedral, was gutted. In a town almost laid waste, thousands became homeless overnight. The raid had the proportions of an atrocity and gave the language a new verb: 'to coventrate', or destroy totally.

This massive concentration of German bombers on one town came close to breaking local morale. Coventry was not a large place, and everyone could claim to know at least one of the many victims. Businesses were destroyed, phone lines were decimated, transport services were all but useless and rationing had to be abandoned. But the Germans failed to follow up their success on the next night. Instead, they turned their attention elsewhere, and despite all the destruction and suffering Coventry endured, no lasting damage was done to the British war effort.

Even so, the mindless decimation and loss of life at Coventry stunned the British people. Worse, though, was the fact that as the war in the air grew ever more sophisticated, the losses suffered at Coventry, horrific as they were, later paled into insignificance. And not only in Britain. The RAF, too, wreaked carnage and ruin, at Dresden, where, in 1945, over 100,000 Germans were killed by squadrons sent by Air Marshal Sir Arthur 'Bomber' Harris, who believed the war could be won simply by bombing Germany to extinction.

Fortunately, the Blitz was finite, and the time came when Londoners and others no longer greeted night-time with fear and trepidation, wondering whether they, or their families and their homes would still be there in the morning. The Blitz was nearing its end by the early summer of 1941, the reason being that Hitler had picked other victims. It was then that he began to look once more to the conquest of Soviet Russia.

Fortunately, the Blitz was finite, and the time came when Londoners and others no longer greeted night-time with fear and trepidation, wondering whether they, or their families and their homes would still be there in the morning

LEFT: AFTERMATH. COVENTRY EMERGES INTO THE DAYLIGHT AFTER A NIGHT THAT WITNESSED THE MOST SUSTAINED AIR RAID OF THE BLITZ. OVER 400 GERMAN BOMBERS EMPTIED THEIR BOMB BAYS, DESTROYING THE CITY AND LEAVING 500 DEAD.

CHAPTER 6

The Balkan Campaign

GERMAN TANKS ROLL THROUGH THE STREETS
OF BUCHAREST, SEPTEMBER 1941, FOLLOWING ROMANIA'S
SIGNING OF THE TRIPARTITE PACT.

THE BALKAN CAMPAIGN

Badly equipped and poorly prepared, the advancing Italian troops walked into a massacre. Not only did they have no idea why they were going to war, they had little combat experience or training. It was an experience that soldiers of the Italian Army would find repeated many times

On 10 June 1940, Benito Mussolini, Fascist dictator of Italy, declared war on France. With Paris about to fall to the Germans, Mussolini wanted to reap benefits from his Axis partner's success. In the week before the French armistice was signed on 22 June, a hastily arranged Italian offensive was launched on French positions in the Alps. The result was a military disaster.

Badly equipped and poorly prepared, the advancing Italian troops walked into a massacre. Not only did they have no idea why they were going to war, they had little combat experience or training. It was an experience that soldiers of the Italian Army would find repeated many times over the next three years, as their leader sought to emulate the astounding string of victories achieved by his ally, Adolf Hitler.

Mussolini had been planning to wage a 'parallel war' alongside Hitler, chiefly to ensure a share of the spoils, ever since the signing of the 'Pact of Steel' between Italy and Germany on 22 May 1939. Just over three months later, as Hitler's forces attacked Poland and, in 1940, northern and western Europe, Mussolini had intended to invade Yugoslavia and Greece. In the event, he was warned off getting involved in the volatile Balkans by Hitler himself.

However, the surrender of France in June 1940 meant the end of the balance of power in the Mediterranean that had previously been held by the French and British navies. This was a situation Mussolini was eager to exploit. Unsure whether or not the French Mediterranean fleet would remain loyal to the Vichy collaborationist government in France, the British had invited the French Admiral Darlan to join forces with them. When

IL DUCE – MUSSOLINI.

BENITO MUSSOLINI

Benito Mussolini, founder of the Italian Fascist Party, became prime minister of Italy in 1922. At that time, Italy was still recovering from the effects of the First World War, and the Italians were desperate for solutions to the problems of their impoverished and crime-ridden nation. After outlawing all other political parties and waging an especially vicious campaign against the communists, Mussolini set about turning Italy into a strong and unified fascist state. He wiped out his enemies at home with his private army of 'Blackshirts' and sought to build a glorious empire abroad. His invasion of Abyssinia (Ethiopia) in 1936 was a challenge to which the League of Nations could offer no practical resistance.

Mussolini's rise to power was an early inspiration to Hitler, who set up his own army of 'Brownshirts' and admired many of Mussolini's policies. However, by the time Germany and Italy formed the 'Axis' in 1936, the positions of the two leaders had been reversed, and Hitler's Germany was by far the stronger of the two nations. In 1939, relations were cemented by the signing of the 'Pact of Steel', which would eventually lead Italy to follow Germany into the Second World War.

LEFT: BRITISH TROOP REINFORCEMENTS BOUND FOR ALEXANDRIA GET THEIR FIRST GLIMPSE OF EGYPT. MANY OF THEM WERE ALSO ABOUT TO GET THEIR FIRST EXPERIENCE OF COMBAT, AS THEY ATTEMPTED TO TURN BACK THE ADVANCING ITALIAN ARMY.

Darlan had refused, Churchill authorised the Royal Navy Commander, Admiral Cunningham, to put the French fleet out of action so as to keep it out of the hands of the Germans. At the port of Alexandria, in Egypt, French ships were captured without problems, but at Mers el Kebir in Algeria the French Fleet was attacked by British guns and, except for one battle cruiser, all ships were either crippled or sunk. Over 1000 French sailors lost their lives and relations between the British and French were severely strained, even though the British had acted with great reluctance. Churchill wept in the House of Commons when he announced the news.

The sudden removal of the French military and naval presence left a vacuum in the Mediterranean that Italy was eager to fill. By default, Mussolini now had the largest air force and navy in the area, and his aims and ambitions were considerable. As far as he was concerned, the Mediterranean Sea – *Mare Nostrum*, or Our Sea – belonged to Italy as a matter of history. In an echo of the Nazi desire for *Lebensraum*, Mussolini spoke of the need to claim living space for the Italians. In private, his ultimate ambition was nothing less than the rebuilding of the ancient Roman Empire. In the Balkans, Albania had been under Italian occupation since 1939. In North Africa, Italy had control of Libya and in 1936, 500,000 Italian troops had invaded Abyssinia (Ethiopia) and Eritrea. Mussolini now expanded his horizons. The French in Algeria and Tunisia were no longer in a position to threaten his Libyan garrison and he felt confident enough to attack British interests in Africa.

On 2 September 1940, Italian troops crossed the border from Libya into Egypt, where two British divisions were stationed in defence of the Suez canal. The canal was a vital link between Britain and her empire in India and the Far East. Through it, men and matériel

At Mers el Kebir in Algeria the French Fleet was attacked by British guns and, except for one battle cruiser, all ships were either crippled or sunk. Over 1000 French sailors lost their lives and relations between the British and French were severely strained

LEFT: FOR THE BRITISH, AUSTRALIAN AND INDIAN TROOPS STATIONED ALONG THE SUEZ CANAL, DEFENCE OF EGYPT MEANT DEFENCE OF THE BRITISH EMPIRE. HERE, TROOPS OF THE BRITISH SOUTH STAFFORDSHIRE REGIMENT TAKE UP POSITIONS ON THE EGYPTIAN BORDER.

ABOVE: ITALIAN TROOPS STATIONED IN LIBYA MAN A LIGHT ANTI-AIRCRAFT GUN. ALTHOUGH THEY COULD BE BRAVE FIGHTERS, THE ITALIAN SOLDIERS WHO FOUGHT IN NORTH AFRICA AND ELSEWHERE WERE LED BY INCOMPETENT COMMANDERS. THIS INCOMPETENCE WAS TO COST THOUSANDS OF LIVES.

from Britain's overseas colonies could be shipped west to support the British war effort. If Mussolini could seize the canal, he would be able to sever Britain's supply lines at a stroke, achieving a military victory that would bring him 'the glory Italy has been seeking for three hundred years'. Led by General Graziani, the Italian Army initially advanced some 60 miles, capturing the town of Sidi Barrani, but despite Graziani's claim that he was leading 'the best colonial army in the world', they could get no further. Some 30,000 Italian soldiers were lost in the advance, while the retreating British suffered only minimal casualties. More significantly, the Italian supply lines were now stretched all the way from Tripoli to Egypt along a single, vulnerable road.

At this juncture, the British Mediterranean Fleet launched a major attack on the Italian Navy. On 11 November 1940, 21 obsolete 'Swordfish' biplanes from the Royal Navy aircraft carrier *Illustrious* attacked 28 ships of the Italian fleet in the naval base at Taranto. Twelve Swordfish carried a single torpedo each. The rest carried bombs or flares. Attacking from less than 35ft, they managed to destroy almost half the Italian ships in less than an hour for the loss of only two planes destroyed and two more damaged. At a stroke, the threat of Italian sea superiority in the Mediterranean had been removed.

A counter-attack against Italian positions in Egypt soon followed. Early in December 1940, the British retook Sidi Barrani, capturing nearly 40,000 Italian prisoners. Although they were outnumbered, the 30,000 British, Indian and Australian troops were both better trained and more mobile than the Italians. The next month, they took Tobruk in Libya and then surrounded the entire Italian 10th Army at Beda Fomm. For Britain, this was a spectacular success and might have meant all-out victory in North Africa if only the British generals Wavell and O'Connor had been allowed to continue their push towards Tripoli. For Mussolini, the adventure in Africa had soon turned into disaster. In Abyssinia, his armies were being attacked by South African and Kenyan troops as well as local partisan groups, and would surrender on 20 May 1941. In the Mediterranean, Mussolini's fleet was all but useless. His only hope for Italian glory now lay in the Balkans.

THE BALKAN CAMPAIGN

(map contents)

THE BALKAN CAMPAIGN

North Bukovina and Bessarabia June 1940 to USSR

Northern Transylvania 1940 to HUNGARY

BUDAPEST

HUNGARY

USSR

RUMANIA

13 December 1940 German enter via Hungary

Bucharest November 1940

South Dobruja 1940 to BULGARIA

Varna

SLOVENIA

CROATIA

Venice

BELGRADE

BOSNIA

YUGOSLAVIA

Dubrovnik

ITALY

ROME

Naples

Sofia

1 March German troops in Sofia and Varna

BULGARIA

28 October 1940–1 March 1941 Italian invasion of Greece

ALBANIA

Annexed to Italy 1 March 1941

MACEDONIA THRACE

GREECE

13 April 1939 Britain and France guarantee security of Greece and Rumania

Lemnos

TURKEY (neutral)

Dodecanese Italian

5 March 1941 British troops arrive

31 October 1941 British occupy Crete and Lemnos

MALTA (British)

MEDITERRANEAN SEA

CRETE

BELOW: WOMEN OF THE GREEK RESISTANCE LEAD A PARTISAN UNIT THROUGH THE MOUNTAINOUS GREEK COUNTRYSIDE. THE GREEK PEOPLE TURNED OUT TO BE FAR MORE FORMIDABLE OPPONENTS THAN MUSSOLINI HAD ANTICIPATED.

THE BALKAN CAMPAIGN

On 28 October 1940, Mussolini launched his invasion of Greece. His justification was the fact that, as Greek independence was guaranteed by Britain, the country was 'un-neutral' and therefore presented a threat to Italy. In secret, Mussolini was still in search of a swift and impressive military victory to compare with the dramatic successes of his German allies, and expected little resistance from small and impoverished Greece. He told his generals that he was ready to 'resign from being an Italian' if his men failed to defeat the Greek Army. Mussolini issued an ultimatum to the Greek King, George II, and his premier, the dictator General Metaxas, demanding that Italy be allowed to occupy Greece until the end of the war. Without waiting for an answer, the 200,000 Italian soldiers stationed in Albania moved into northern Greece. Despite Hitler's warnings not to, Italy had started a war in the Balkans.

Having seen Germany overrun western Europe in a matter of weeks, Mussolini confidently expected his own war with Greece to be over within days. He was soon proved totally wrong. The first problem the Italian Army encountered was the mountainous Greek terrain. There were few proper roads and those that did exist were in poor repair. What was more, the Italians had no maps. To make matters even worse, the winter

ABOVE: A CAPTURED GERMAN PRISONER IS SEARCHED BY LIEUTENANT COLONEL REG JONES OF THE BRITISH EXPEDITIONARY FORCE AS AN ALBANIAN FARMER LOOKS ON.

RIGHT: A BRITISH COMMANDO PATROL SETS OFF THROUGH THE MORN-ING MISTS INTO THE MOUN-TAINS OF ALBANIA . THE DIFFICULT TERRAIN AND HARSH CONDITIONS IN THE BALKANS LED TO DISASTER FOR THE ITALIANS, WHO WERE COMPLETELY UNPREPARED TO FIGHT A WAR IN SUCH CIRCUMSTANCES.

rains had begun days before the invasion was launched, and the temperature soon dropped to freezing point. Mussolini had been so confident of quick success that his troops had not been supplied with winter clothing. Thousands froze to death in the first weeks of the campaign. Mussolini then discovered that the support for the invasion that he had expect-ed, though not sought, from the Fascist-inclined government of neighbouring Bulgaria was not forthcoming, and his secret campaign of bribing Greek politicians and generals had been for nothing. In this way, Mussolini had hoped to 'fix' a speedy surrender, but his attempts at cheating had failed.

In fact, with support from the RAF, the Greeks turned out to be truly formidable oppo-nents. Aided by Albanian mercenaries, many of whom had been originally employed by the Italians, and led by the seasoned General Papagos, the Greeks counter-attacked almost immediately. Within a week, the Italian troops, already demoralised by the weather and the terrain, were being pushed back into Albania.

At that, the Italian Army command began to panic. Marshal Badoglio, the Italian Chief of Staff, was sacked for accusing Mussolini of mounting the invasion for purely political purposes. Mussolini himself went to the front to rally his troops, but could do little to halt the Italian retreat. At sea, what was left of the Italian fleet was suffering further defeats from the Royal Air Force. Mussolini's plans were coming apart. It was at this point that Hitler's patience with his Fascist ally ran out. Fearing that the British air bases established in Greece would eventually be used to threaten Germany and the oilfields in neighbouring Romania, Hitler decided to take control of the situation and invade Greece himself. In January 1941, he announced that 'for reasons of strategy, politics and psychology', Germany would come to the Italian Army's aid.

However, before his armies could march on Greece, Hitler needed to secure the support of the country's neighbours, a move that would also have the effect of securing his southern flank for the coming invasion of Russia. To this end, Yugoslavia, Hungary, Romania and Bulgaria were 'invited' to join the Tripartite Pact signed on 27 September 1940 by Germany, Italy and Japan. Hungary and Romania, both already dominated by Germany politically and economically, agreed

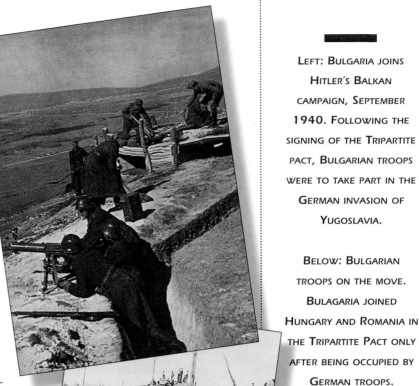

LEFT: BULGARIA JOINS HITLER'S BALKAN CAMPAIGN, SEPTEMBER 1940. FOLLOWING THE SIGNING OF THE TRIPARTITE PACT, BULGARIAN TROOPS WERE TO TAKE PART IN THE GERMAN INVASION OF YUGOSLAVIA.

BELOW: BULGARIAN TROOPS ON THE MOVE. BULAGARIA JOINED HUNGARY AND ROMANIA IN THE TRIPARTITE PACT ONLY AFTER BEING OCCUPIED BY GERMAN TROOPS.

MEN OF THE SOE AIDED PARTISAN GROUPS IN FRANCE, EUROPE AND THE BALKANS.

THE SPECIAL OPERATIONS EXECUTIVE (SOE)

Set up in July 1940 with instructions from Winston Churchill to 'set Europe ablaze', the Special Operations Executive aided partisan groups in France, western Europe and the Balkans in their resistance to German or Italian occupation throughout the war. As well as supplying manpower and expertise to guerrilla operations, the SOE also co-ordinated air drops of arms and explosives. In Greece, SOE agents infiltrated partisan villages and in Yugoslavia they struck up alliances with the Chetniks and afterwards the communist partisans led by Tito. Tito's partisans were also supplied with a wide variety of arms, from guns to tanks, by the Americans, and this assistance proved instrumental in the eventual liberation of Belgrade from German troops in 1945. Tito himself would go on to become leader of Yugoslavia after the war, maintaining an uneasy relationship with Soviet Russia.

at once. Bulgaria joined them after being occupied by German troops who had marched through Romania. Only Yugoslavia, where a military coup replaced the pro-German government within days of the country joining the Pact, signalled defiance to Germany's intentions.

Hitler was reported to be enraged. He immediately ordered that an invasion of Yugoslavia would accompany that of Greece, even though this meant putting off his plans for the assault on Russia. He called for the complete political and military destruction of Yugoslavia. On 6 April 1941, Operation Punishment began. Thirty-three German divisions marched into Yugoslavia, accompanied by a massive bombing campaign against the capital, Belgrade. Soldiers of the Yugoslav Army, many of them on horseback, fought valiantly, but could put up little effective resistance. In the 10 days before the Yugoslav Government surrendered, nearly 20,000 people were killed by Luftwaffe bombing raids alone.

Meanwhile, German troops, tanks and planes had begun pouring into Greece, where they were to have far more success than the Italians. With the Greek Army committed to fighting the retreating Italians in Albania, the country was poorly defended, despite the pres-

ence of large numbers of British troops. As soon as the German plans for the invasion of Greece became clear, Winston Churchill authorised the diversion of British forces from the North African campaign. However, this turned out to be a disastrous decision. Despite Churchill's enthusiasm for the chance to engage Hitler in Europe, the move meant losing the initiative in North Africa, where Britain was on the verge of victory. By contrast, the British Expeditionary Force that landed in Greece could do little to stem the German advance. Woefully outnumbered and outgunned, the British were obliged to retreat within days of the German invasion.

Athens fell to German troops in less than three weeks. In an echo of Dunkirk, almost 50,000 British troops were evacuated from Greece by sea under heavy fire from German aircraft. Once again, they had been forced to flee, leaving their arms and equipment behind. On 21 April, the Greek Army surrendered. Only the island of Crete, held by the RAF and a garrison of British and New Zealand troops since the beginning of

LEFT: THE YUGOSLAV ARMY
CONTAINED OVER ONE
MILLION MEN BUT WAS
BADLY EQUIPPED AND RIVEN
BY DISSENT AND OPPOSING
ETHNIC AND POLITICAL
FACTIONS.

BELOW: THE CONQUERING
GERMAN FORCES PARADE
THEIR ARMOUR THROUGH
THE STREETS OF ATHENS.
DEVASTATED BY THE LOSS
OF HIS COUNTRY, THE
GREEK PRIME MINISTER
ALEXANDER KORYZIZ
COMMITTED SUICIDE THREE
DAYS BEFORE THE GREEK
SURRENDER.

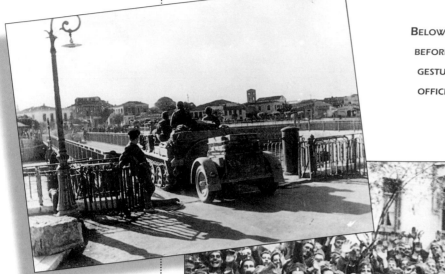

BELOW: GREEK TROOPS POSE FOR A PHOTOGRAPH IN THE DAYS
BEFORE THE SURRENDER. HITLER, IN A BIZARRELY CHIVALROUS
GESTURE, PERSONALLY ORDERED THAT SURRENDERING GREEK
OFFICERS BE ALLOWED TO KEEP THEIR CEREMONIAL SWORDS.

ABOVE: GERMAN TROOPS
MOVE QUICKLY TO OCCUPY
THE GREEK ISLANDS,
INCLUDING EUBOA,
SEEN HERE.

ABOVE: A GERMAN PARA-
TROOPER GETS THROUGH.
MANY, HOWEVER, WERE
PICKED OFF BY BRITISH
GUNS BEFORE THEY EVEN
REACHED THE GROUND.

the Italian campaign, remained briefly free from Axis control. In order to take
Crete, the German armed forces launched a massive airborne attack. Following
Luftwaffe assaults on the island's defences, the largest parachute force the world had
yet seen began dropping over Crete. They were supported by more troops following in gliders. Once these troops had captured the island's airfield, the Luftwaffe was
able to establish complete command of the area. The losses on both sides were very
great. The German parachute forces were so severely decimated that they were
never again used in significant numbers. Over 25,000 British, Australian and New
Zealand troops were lost trying to hold Crete. Again, the Royal Navy evacuated
those it could get out, losing over 30 ships and 2000 men in the process.

The Axis powers now held all of the northern Mediterranean coastline. Once
again, the German blitzkrieg had proved unstoppable. Mussolini, anxious to
make up for his military humiliation, attempted to claim as much territory as he
could from the German victory. This, in fact, suited Hitler, who had never wanted to become militarily involved in the Mediterranean in the first place. He was soon to
turn his attentions elsewhere. Nevertheless, it was made clear to the Italian dictator that,
from now on, he would be taking his orders from Berlin. The Italians were handed large
areas of Greece and Yugoslavia and soon found themselves embroiled in a guerrilla war. In
Yugoslavia, two resistance organisations, the royalist Chetniks and the communist partisans under Josip Broz, better known as Marshal Tito, declared war on both the occupying
forces and on each other. The fact that Hungary, Bulgaria and Germany were also

administering parts of Yugoslavia made the situation even more complicated. The situation in Greece was similar. There, the nationalist EDES and the communist ELAS spent as much time fighting each other as they did the occupiers. After the eventual Italian surrender in 1943, ELAS, tacitly supported by the Soviet Union, would go on to do battle with British troops flown in to prevent a communist take-over in Greece. In the meantime, Mussolini's answer to the guerrilla threat was to declare that for every Italian soldier killed, 20 hostages would be executed. Infinitely more damaging to the Greek people, though, was the mass starvation that swept the country during the occupation, killing hundreds of thousands. Mussolini's response was to claim that the Greeks had brought the situation on themselves.

The long-term consequences of Italy's ill-fated Balkan campaign were considerable. At home, Mussolini's standing would never recover from the Italian Army's humiliation at the hands of a few Greek and Albanian 'peasants'. However, by diverting the British from certain victory in North Africa, the Greek campaign gave Hitler time to send an armoured division, under the leadership of Field Marshal Erwin Rommel, to assist the Italians at Tripoli, in Libya. This would change the course of the desert war. Most significantly of all, the delay caused by the distractions in Yugoslavia and Greece would turn out to have a major effect on Hitler's next campaign: the invasion of Russia.

LEFT: JOSIP BROZ, BETTER KNOWN AS 'TITO', LED THE YUGOSLAVIAN COMMUNIST PARTISAN MOVEMENT, WHICH CONTAINED OVER 20,000 MEMBERS AT ITS HEIGHT. HOWEVER, FROM 1942 ONWARDS, TITO'S PARTISANS DEVOTED MOST OF THEIR ENERGIES TO FIGHTING RIVAL ROYALIST CHETNIKS RATHER THAN THE GERMANS.

ABOVE: SS PARATROOPS MAN LOOKOUT POSITIONS DURING A FAILED OPERATION TO TRY AND CAPTURE TITO.

LEFT: A JEWISH PARA-TROOPER TAKES UP CAMP WITH A GROUP OF PARTISANS.

CHAPTER 7

Barbarossa

THE WEHRMACHT IN ACTION TWO WEEKS BEFORE THE LAUNCH
OF OPERATION BARBAROSSA, HITLER'S ATTEMPT AT THE
CONQUEST AND TOTAL SUBJUGATION OF THE PEOPLES OF
THE SOVIET UNION.

BELOW: THE DEMORALISED
FACES OF SOVIET POWS.
BRAVE BUT POORLY
EQUIPPED, THE BELEA-
GUERED RED ARMY COULD
PUT UP LITTLE
EFFECTIVE RESISTANCE.

OPERATION BARBAROSSA

In the early hours of Sunday, 22 June 1941, a frantic radio message was received by the Soviet Army command in Moscow. Troops along the Soviet Union's western border were reporting: 'We are being fired on. What do we do?' Germany had launched the invasion of the Soviet Union, and the two greatest armies in Europe were about to confront each other in savage combat.

As early as December 1940, Adolf Hitler had told his generals his plan for Operation Barbarossa, which was 'to crush Soviet Russia in a rapid campaign'. With the failure of the invasion of Britain, he told them, Germany would instead look east to the vast spaces beyond the Soviet border. Not only would victory over the Soviet Union secure further *Lebensraum* – living space – for the expansionist *Volksreich*, the German peoples, it would also provide the German military machine with almost unlimited new resources. Following the capture of the industrial Don Valley and the oilfields of the Caucasus in the south, Germany would soon be ready to launch a new offensive against Britain.

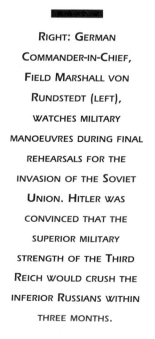

BELOW: THE DEMORALISED FACES OF SOVIET POWS. BRAVE BUT POORLY EQUIPPED, THE BELEAGUERED RED ARMY COULD PUT UP LITTLE EFFECTIVE RESISTANCE.

RIGHT: GERMAN COMMANDER-IN-CHIEF, FIELD MARSHALL VON RUNDSTEDT (LEFT), WATCHES MILITARY MANOEUVRES DURING FINAL REHEARSALS FOR THE INVASION OF THE SOVIET UNION. HITLER WAS CONVINCED THAT THE SUPERIOR MILITARY STRENGTH OF THE THIRD REICH WOULD CRUSH THE INFERIOR RUSSIANS WITHIN THREE MONTHS.

OPERATION BARBAROSSA

SWEDEN   FINLAND

BALTIC SEA

Leningrad · Volkhov

Tallinn

Novgorod

Riga

Velikiye Luki

MOSCOW

Memel

Kaunas

Smolensk

EAST
PRUSSIA

Minsk

Gorodishche

Bryansk

WARSAW

Brest-Litovsk

Pripet Marshes

POLAND

Kiev

Lokhvitsa

Slovakia

Vinnitsa

Dnepropetrovsk

HUNGARY

→ German attacks
– – Stalin Line
Front Line 21 June 1941
Front Line 9 July 1941
Front Line 1 September 1941
Front Line 30 September 1941
Trapped Russian troops
Russian counter-attacks

Pervomaysk

Zaporozhye

Odessa   Perekop

0   Miles   200
0   Kilometres   300

BLACK SEA   CRIMEA

Barbarossa was not universally supported by the German army command. Many pointed out the dangers of fighting a war on two fronts, especially if Britain decided to mount its own invasion in the west. Hitler, however, maintained that blitzkrieg in Russia would produce victory in three months at most. The Russians, he was convinced, were an inferior race incapable of resisting superior German military might. Like the rest of Europe, they would crumble before the onslaught.

By dawn on the morning of 22 June, the massive scale of the German invasion force had become clear. 'When Barbarossa opens,' Hitler had told his generals, 'the world will hold its breath.' Some three million men, over 3000 tanks and 2000 planes were soon pouring into Soviet territory. They were divided into three separate army groups: Army Group 'North' was to head north-west, for the Baltic states and Leningrad; Army Group 'South' was to move southwards to the Crimea, securing the agriculturally rich Ukraine, the Don Valley and the Caucasus on the way; and Army Group 'Centre', led by the panzer tanks of General Heinz Guderian, would head directly for Moscow, the Soviet capital. They would be supported by Romanian forces advancing from the south, as well as by Italian, Croatian, Hungarian and Slovakian divisions. The Finns, too, would be advancing from the north, hoping to use the German invasion as a means of retrieving their losses in the war with Russia in 1939–40. All in all, this was the largest invasion force the world

ABOVE LEFT: WITHIN HOURS OF THE COMMENCE-MENT OF BARBAROSSA, THE SOVIET DEFENCES WERE CUT TO PIECES BY GERMAN PANZER DIVISIONS. BY COMPARISON, THE 20,000 SOVIET TANKS WERE HOPELESSLY OUT OF DATE AND COMPLETELY OUT-MANOEUVRED.

had yet seen, and it had taken the Soviet Union completely by surprise.

Since January 1941, the Soviet Union had been supplying food, fuel and materials to Germany as an extension of the Nazi–Soviet pact signed in 1939. The last shipment, in fact, had been delivered on the evening of 21 June. Long before then, though, Soviet Intelligence had suspected a German attack, but the Soviet dictator, Josef Stalin, had rejected their recent reports that an invasion was imminent. Despite the evidence of German troop concentrations along the Soviet border, Stalin refused to believe that Hitler was about to break their treaty. As a result, his forces were almost totally unprepared to face the Nazi blitzkrieg. Within the first

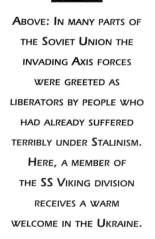

ABOVE: IN MANY PARTS OF THE SOVIET UNION THE INVADING AXIS FORCES WERE GREETED AS LIBERATORS BY PEOPLE WHO HAD ALREADY SUFFERED TERRIBLY UNDER STALINISM. HERE, A MEMBER OF THE SS VIKING DIVISION RECEIVES A WARM WELCOME IN THE UKRAINE.

RIGHT: SS SOLDIERS IN A VILLAGE IN THE KURSK REGION. THROUGHOUT THE RUSSIAN COUNTRYSIDE THE SS EMBARKED ON A CAMPAIGN OF TERROR, TORTURING AND KILLING MORE THAN THREE MILLION MEMBERS OF A RACE OF PEOPLE THEY CONSIDERED 'SUB-HUMAN'.

few hours, the Luftwaffe destroyed over 2000 Soviet planes, most of them before they had even left the ground. The city of Brest-Litovsk, site of the treaty that had ended Russian involvement in the First World War, fell before the day was out. Racing across the Russian countryside, German panzers cut the Soviet defences to pieces.

At this juncture, the Red Army could put up little effective resistance. Despite being able to call on some 10 million men, it was woefully disorganised and communications between divisions were poor. Even the initial order to fire back at the invaders had, reportedly, taken over four hours to reach the front line. Mobility was also a problem, especially in the face of the highly mobile Nazi armour. By comparison, the Soviet Union's 20,000 tanks were hopelessly outdated, and the pilots of their 7500 planes were poorly trained. Much of the blame for these problems lay with the savage purge of the military that Stalin himself had ordered in 1936–8. It also accounted for the Russians' initial reverses in Finland. Most of the Red Army's best and most experienced officers had been executed on trumped up charges of treason, inflicting lasting damage on the army's command structure.

Even so, the Red Army troops were hardy and courageous. Their devotion to Mother Russia had all the force of a deep emotional attachment, and death was a small price to pay for preserving her. Without any clear strategy, though, the Russians simply threw everything they had against the invading Nazis. They sustained horrendous losses. Reports described tank brigades queueing up to go into battle, only to be wiped out in hours.

By contrast, the German blitzkrieg seemed unstoppable. Within less than a week, the Wehrmacht had captured more than 100,000 Russians and over 1000 tanks. Minsk, capital of Belarus, was on the brink of falling. In the north, the Wehrmacht had already swept through the Baltic states and was heading for Leningrad. On the morning of 3 July, the Soviet people turned on their radios to hear a sombre Stalin as he addressed the nation. It was the first time he had done so in over three years. Stalin told his people: 'Our country has entered into a life and death struggle with its most wicked enemy.' The situation was desperate, he admitted, and demanded the complete mobilisation of every available resource that could be used against the enemy. This was to be 'a patriotic war of liberation', and the Soviet people could afford to give no quarter. Where the Red Army was defeated, ordinary people should take up arms and wage guerrilla warfare in their place. If forced to retreat, they were to adopt a 'scorched earth' policy, burning, destroying and wrecking their own homes and property to deny the Nazis 'a single kilogram of grain or a single litre of petrol'.

Much of the blame for these problems lay with the savage purge of the military that Stalin himself had ordered in 1936–8. It also accounted for the Russians' initial reverses in Finland. Most of the Red Army's best and most experienced officers had been executed on trumped up charges of treason, inflicting lasting damage on the army's command structure

JOSEF STALIN

The real name of Josef Stalin – the assumed name meant 'Man of Steel' – was Dzhugasvili. A devious and cunning Georgian, Stalin had been ruler of the Soviet Union since the death of Vladimir Ilych Lenin, leader of the Bolshevik revolution, in 1924. In the 17 years between then and the Nazi invasion in 1941, he had turned the backward, largely peasant-based Soviet Union into an industrial superpower by imposing a series of harsh Five Year Plans for economic development. To this end, the Russian people were denied virtually everything that made for a comfortable life.

In order to secure his position against those he suspected of being enemies of the state, Stalin had conducted a campaign of terror in which millions of citizens were executed or were hauled off to die in Siberian labour camps.

Although he was a sworn enemy of both Nazism and Germany, Stalin had agreed to the signing of the Nazi–Soviet pact in 1939 as a cynical ploy to prevent Germany from attacking the Soviet Union. Hitler's own motives had not been dissimilar.

When the ploy failed and Hitler invaded, Stalin was forced to turn for assistance to the British and US governments. His ideological distance from them was even greater than it was from the Nazis, and the feeling was mutual. Both the British and the Americans, who were not yet in the war when Russia was invaded, loathed communism as a threat to democratic freedom. Nevertheless, what mattered was the defeat of Hitler, and so the uneasy alliance held for as long as that took. If Anglo–American friendship with Stalin barely outlived the war, it was inevitable, but the 'marriage' served to save Russia and the world before the divorce became absolute.

ALTHOUGH RESPONSIBLE FOR TERRIBLE CRIMES AGAINST HIS OWN PEOPLE IN PEACETIME, STALIN PROVED TO BE AN INSPIRING WARTIME LEADER.

The speech electrified the Russians, and was to prove an inspiration to resistance groups across Europe. But was it too late? Prime Minister Winston Churchill, though a fervent anti-communist, had pledged support for Stalin and the Soviet Union. The two countries now had a common enemy, Churchill explained, adding that 'if Hell declared war on Hitler, I would at least give the Devil a favourable mention in the House of Com-

mons'. Churchill, however, was not alone in his distaste for Stalin and the communist creed. In many parts of the Soviet Union, the invading German armies had actually been welcomed as liberators. Millions had suffered during the Stalinist terror of the 1930s and longed for an end to the Moscow government. In the southern Soviet Union, Georgians – ironically, Stalin's home state – as well as Armenians and other ethnic groups traditionally opposed to Soviet rule were recruited into the German war effort. In the Baltic states of Latvia and Lithuania, only recently absorbed into the Soviet Union against their will, new SS divisions were formed to fight alongside the German Army. Many ethnic Russians had looked forward to the downfall of the communist regime, and if this was the way it would happen, they wanted to help.

Little did they realise that they were, in fact, offering themselves for slavery and sacrifice. The consequences of the Nazi plan to 'conquer, rule and exploit' the Soviet Union soon became clear, however, as captured peasants and prisoners of war alike were forced to work for the Nazis. The treatment they received at the hands of the Nazi occupiers was atrocious. Heinrich Himmler, head of the SS, once said that he was not interested in how many thousand Russian women died digging an anti-tank ditch, as long as the ditch was dug. Special mobile police units, the *Einsatzgruppen*, were attached to the advancing armies with the sole responsibility of rounding up Jews and communists for deportation or summary execution. In one operation at Kiev, 33,000 Jews were shot dead. Others were transported back to labour camps in Germany as the first stage in clearing western Russia for settlement by 'pure Aryans'. This plan had been worked out as far back as 1935, when Hitler had set up a Race and Settlement Office to co-ordinate German expansion in the east. Now, he spoke of the need to 'Europeanise' Russia, a process that was to be carried

Special mobile police units, the Einsatzgruppen, were attached to the advancing armies with the sole responsibility of rounding up Jews and communists for deportation or summary execution. In one operation at Kiev, 33,000 Jews were shot dead

out with 'no remorse'. The German people, Hitler explained, were 'absolutely without obligation' as far as their treatment of the Slavic *Untermensch* were concerned. 'Slav' after all meant 'slave' and slaves they would be. The only responsibility the invaders had towards the subdued population would be to 'let them know just enough to understand our highway signs, so that they won't get themselves run over by our vehicles'.

Throughout the summer of 1941, the German advance continued across the Soviet Union at an astonishing rate. By the end of September, the German Army had taken the Ukrainian capital of Kiev and in the north seemed poised to crush Leningrad, the birthplace of the Bolshevik revolution of 1917. In the south, most of the Crimea had fallen. Over half of the Red Army had been either killed or captured and Soviet tank numbers had been reduced to less than 1000. It was surely only a matter of time before Moscow itself fell and the Russians surrendered. Nazi Germany was on the verge of its greatest victory, or so the Germans felt able to persuade themselves.

On the face of it, the Russian cause certainly seemed hopeless. The face of it, however, was deceptive. Despite their appalling losses, the Russian spirit remained unbroken. Russia had long been an excessively hard, demanding country. The rule of the tsars had always been severe, and the communist government that succeeded it had proved not much better. Russia was not a place for soft living and was without even the minimal comforts thought to be essential in the West. Suffering and deprivation were everyday experiences that toughened the ordinary Russian beyond the norm. It was no coincidence that of all those who fought against the Nazis, Russia was the only country that recruited women into its frontline fighting forces. In the circumstances of 1941, it was fortunate that this was so. It came naturally to the Russians to fight back, and to the death.

Consequently, in the towns and villages, Stalin's call for resistance had been readily answered by newly formed Partisan Brigades, who waged a guerrilla war against the invaders by planting bombs, sabotaging equipment and destroying bridges and

A SOVIET PROPAGANDA POSTER BARELY COMES CLOSE TO DEPICTING THE HORRORS OF 'MASTER PLAN EAST'.

MASTER PLAN EAST

Drawn up months before the German invasion of the Soviet Union, the 'Master Plan East' formulated by the SS was the culmination of Nazi hatred for their supposedly inferior Slavic neighbours. The document for the Plan laid out the long-term German arrangements for the conquered Soviet people and the future of the Russian nations. It called for the extermination of at least 30 million Russians, to take place before German citizens could move in and settle what was left of their country. The Soviet Union was then to be divided into agricultural 'provinces' ultimately ruled by the head of the SS, Heinrich Himmler himself. While attempting to carry this plan to its conclusion, Himmler's SS was responsible for the murder of millions of Soviet citizens.

telephone lines. The Red Army itself continued to fight with a bravery, and a savagery, that both impressed and terrified the Germans. The troops seemed to have a total disregard for the huge numbers of men they were losing to the enemy's superior firepower. As one German commander noted: 'The Russians' behaviour in action is simply incomprehensible.' Nevertheless, they succeeded in slowing the German advance, and soon the Soviet people would have a new ally and a familiar one: the remorseless, bone-freezing Russian winter. By the time Hitler's three months to victory was up, autumn had already arrived. From then on, it got worse, much worse.

THE SAVAGE WINTER

The first driving rains began to fall in early October. Within days, road and fields had become impassable as the German war machine found itself bogged down in mud. For almost a month, the movement of tanks and artillery was completely stalled by the wretched conditions, as commanders waited for a frost to harden the ground. The delay proved disastrous. With the arrival of the first snows at the beginning of November, the temperature began to plummet. The same climate that had defeated Napoleon's invasion of Russia in 1812 was about to be visited on the German Army. Convinced that the Russian campaign would be over in three months, as Hitler had planned, the German military had made no preparations for fighting a winter war. The German Army was unprepared for the severity

The rule of the tsars had always been severe, and the communist government that succeeded it had proved not much better. Russia was not a place for soft living and was without even the minimal comforts thought to be essential in the West. Suffering and deprivation were everyday experiences

ABOVE: WEHRMACHT SOLDIERS STRUGGLE IN THE MUD BROUGHT BY THE AUTUMN RAINS. SOON, 'GENERAL WINTER' WOULD TURN OUT TO BE ONE OF THE GERMAN ARMY'S MOST POWERFUL ADVERSARIES.

LEFT: WOMEN IN A SOVIET ORDNANCE FACTORY WORK ROUND THE CLOCK TO PROVIDE AMMUNITION FOR THE FRONT.

of the conditions it now faced, and as the temperature dropped to minus 20 and minus 30 degrees, tanks and lorries started breaking down. Weapons and artillery jammed; batteries froze solid, rendering radio equipment useless. The Luftwaffe was grounded, cutting off supplies and support to the front. And the men, who had not been issued with winter clothing, began to freeze to death.

Thin leather boots and gloves were no defence against the relentless cold. During December 1941, one panzer

НА ЗАЩИТУ ГОРОДА ЛЕНИНА!

ABOVE: THE SOVIETS ALSO UNDERSTOOD THE POWER OF PROPAGANDA WHEN IT CAME TO THE DEFENCE OF THE MOTHERLAND

RIGHT: A WOMAN FROM A SOVIET VILLAGE LIBERATED BY THE RED ARMY CLINGS TO ONE OF HER SAVIOURS. THE COMING OF WINTER SAW THE BEGINNING OF THE RUSSIAN FIGHT-BACK, AS THE HARSH WEATHER DECIMATED GERMAN MORALE.

division reported that it was losing five times as many men to frostbite as were dying in combat. Supplies of fuel ran out as tank crews kept their engines running all night rather than risk trying, but failing, to restart them in the morning. Others simply burned petrol to keep warm. The Russians, meanwhile, seemed immune to the freezing temperatures. Not only were they accustomed to such conditions, they were far better equipped to deal with them, having learned their lesson in Finland in 1939–40. As well as winter clothing, they had anti-freeze for their tanks and winter oil for their guns. German officers reported seeing Russian soldiers capture weapons that their own units had abandoned as useless, oil them, and then turn them on their previous owners. Even the ponies they used to haul their artillery were better suited to the climate than their German counterparts, which were dying in droves. All of a sudden, the rules of warfare seemed to have been turned on their head.

The effect on German morale was shattering. Field Marshal von Bock reported back to Hitler that his men were on the verge of mutiny. For the first time, troops who had been told they were invincible members of a master race had started to entertain the possibility of defeat. They were supposed to be fighting a glorious war for *Lebensraum*, not freezing to death 200 miles from Moscow. They had been led to believe that the Russians were subhuman *Untermensch* and ignorant peasants who would put up little or no resistance. Had not Hitler promised that the Soviet people would fold quickly after the initial German advance? Had he not told his men that 'you only have to kick in the door and the whole rotten structure will come crashing down'? Stalin was supposed to have surrendered by September, but he was still in the Kremlin, refusing to flee, despite the enemy's close approach. In the north, Leningrad was still holding out against the German onslaught. The Red Army had at last begun to organise and marshal its tremendous resources, and they were also starting to throw new equipment against the invaders: the new T-34 tanks, for instance, which were both better armoured and more manoeuvrable than the German panzers.

> Had not Hitler promised that the Soviet people would fold quickly after the initial German advance? Had he not told his men that 'you only have to kick in the door and the whole rotten structure will come crashing down'? Stalin was supposed to have surrendered by September, but he was still in the Kremlin

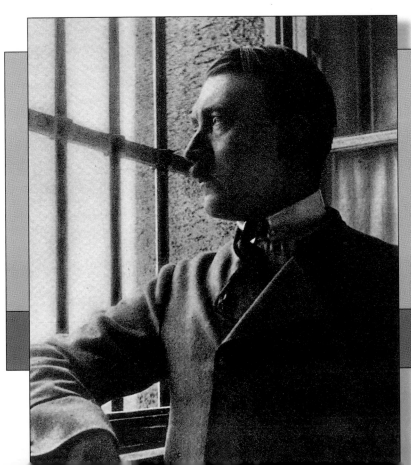

HITLER'S CONSPIRACY THEORIES

Although Hitler spoke of the need to invade the Soviet Union to secure Lebensraum and new resources for the German people, his reasons for launching Operation Barbarossa ran much deeper. As he wrote in his book, Mein Kampf (1925–1927), – 'My Struggle' – Hitler believed that Germany had been betrayed at the end of the First World War by a conspiracy of Jews and communist Bolsheviks, who had come close to ruining his adopted country. Hitler was determined to destroy utterly the source of what he called 'Jewish Bolshevism', and along with the attempted extermination of the Jewish people, this meant the total destruction of the communist Soviet Union.

HITLER IN PRISON IN LANDSBERG JAIL, WHERE HE DEVELOPED HIS RACIST THEORIES IN THE BOOK MEIN KAMPF.

THE MOVEMENT OF FACTORIES EAST OF THE URALS

Throughout the summer of 1941, the Soviets experienced a 'second industrial revolution' as the German war machine rolled across Soviet Russia. From Leningrad to the Crimea steel and chemical works, oil refineries, power stations and tank factories were being dismantled screw by screw and transported to the relative safety of the vast Russian interior. Over 2000 factories vital to the war effort were taken apart and, along with equipment, material and workers, loaded onto trains bound for the far side of the distant Ural mountains. There they were reassembled and were ready to restart production within days. Over 80 per cent of all war-related Soviet industry was moved east in this way in a matter of weeks, a mammoth undertaking.

At Sverdlovsk in the Urals one witness described how locals were given two weeks to build a factory from scratch after being told that new equipment was on its way from the west. Armed with spades and pick-axes they set to work on a patch of empty ground:

> students, typists, accountants, shop assistants, housewives, artists, teachers...In the light of arc-lamps people hacked at the earth all night. They blew up the stones and the frozen earth, and they laid the foundations...people's hands and feet were swollen with frostbite, but they did not leave work. Hundreds of trucks kept rolling up with building materials...on the twelfth day, into the new buildings with their glass roofs, the machinery, covered with hoar-frost, began to arrive. Braziers were kept alight to unfreeze the machines...two days later the war factory began production.

(Quotes taken from first person account quoted in The Year of Stalingrad by Alexander Werth. Hamilton, 1946)

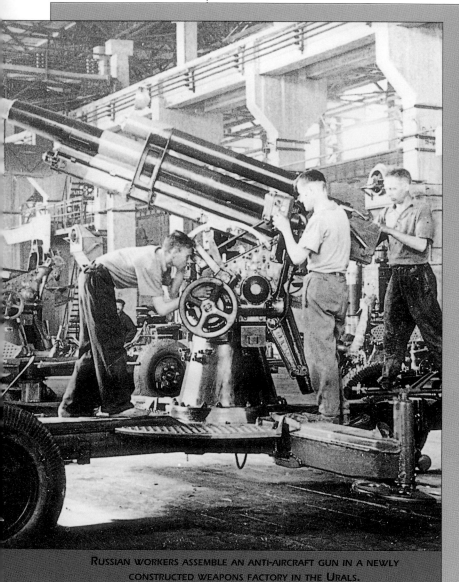

RUSSIAN WORKERS ASSEMBLE AN ANTI-AIRCRAFT GUN IN A NEWLY CONSTRUCTED WEAPONS FACTORY IN THE URALS.

The effect of the reversal of Nazi fortunes, their first appreciable defeat on land, had been felt around the world. The idea began to filter through that the Germans were not as invincible as their early successes had made them appear. Faced with a really resolute foe...they, too, could taste defeat

Meanwhile, Soviet factories were beginning to pour out equipment, planes and guns as fast as the Germans could destroy them. They were supported by supplies from Great Britain and the USA, both of whom had now pledged assistance to the Soviet Union. Across the Soviet Union, women were reporting for work on production lines to turn out everything from sheet steel to artillery pieces. Others had actually gone to the front as doctors, surgeons and Red Cross volunteers. Some 800,000 women joined up for combat duty in the Red Army. Others joined the air force. Industries vital to the war effort were being literally dismantled and transported east to the safety of the Ural mountains, Kazakhstan and central Asia. As the German army advanced on Moscow, over one million people and 500 factories simply upped and moved out of enemy reach.

The crunch was to come in early December, as the German forces reached the outskirts of Moscow. For months, the Luftwaffe had been bombing the city in an attempt to weaken and demoralise the inhabitants. Now, led by Marshal Georgi Zhukov, who had

already mounted a defence of Leningrad, the Red Army launched its first major counter-attack. In December, from Kalinin in the north to Rostov in the south, Soviet troops moved against the demoralised Germans. Despite direct orders from Hitler that they stand and fight, the Germans were forced into retreat. The success of the Soviet offensive, though limited, was nevertheless astounding for an army that had lost almost four million men in the previous few months. Crucial was the arrival at the front of 20 divisions of crack winter troops from Siberia. These 250,000 highly trained men, used to defending the arctic Russo–Japanese border, repeatedly cut through the German lines. They had become available for action in the west only after a timely discovery by a spy, Richard Sorge, that Japan had no plans to attack the Soviet Union.

Apart from the mortifying shock to their master race ego, the retreat cost the lives of 100,000 German troops before they managed to halt the Soviet advance. By this time, though the Red Army had made few decisive territorial gains, the effect of the reversal of Nazi fortunes, their first appreciable defeat on land, had been felt around the world. The idea began to filter through that the Germans were not as invincible as their early successes had made them appear. Faced with a really resolute foe, like the British or the Russians, they, too, could taste defeat. Even more pertinently in this context, Moscow had been saved from Nazi clutches, even if it might be for only a short while.

Outraged, Adolf Hitler ordered his troops to hold their positions and forbade any further withdrawal. He then sacked Guderian and a number of his other most important generals before appointing himself commander-in-chief of the German armed forces. From now on, the man who had never risen above the rank of corporal would run the war himself. In the long run, there was no more disastrous decision that Hitler could have made.

ABOVE: THE CITIZENS OF MOSCOW DIG ANTI-TANK TRENCHES TO DEFEND THEIR CITY AGAINST THE ADVANCING GERMAN FORCES. MOBILISED BY MARSHALL GEORGI ZHUKOV, 250,000 ORDINARY PEOPLE WERE CALLED UP TO DEFEND MOSCOW.

CHAPTER 8

Pearl Harbor

The USS West Virginia and the USS Tennessee lie ablaze after the Japanese surprise strike against Pearl Harbor, 7 December 1941. Following Japan's strike on Pearl Harbor the USA entered the war on the Allied side and the now global conflict was to spread throuhout the vast reaches of the Pacific.

THE 'ARSENAL OF DEMOCRACY' UNDER ATTACK

At 7.02 a.m. on Sunday, 7 December 1941, Private Joseph Lockhard, on duty at the US naval base at Pearl Harbor on Oahu island, Hawaii, was surprised to find a massive blip on his radar screen. Something large was approaching Pearl Harbor from the north. It was 137 miles away and closing. Excited by the largest signal the new radar equipment had yet picked up, Lockhard reported it to his superior, Lieutenant Kermit Tyler. Tyler, placing little faith in radar, a new-fangled piece of equipment as far as he was concerned, told Lockhard to ignore it and took no further action. Tyler was in any case expecting a flight of B-17 bombers to land on Oahu, so the freak signal could easily be put down to their approach. Even so, Lockhard continued to track the signal until he lost it as it neared Hawaii, where it broke up. His shift over, Lockhard and his partner, Private Elliott, left for breakfast. The meal was not to be uninterrupted.

At 7.55 a.m., the first wave of Japanese bombers hit Pearl Harbor. Admiral Isoruku Yamamoto, Commander-in-Chief of the Imperial Japanese Navy, had chosen the perfect time to launch his surprise attack. It was Sunday morning, the quietest time of the week. Few officers were at their posts. Many of the marines in the base were in the mess hall sitting down to breakfast, while the band on the *USS Nevada* was striking up 'The Stars and Stripes'. The band continued to play as 183

BELOW: THE US NAVAL BASE AT PEARL HARBOR, HAWAII. AS THE USA AND JAPAN MOVED CLOSER TO WAR THE US NAVY BEGAN TO MAKE PREPARATIONS AGAINST SURPRISE ATTACKS ON ITS PACIFIC BASES. BUT NO ONE IN THE NAVY DEPARTMENT EXPECTED THE HAMMER BLOW TO FALL ON PEARL HARBOR.

RIGHT: US SAILORS OF THE NAS KANEOHE HONOUR THEIR DEAD COMRADES WITH A TRADITIONAL HAWAIIAN CEREMONY, PLACING WREATHS OVER THEIR TOMBSTONES. OVER 2400 SOLDIERS AND CIVILIANS WERE KILLED DURING THE JAPANESE ATTACK ON PEARL HARBOR.

THE ATTACK ON PEARL HARBOR

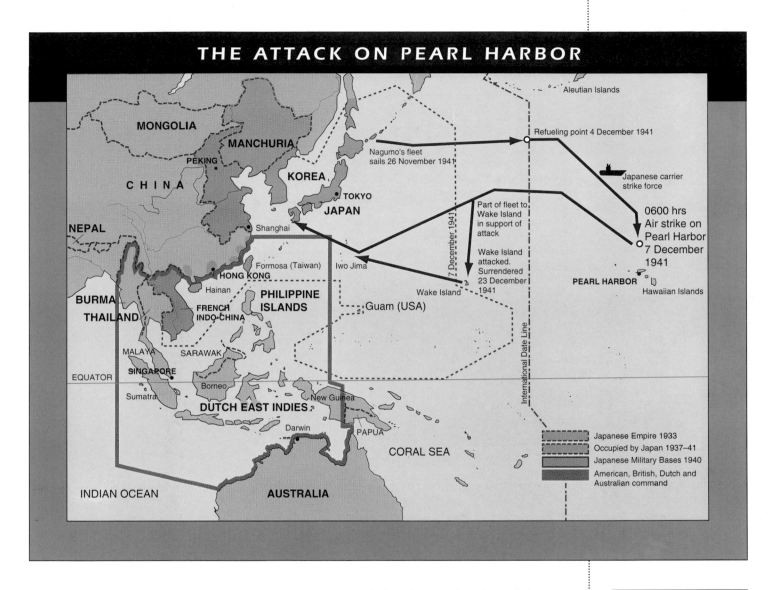

Aleutian Islands

MONGOLIA

MANCHURIA

PEKING

Refueling point 4 December 1941

Nagumo's fleet
sails 26 November 1941

Japanese carrier
strike force

CHINA

KOREA

TOKYO

JAPAN

NEPAL

Shanghai

Part of fleet to
Wake Island
in support of
attack

0600 hrs
Air strike on
Pearl Harbor
7 December
1941

Formosa (Taiwan)

Iwo Jima

Wake Island
attacked.
Surrendered
23 December
1941

HONG KONG

Hainan

BURMA

PHILIPPINE
ISLANDS

Wake Island

PEARL HARBOR

Hawaiian Islands

FRENCH
INDO-CHINA

THAILAND

Guam (USA)

MALAYA

SARAWAK

SINGAPORE

EQUATOR

Borneo

Sumatra

New Guinea

DUTCH EAST INDIES

Darwin

PAPUA

CORAL SEA

Japanese Empire 1933
Occupied by Japan 1937–41
Japanese Military Bases 1940
American, British, Dutch and
Australian command

INDIAN OCEAN

AUSTRALIA

7 December 1941

International Date Line

Japanese aircraft – 49 bombers, 51 dive bombers, 40 torpedo bombers and 43 Zero fighters – began their assault on the Hickham and Wheeler airfields and on 'battleship row', Ford Island, where the cream of the US Navy was basking in the bright Pacific sunlight.

The unseen, unsuspected voyage from Japan had been a masterpiece of strategy and deception. Using a circuitous route and strict radio silence, Yamamoto had managed to send a task force of six aircraft carriers, two battleships, with cruisers and destroyers in support, across the 3400 miles of ocean that separated Hawaii from Japan, and he had done so in total secrecy. The fleet was under the command of Vice-Admiral Chuichi Nagumo, who was given the task of destroying the US fleet at anchor. The fleet had to be knocked out if the Japanese Army and Navy were to proceed with their planned conquest of the British and Dutch colonies in South-East Asia and US possessions in the Pacific, and in their place construct the 'Greater South-East Asia Co-Prosperity Sphere'. This was the equivalent of Hitler's *Lebensraum* in Europe, as the Japanese looked outward from their cramped, poorly resourced islands to the plump, rich prizes across the ocean.

Although Japan and the USA had been moving closer and closer to war over the previous months, the surprise was complete. Many of the US fighters on Oahu were unfuelled and parked close together on the airfields, perfect targets for the Japanese bombers.

Admiral Isoruku Yamamoto, Commander-in-Chief of the Imperial Japanese Navy, had chosen the perfect time to launch his surprise attack. It was Sunday morning, the quietest time of the week. Few officers were at their posts. Many of the marines in the base were sitting down to breakfast

FRANKLIN DELANO ROOSEVELT

During the 1930s, Franklin Delano Roosevelt, who was first elected president of the USA in 1932, watched with increasing concern as Nazi Germany and Fascist Italy moved closer and closer to war with the world's democracies. Roosevelt's own sympathies lay with the British and the French in their stuggle to deal with Nazi aggression, but he was a consummate politician and a genuine democrat who would never take the USA into war without the backing of the majority of his people. This majority was not, at first, forthcoming.

In 1939, most Americans were on the side of the Allies, who were, after all, fighting for the triumph of the democracy to which the Americans were themselves devoted. But this did not yet amount to a willingness to go to war on their behalf, largely due to America's isolationist tradition, which had been a strong influence ever since the Monroe Doctrine of non-involvement in European affairs was issued in 1823. American experience in the First World War was one of bitter disillusionment. Consequently, there was no eagerness to repeat the experience. In the presidential election of 1940, in which Roosevelt stood for a third term as president, he had pledged that the USA would not enter the war. Roosevelt was, however, keen to aid the Allies.

Although isolationism and anti-war sentiments hamstrung him, he did his best to find a way round the problem. He extended as much US aid to the British as was possible. By 1941, the USA was doing much to finance the British war effort and the US Navy, despite its non-combatant status, was taking greater and greater risks safeguarding Allied convoys in the Atlantic. Despite several German attacks on US ships, Roosevelt still refused to bring the USA into the war, until, that is, the events of 7 December 1941 brought about a complete change of heart.

The attack on Pearl Harbor left Roosevelt no choice but to declare war on the Japanese Empire, and the American people, outraged at this cynical stroke of bad faith, backed him up.

It was evident, though, that the main peril to the future of the world lay in Europe, where Hitler had created a continent-wide empire. This was why the Pacific theatre

PRESIDENT ROOSEVELT SIGNS THE US DECLARATION OF WAR AGAINST JAPAN.

was made subordinate to Europe. Throughout the war, however, Roosevelt remained true to the anti-imperialist traditions of the USA and was careful not to involve US troops in operations intended to preserve the British Empire.

Anti-aircraft positions were unarmed and unmanned and the American sailors watching the approaching torpedo bombers assumed they were US aircraft on a practice exercise. By the time the first wave left Hickham and Wheeler fields and 'battleship row', all three locations were a mass of burgeoning flame and twisted wreckage.

At 8.50 a.m., the second wave of the Japanese attack tore across the skies above Oahu. By this time, of course, the Americans were wide awake and put up an impressive flak barrage. But it was not enough to stop disaster from continuing to unfold. By the time the Japanese planes had finished, over 2000 US servicemen had been killed, nearly 200 planes had been destroyed and, most crucially, six battleships had been sunk, including the *USS Arizona*, which lost over one thousand crewmen. A further two battleships were damaged. Three cruisers and three destroyers were sunk. At a stroke, it appeared, Japan had gained naval superiority in the Pacific, for the loss of only 29 planes. There had been no declaration of war.

As the second wave of planes arrived back on their carriers, Nagumo had to decide whether or not to make a third strike. If he were to send his planes in a third time, he could ensure the destruction of the harbour facilities and their oil reserves, so making the base unusable for several months or even years. But, by now, the Americans would be ready and waiting for them, so Nagumo erred on the side of caution and decided instead to withdraw. He had no knowledge of where the rest of the US fleet was, and, fearing a surprise attack, decided it was wiser to conserve his carriers than to risk them with a third strike. After all, they would be needed as the Japanese began reaching out across the Pacific, which they were determined to transform into a new Japanese empire. It was fortunate for the Americans that Nagumo failed to launch that third strike. It was luckier still that he failed to locate the vital US aircraft carriers that had not been in harbour at Oahu that morning.

These carriers did not simply escape to fight another day. In the Pacific conflict that followed the sneak attack on Pearl Harbor, carrier warfare was to be the lynchpin of US naval operations as groups of US vessels, like the posses of the old West, ranged the ocean picking off their Japanese victims while remaining near invincible themselves by blasting a barrage of firepower at any aircraft or ship that dared to challenge them.

Pearl Harbor, however, was only the most famous, or rather infamous, strike in an ocean-wide campaign that was astounding in its ambition and extent. All the more so for an island nation that had only one-tenth the industrial capacity of the foe it so impudently assaulted on Oahu. The government of General Hideki Tojo aimed at nothing less than the destruction of the British, French and Dutch empires in the East as well as the American Commonwealth of the Philippines. The rule of the white man would then be replaced by the Co-Prosperity Sphere, which would see Asia ruled by the Asians. The Japanese believed they had a divine mission to lead Asia into this new era. Furthermore, they had convinced themselves that the Americans had pushed them into war by their apparent determination to crush the Japanese economy and prevent it from expanding as it was 'destined' to do. The war, the Japanese argued, had been undertaken for the purposes of 'self-preservation'.

Less than a century earlier, Japan had been a medieval state, cut off from the world by the Isolation Decree of 1636. The purpose of this was, mainly, to keep out the insidious influence of Christian missionaries, but it did not mean that the leaders of Japan were unaware of the way the outside world was progressing as their country rejected contact from outside. When the American Commodore Matthew Perry arrived in Kyoto harbour in 1853, with a steamship belching fire, ordinary peo-

POSTERS, LEFT TO RIGHT:
A POSTER COMMEMORATING
THE DEAD OF PEARL HAR-
BOR, ISSUED EARLY 1942.

ROSIE THE RIVETER CALLS
AMERICAN WOMEN ONTO
THE FACTORY FLOOR.

HER MALE COUNTERPART
URGES AMERICA'S YOUTH TO
JOIN THE ELITE UNITED
STATES MARINE CORPS.

PATRIOTIC AMERICANS ARE
URGED TO STRETCH
RESOURCES AND 'CAN ALL
YOU CAN'.

AMERICAN WORKERS ARE
WARNED OF THE NEED TO
BE SECURITY CONSCIOUS –
YOU NEVER KNOW WHO'S
LISTENING!

ple, who did not even know what an ocean-going
sailing ship was, thought the world had come to an end. In a way, it had.
Perry came to demand that the Japanese end their isolation and open
up their ports to foreign trade. The rulers of Japan were no fools and
realised that their medieval number was up. If they did not agree voluntarily,
they would be forced to do so, as their neighbour, China, had been forced only
a few years before.

Subsequently, after 1867, Japan began to modernise and did so at such a
phenomenal rate that the process took one-tenth of the time it had taken in Europe.
Unfortunately, along with modern technology, financial systems and other appurtenances
of the modern world, the Japanese also acquired a modern appetite for overseas conquest
and before long decided to expand out of their cramped home islands. In particular, the
Japanese, lacking sufficient raw materials for industry, cast covetous eyes on other Asian
territories where these vital supplies were plentiful. Malaya, a British possession, and the
Dutch East Indies (Indonesia) were particular treasure troves, rich in oil, rubber and tin.

Until 1940, the Japanese had focused their main overseas expansion on China, where they
had been successfully occupying the richest parts of the country since 1931. In 1932, they
even set up a puppet state in Manchukuo, with the last Chinese emperor, Pu Yi, as its ruler.

However, Hitler's successes in Europe turned Japanese attention to the European
colonies in Asia, which, in the case of the French and Dutch were now 'orphans' with their

BUSHIDO

The ferocious militarism displayed by Japanese soldiers throughout the war had its roots in the ancient Samurai code of Bushido, or 'The Way of the Warrior'. Under this code, Japanese soldiers pledged undying loyalty to their Emperor, Hirohito, and the honour of Japan. According to Bushido, death was preferable to capture, and if a Japanese soldier was caught in the act of surrender, he was liable to the death penalty. Strict implementation of the code often led to suicidal resistance to the Allies, in such moves as the Banzai charge. This occurred when all ammunition was exhausted and Japanese troops would charge with bayonets, inflicting horrible injuries on their enemies and on themselves. Those who survived the Banzai charge, or those present at a defeat, were expected to commit suicide and often did so.

The practice, popularly known as 'hara kiri', was more correctly termed 'seppuku' and involved self-disembowelling, one of the most painful of deaths. Traditionally, a swordsman stood by ready to behead the suicide.

Bushido and adherence to it led to many cultural misunderstandings between Westerners and the Japanese, particularly when it came to the treatment of prisoners of war. The Japanese were routinely brutal to prisoners, because they had allowed themselves to be captured. In Japanese eyes, they were therefore despicable. The Allies, however, strictly implemented the Hague Convention and the decent treatment of prisoners it required. This included those Japanese who themselves became prisoners of war, and survived. This was quite incomprehensible to the Japanese, however, and rather than acknowledge it as a sign of civilised behaviour, they concluded that the Allies were weak.

IN STRICT ADHERENCE TO THE CODE OF BUSHIDO, TWO JAPANESE SOLDIERS COMMIT 'HARA-KIRI' RATHER THAN FACE THE SHAME OF BEING TAKEN ALIVE.

CAN ALL YOU CAN

IT'S A REAL WAR JOB!

QUIET!

LOOSE TALK COST LIVES

WAR EXTRA

WAR DECLARED!
U. S. FLEET SAILS!
BATTLESHIP BOMBED
2ND RAID ON HONOLULU!

America's Best Evening Newspaper

The Seattle Daily Times 3RD SUNDAY EXTRA!

PRICE FIVE CENTS

SEATTLE, WASHINGTON, MONDAY, DECEMBER 8, 1941.

ABOVE: THE SEATTLE DAILY TIMES FRONT PAGE SPLASH ON THE DAY AFTER PEARL HARBOR. IN A PIECE OF TYPICAL WARTIME CENSORSHIP THE FULL EXTENT OF THE DESTRUCTION OF THE US NAVY WAS KEPT FROM THE AMERICAN PEOPLE. THE AUTHORITIES FEARED THAT REVEALING THE TRUTH MIGHT SAP THE AMERICAN WILL TO FIGHT.

mother countries under occupation. The 'fall' of Britain, which once seemed likely, also put the British colonies on the Japanese acquisition list. Even after the RAF won the Battle of Britain and it was clear that the British were going to survive, it seemed evident that the inevitable life-or-death struggle with the Nazis would prevent the British from stretching their resources in order to put up a stiff fight in the East as well.

The Japanese, therefore, began to cast covetous eyes on Hong Kong, Singapore, Malaya, the Dutch East Indies, French Indochina and other colonial territories. Even before Pearl Harbor, in July 1941 the Japanese had been pressurising the French in Indochina, and had wrung bases out of them for their own forces. Next, on 26 July 1941, the Japanese moved into Thailand and Cambodia and seized Saigon.

Long before that, though, US President Roosevelt had become increasingly alarmed about Japanese ambitions in the Pacific. If they were to prey on European possessions in Asia, they would inevitably, also, have to seize the strategically placed Philippine Islands, which had come under US rule after the Spanish–American War of 1898.

In September, 1940, the Japanese joined the Triple Alliance with Germany and Italy, so expanding the group known as the Axis powers. This was an extremely ominous move. Roosevelt responded with trade sanctions against Japan, a weapon to which she was especially vulnerable. Relations between the two nations continued to deteriorate from then on, and a crucial turn was taken with the USA's response to Japanese aggression in French Indochina. The USA implemented an oil embargo and froze Japanese assets in the USA, an action in which the British and Dutch joined.

The countdown to war had begun. Japan's own oil reserves would last not much longer than a year, which made taking possession of the Dutch East Indies essential if the country was not to grind to a halt. Talks opened between Japan and the USA, but the two sides never really neared a compromise. The Japanese had decided by September 1941 that if the talks with the Americans were not successful by the beginning of December at the latest, they would have no choice but to go to war. As the talks continued to falter, war seemed more and more likely, and in mid-November Nagumo's fleet set sail for Pearl Harbor.

After the attack of 7 December 1941, which took place while Japanese envoys were still engaged in talks in Washington, an enraged President Roosevelt declared war over what he termed 'a day that will live in infamy'. The occasion was of such grave import that the president, who had been paralysed by an attack of polio in 1921, was wearing his heavy metal callipers so that he could stand up to make the announcement. In Germany, Adolf Hitler declared war on the USA. In Britain, Winston Churchill was relieved. The USA, the 'arsenal of democracy' and the mightiest industrial power in the world, was in the war at long last. However, for Isoruku Yamamoto, it was a sombre moment. After Pearl Harbor, he had commented: 'I fear that all we have done is to waken a sleeping tiger.' As he had feared, the tiger was now wide awake.

MALAYA

While Pearl Harbor burned and the Americans there reeled at the shock of the sneak attack, the Japanese 25th Army under Lieutenant General Yamashita crossed into Thailand and pressed on to the British colony of Malaya. Yamashita was planning to fight his way down the 600 miles of the Malayan peninsula to capture the British naval base at Singapore, a key stronghold of the British Empire in the Far East. With Singapore in Japanese hands, British strength in the Pacific would be broken. Meanwhile, Japanese bombers launched attacks on Hong Kong and the Philippines.

Things went wrong for the British in Malaya from the outset. Confusion prevented them from launching the long-prepared counter-attack, code-named Matador, against the Japanese. Within days of the enemy landings at Dingora, Patani and Kota Bharu, the British were beginning a retreat that would not stop until they reached Singapore and the sea.

The British were singularly complacent about the threat to their empire posed by the Japanese, whom they totally underrated as fighting force. The Japanese, in fact, were regarded contemptuously, as bow-legged little yellow men who could only ape their European 'betters' and were unable to manoeuvre aircraft in the air because their slit eyes obscured their vision. In fact, some of the most celebrated air aces of the war were Japanese, including Saburo Sakai, who, among other feats, used to fly his plane close to stalling speed to conserve fuel. Nevertheless, the dismissive view of the Japanese was so prevalent at the start of the war in the Pacific that when one British official in Singapore was told the Japanese had landed, he told his military opposite number to 'push the little men off'.

However, the Japanese in Malaya proved themselves better led, better trained and better

> The Japanese, in fact, were regarded contemptuously, as bow-legged little yellow men who could only ape their European 'betters'... when one British official in Singapore was told the Japanese had landed, he told his military opposite number to 'push the little men off'

HIT HARD! HIT FAST! HIT OFTEN!

Produce for Your Navy

VICTORY BEGINS AT HOME!

LEFT: A US NAVY POSTER URGES GREATER PRODUCTIVITY TO SECURE A SPEEDY VICTORY.

BELOW LEFT: YAMASHITA'S MEN BEGIN THEIR CHARGE IN PENANG, WHERE THEY WERE TO ENJOY YET ANOTHER DAZZLING VICTORY. JAPANESE TROOPS IN MALAYA CONSISTENTLY TOOK THE INITIATIVE WHILE BRITISH AND EMPIRE FORCES FELL VICTIM TO THEIR SWIFT AND SKILFUL ATTACKS. YAMASHITA'S MEN HASTENED THEIR ADVANCE DOWN THE MALAY PENINSULA WITH BIKES, SOME OF WHICH CAN BE SEEN IN THE FOREGROUND.

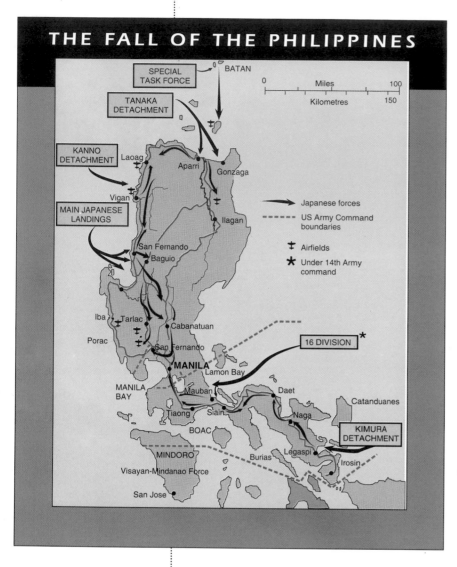

THE FALL OF THE PHILIPPINES

SPECIAL TASK FORCE

BATAN

TANAKA DETACHMENT

KANNO DETACHMENT

MAIN JAPANESE LANDINGS

0   Miles   100

0   Kilometres   150

Laoag

Aparri

Gonzaga

Vigan

Ilagan

→ Japanese forces

- - - US Army Command boundaries

✠ Airfields

✱ Under 14th Army command

San Fernando

Baguio

Iba   Tarlac

Porac   Cabanatuan

San Fernando

16 DIVISION ✱

MANILA

Lamon Bay

MANILA BAY

Mauban   Daet

Catanduanes

Tiaong   Siain   Naga

BOAC

KIMURA DETACHMENT

Burias   Legaspi

MINDORO   Irosin

Visayan-Mindanao Force

San Jose

equipped than the British. Yamashita was so confident of victory that he elected not to take all the troops available to him on his Malayan campaign. With only 60,000 men, he was outnumbered by the British, Indian, Malay and Australian troops that the British Commander in Malaya, Lieutenant-General Sir Arthur Percival, had at his disposal. But Yamashita, who quickly captured forward British airfields, had air superiority throughout the campaign. It was a crucial advantage for the Japanese and it cost the British dearly.

Winston Churchill was not unaware that the Japanese had designs on Britain's empire. In order to discourage them from attacking Malaya, he dispatched the battleship *Prince of Wales* and the cruiser *Repulse* to Singapore. They arrived just in time to attempt the destruction of the Japanese invasion force landing in northern Malaya. Admiral Sir Tom Phillips sent his two warships north from Singapore, but they were soon spotted by the Japanese, and Phillips, seeing that the element of surprise was lost, turned for home. He never got there. Phillips's position was extremely perilous. His ships had no air support and were crucially vulnerable to attack from dive- or torpedo-bombers. Before he could reach his base, misleading signals sent him off on a wild goose chase to stop a nonexistent Japanese ship near his current position. It was then that the warships were again spotted by the Japanese, in the Gulf of Siam. On 10 December 1941, assaulted by Japanese bombers, the two ships were sunk and over 800 men were lost. Among them was Admiral Phillips. Churchill described the disaster as 'the most direct shock' he received during the whole of the war. British power in the Far East was in tatters.

Less than two months later, on 1 February 1942, the British had surrendered the whole of the Malayan peninsula and had withdrawn to the island fortress of Singapore. The Japanese had outflanked the British down the whole length of the peninsula. Using their superior mobility, the Japanese ran behind British positions and attacked them from the rear. Many of the British forces were inexperienced, especially the Indian brigades, some of whom had never seen a tank before, since the British had no tanks for defence in the entire territory. Once the British had begun to retreat, they found it hard to stop, though military communiqués, employing the euphemisms of 'warspeak', reported that their forces had once again 'successfully disengaged the enemy'.

The Japanese crossed the Straits of Johor, which separated Singapore from the mainland, on 8 February. This, if anything, was even more of a 'direct shock'. The British had presumed that the tangled jungle country made Singapore impossible to assault from the landward side. Yet, the Japanese achieved the seemingly impossible and a week later, on 15 February, Singapore was in Japanese hands and Lieutenant-General Percival, who had risen from the ranks to the Malaya Command, was a picture of misery and shame as he yielded to his conquerors. Well might he look grim and grey-faced. Percival had just presided over the greatest military defeat in British history. Over 60,000 men were taken prisoner, half of them Indians. Many of these were recruited into the Japanese-sponsored Indian National Army set up by the Indian nationalist Subhas Chandra Bose for the purpose of driving the British out of the sub-continent.

The British had experienced a series of crushing defeats in the Far East within a few weeks. Hong Kong, Malaya and Singapore had fallen. They were also hard pressed in Burma, where the Japanese were hoping to force the closure of the Burma road, the only supply route into Nationalist China. If Burma were to fall, then the Japanese would be at the eastern gates of India, the 'jewel in the crown' of the British Empire.

But the British were not the only ones involved. The Australians, seeing the collapse of Singapore and sensing their own danger, began looking to the Americans to stop the Japanese. The Americans, though, were having problems of their own.

THE PHILIPPINES

The full-scale Japanese invasion of the Philippines began on 22 December 1941. By then, General Douglas MacArthur, the Commander of the US forces, had already had half of his air force destroyed on the ground due to a hesitant reaction, on his part, to the bombing of Pearl Harbor. The little air support left for US naval forces in the Philippines effectively neutralised them. The Japanese troops landed swiftly and made their approach towards the capital, Manila.

MacArthur declined the invitation to defend the city, and instead skilfully withdrew to strong defensive positions in the Bataan peninsula and the island fortress of Corregidor. Here, the Americans were to endure several months of savage and bitter fighting. MacArthur had managed to salvage few rations for his force of over 60,000 Filipino and 15,000 US troops. This shortfall was to have serious consequences.

The 'battling bastards of Bataan', as the Americans became known, held off the Japanese advance for several months, but they were to suffer horribly from tropical diseases whose impact was made worse by the Americans' lack of food and medical supplies. Despite pleas from MacArthur, Washington was unable to sent

BELOW: AFTER STUBBORN RESISTANCE BY THE ALLIES, THE PHILIPPINES FINALLY FELL IN MARCH 1942. IT WAS NOT, HOWEVER, UNTIL THE SECOND WORLD WAR FINALLY ENDED THAT THE FEROCIOUS BRUTALITY METED OUT TO ALLIED POWs WAS REVEALED. THE UNEQUIVOCAL SENTIMENTS EXPRESSED HERE LEAVE NO DOUBT AS TO THE SENSE OF AMERICAN OUTRAGE.

Hundreds of Wainwright's weakened men were to die from the harsh treatment they received as Japanese prisoners of war. This brutality sprang largely from the Japanese Samurai military code of Bushido, which made being taken prisoner a disgrace worse than death

RIGHT: THE RISING SUN FLIES OVER THE PHILIPPINES. JAPANESE TROOPS CELEBRATE THEIR HARD-WON VICTORY IN AMERICA'S FORMER COLONY. BUT OF ALL THE TERRITORIES THE JAPANESE OCCUPIED, THE LOCAL FILIPINOS PUT UP THE STIFFEST GUERRILLA RESISTANCE TO THEIR NEW MASTERS.

reinforcements to his hard-pressed men. The 'Europe first' strategy agreed with the British after the US declaration of war meant that all available US resources were being concentrated on the defeat of Hitler. The Pacific theatre, though closer to home, had to take second place.

THE FALL OF SINGAPORE, 15 FEBRUARY 1942

The capture of Singapore by the Japanese is still regarded, over 50 years later, as the British Army's single most crushing defeat. The island naval base had been built between the two world wars and had developed a reputation as a rock-like fortress. It was considered so resilient to enemy attack that it was nicknamed 'the Gibraltar of the East' after the Rock in the Mediterranean with an age-old history of survival in the face of attack.

Yet, Singapore was taken by outnumbered Japanese soldiers after only a week's fighting. Its loss was one of the events that led to the dismantling of the British Empire after the war. The fact that the British had been beaten so soundly and were unable to rise to the challenge of Japanese attack in Asia was a fatal blow to British prestige in the East.

In British plans, any attack on Singapore was bound to come from the sea, which explained the big naval guns that were installed there. They were useless, however, when the Japanese approached instead by land. In addition, British forces had been spread far too thinly to resist the invaders. Within days, Singapore's water supply had been seized, provoking desertions and unrest among the island's Malay and Chinese inhabitants. Days later, on 15 February 1942, Lieutenant-General Sir Arthur Percival surrendered to the Japanese, confirming what Winston Churchill called the 'worst disaster and biggest capitulation in British history'.

EMPIRE DOWN. PERCIVAL SURRENDERS TO YAMASHITA IN SINGAPORE, FORMALLY ACKNOWLEDGING THE BIGGEST MILITARY DISASTER IN BRITISH HISTORY.

As the dire situation became desperate, MacArthur was ordered to quit the Philippines on 11 March 1942 and regroup in Australia. Before departing, MacArthur pledged to the Filipino people: 'I will return.' The only US forces in the island chain were now left under the command of Major-General Jonathan Wainwright, who continued stubborn resistance on Bataan until 9 April. The fortress of Corregidor held out until hunger, constant air raids and a landing of Japanese troops made further resistance untenable by 6 May. Hundreds of Wainwright's weakened men were to die from the harsh treatment they received as Japanese prisoners of war. This brutality sprang largely from the Japanese Samurai military code of Bushido, which made being taken prisoner a disgrace worse than death. Consequently, the Japanese had no consideration at all for those so shamed. This was how the forced march to prison camps made by the defenders of Bataan became notorious after the war as the 'death march'.

Before the final collapse of resistance in the Philippines, the Japanese were able to begin their thrust to the south and begin the capture of the oilfields in the Dutch East Indies. In December 1941 and January 1942, Japanese landings began securing these prize resources. Resistance was offered by what remained of the Allied forces in the Pacific but, though brave, it was futile. The combined remnants of the US, British, Dutch and Australian (ABDA) navies made a final bid to halt the Japanese in the Battle of the Java Sea, but they failed. The Japanese defeated the allies, and their Dutch commander,

RIGHT: THE DESPAIR OF DEFEAT. THESE US SOLDIERS HAVE JUST BEEN TAKEN CAPTIVE BY THE JAPANESE IN BATAAN AFTER PUTTING UP A STIFF FIGHT FOR OVER 100 DAYS. THEY ARE ABOUT TO BEGIN A 100KM JOURNEY ON FOOT TO THE PRISONER OF WAR CAMPS PREPARED FOR THEM IN SAN FERNANDO. THE TREK WAS A TORTUOUS ONE. THE SOLDIERS, ALREADY WEAK FROM MALNUTRITION, WERE BEATEN AND CLUBBED BY THEIR CAPTORS.

RIGHT: TWO WOMEN, ONE AMERICAN AND ONE DUTCH, DO THEIR BEST TO ADD A FEW TOUCHES OF HOME COMFORT TO THE LESS THAN IDEAL CONDITIONS OF A JAPANESE WOMEN'S PRISON CAMP.

Rear-Admiral Karel Doorman, went down with his ship. Resistance in the Dutch East Indies ceased on 8 March and, consequently, 100,000 Allied soldiers were to spend the rest of the war in the unspeakable conditions of Japanese captivity.

RIGHT: THE PILOTS OF A FIGHTER CREW OF THE USS LEXINGTON ARE BRIEFED BEFORE GOING INTO ACTION. THE LEXINGTON WAS SUNK BY THE JAPANESE IN THE BATTLE OF THE CORAL SEA.

BATTLE OF THE CORAL SEA, 4–8 MAY 1942

The Japanese continued their progress south, building an air base at Guadalcanal in the Solomon Islands, another British colony. They hoped to move on to capture Port Moresby in Papua New Guinea, for a base there would put Australia within striking distance of Japanese bombers. The Allies learned of Japan's intentions, and their determination to stop their advance led to the first-ever battle between two carrier fleets, fought entirely in the air. The two fleets never sighted each other. Although the battle was effectively a draw, the Japanese had the better of the fighting, sinking the US carrier *Lexington* and damaging the *Yorktown*. While the US planes damaged two Japanese carriers, they sank none. But for the first time since Pearl Harbor, the Japanese advance had been checked. Port Moresby remained out of reach and Australia, for the time being, was safe.

ABOVE: FIGHTER SQUAD 16 OF THE USS LEXINGTON RECEIVES THE GAME-PLAN BEFORE TAKING TO THE SKIES TO HUNT OUT THE JAPANESE FLEET DURING THE BATTLE OF THE CORAL SEA. TORPEDO PLANES AND BOMBERS LATER SANK HER.

CHAPTER 9

The War at Sea

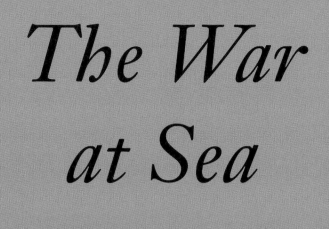

A US NAVY SHIP BATTLES ITS WAY THROUGH
HIGH SEAS IN THE NORTH ATLANTIC. AFTER THE LEND-LEASE
ARRANGEMENT BETWEEN BRITAIN AND THE USA HAD OUTLIVED
ITS USEFULNESS, PRESIDENT ROOSEVELT, FOLLOWING HIS
SECOND RE-ELECTION, LOANED 50 US WARSHIPS TO BRITAIN
TO PROTECT HER MERCHANT SHIPPING.

BATTLE OF THE ATLANTIC

On 3 September 1939, the day Britain declared war on Nazi Germany, the German submarine U-30 torpedoed the ocean liner *SS Athenia* in the north Atlantic. The 112 British and American passengers who were killed were the first Allied casualties of the war. Over the next six years, German and British vessels were to fight a desperate battle for supremacy in the Atlantic that would cost the lives of nearly 100,000 British sailors and lead to the almost total destruction of the German Navy.

As an island, Britain had always looked to the sea for her defence. At the beginning of the war, the Royal Navy had 12 battleships, seven aircraft carriers and over 200 cruisers and destroyers in service. This was considerably more than the German fleet, the Kriegs-marine, although Germany's ships, all built since 1918, were generally better equipped. The Straits of Dover were protected by thousands of mines, and German ships bound for the Atlantic were forced to sail north, around Scotland, to find safe passage. As the Battle of Britain would illustrate in 1940, without air superiority Germany could do little directly to threaten the British mainland by sea. Yet, in order to fight a war, Britain relied on

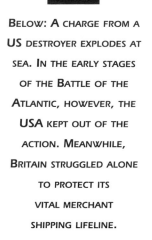

BELOW: A CHARGE FROM A US DESTROYER EXPLODES AT SEA. IN THE EARLY STAGES OF THE BATTLE OF THE ATLANTIC, HOWEVER, THE USA KEPT OUT OF THE ACTION. MEANWHILE, BRITAIN STRUGGLED ALONE TO PROTECT ITS VITAL MERCHANT SHIPPING LIFELINE.

RIGHT: THE SECOND ESCORT
GROUP SCORES A SUCCESS
AGAINST A U-BOAT. THREE
OF THE GROUP'S SIX U-BOAT
KILLS WERE MADE WITHIN
AN HOUR.

LEFT: VITAL SUPPLIES FROM
THE USA AND
CANADA ARRIVE IN BRITAIN.
IN 1939 BRITAIN IMPORTED
55 MILLION TONS OF ITS
GOODS AND HALF OF ITS
FOOD FROM OVERSEAS. IF
HITLER COULD SEVER THIS
LIFELINE, THE BRITISH
PEOPLE WOULD BE FORCED
TO SURRENDER.

importing fuel, materials, even food, without which she could not build tanks artillery or aircraft, or even feed soldiers and civilians and keep them warm in winter.

Britain's chief suppliers in the early stages of the war were her overseas colonies, India and Canada chief among them, and the USA. Despite US neutrality, President Roosevelt had agreed to succour the British war effort on a 'cash and carry' basis. This meant that the British Government could buy whatever it needed from the USA for as long as its stocks of US dollars lasted, and it had the ships to transport the material. Governments in both London and Berlin knew that if the merchant navy were prevented from carrying out this task, Britain could be starved out of the war. As Churchill put it: 'Without ships, we cannot live.' In the first months of the war, Germany attempted to disrupt British shipping in a number of ways.

Firstly, thousands of magnetic mines – Hitler's 'secret weapons' – were laid by German aircraft around the British coast and the entrance to the River Thames. They successfully sank 27 British ships during October and November 1939. The danger was defused only after a British explosives expert, Lieutenant-Commander J.D. Ouvry, bravely took apart a live mine in order to study the way it worked. With his help, the Royal Navy was able to

Governments in both London and Berlin knew that if the merchant navy were prevented from carrying out this task, Britain could be starved out of the war. As Churchill put it: 'Without ships, we cannot live'

design an electronic defence system, to be carried by each ship, that would prevent the mines from detonating. Meanwhile, from the first day of the war, German warships had been scouring the Atlantic sea lanes for unescorted shipping. Between September and December 1939, the German pocket battleship *Admiral Graf Spee* attacked and sank nine British merchant ships before being challenged by three British cruisers off the coast of South America. In the ensuing battle of the River Plate, *HMS Exeter* was crippled, but despite being outgunned, the captains of the *Ajax* and *Achilles* managed to force the more powerful *Graf Spee* to run for Montevideo, in neutral Uruguay, where the *Graf Spee*'s captain, Hans Langsdorff, was told he could have only three days to make repairs to his ship before having to put to sea again. Meanwhile, *Ajax* and *Achilles* were waiting for him outside Uruguayan territorial waters. Three days later, on 17 December, after declaring 'You English are hard. You do not know when you are beaten', Langsdorff scuttled his own ship in the River Plate estuary rather than let it fall into British hands. He committed suicide two days later in Argentina.

RIGHT: LIEUTENANT COMMANDER GÜNTHER PRIEN, CAPTAIN OF THE GERMAN SUBMARINE U-47 **AND ONE OF THE GERMAN KRIEGSMARINE'S GREATEST SUBMARINE ACES.**

BELOW: OFFICERS FROM THE U-47 **LINE UP FOR INSPECTION BY GRAND ADMIRAL DÖNITZ, THE ARCHITECT OF THE GERMAN U-BOAT CAMPAIGN.**

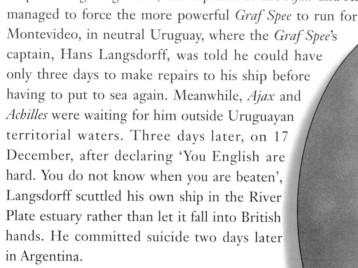

A HEAVILY ICED-UP HMS BELFAST IN THE TREACHEROUS WATERS OF THE ARCTIC CIRCLE EN ROUTE FOR THE SOVIET UNION.

ARCTIC CONVOYS PQ17 AND PQ18

In July 1942, the ships of Arctic convoy PQ17 were en route for the north Russian port of Archangel when warning was received that the German battleship Tirpitz was heading their way. Fearing the convoy's escort ships would be no match for the Tirpitz's guns, Admiral Sir Dudley Pound, the British First Sea Lord, ordered the convoy to scatter. This was a disastrous mistake. The U-boats, aided by the Luftwaffe, picked off the isolated merchant ships one by one, and 24 ships, two-thirds of the original convoy, were lost. Over 150 men perished in the icy waters. The convoy leader, Captain John Broome, later told a court of enquiry that Pound's order should never have been given.

The grim lesson was well learned. Two months later, convoy PQ18 was also attacked in the same area, but this time, the ships remained together and their escort vessels managed to shoot down over 40 Luftwaffe planes. Although 13 merchant ships were lost over six days of fighting, 27 were safely delivered to the Soviet Union.

The victory over the *Admiral Graf Spee* was an inspiration to the British at home, but it was, in reality, only a distraction from the real threat to come. On 14 October 1939, the German submarine *U-47* had sailed unobserved into the British naval base at Scapa Flow in the Orkney Islands and sank the battleship *Royal Oak*, killing nearly 800 men. *U-47*, captained by Lieutenant-Commander Günther Prien, escaped undamaged. Submarines had previously been used in combat during the First World War, but their operations had since been largely outlawed by the Hague Convention, which demanded that attacks on shipping should take place only where provision could be made for picking up survivors. The German decision to ignore the Convention and renew the use of submarines came as a nasty surprise to the British.

The German U-boat campaign that was to follow was principally the responsibility of Admiral Karl Dönitz, a U-boat commander during the First World War, who sincerely believed that submarines could win the war for Germany. Despite having fewer than 60 U-boats under his command at the start of the war – only one-third of them capable of operating in the north Atlantic – Dönitz persuaded Hitler to sanction his hand-picked crews to launch a major offensive against British shipping. Although the Royal Navy had at this stage at least as many submarines as the Germans, only Dönitz had recognised the potential of their peculiarly furtive form of warfare for the task of destroying Britain's supply lines. The British, however, would soon come to realise the enormity of the threat, and Winston Churchill would later write: 'The only thing that ever really frightened me during the war was the U-boat peril.'

In September 1939 alone, German U-boats sank 26 British merchant ships in the Atlantic. By the end of the year, the figure had risen to over one hundred. Before every mission, Dönitz personally saw his men off from their bases in Germany, and was there to congratulate them on their return. His personal touch inspired the U-boat crews, despite the

Although the Royal Navy had...as many submarines as the Germans, only Dönitz had recognised the potential of their peculiarly furtive form of warfare...Churchill would later write: 'The only thing that ever really frightened me during the war was the U-boat peril'

RIGHT: A SIGNAL MAN ON A ROYAL NAVY WARSHIP TRANSMITS A MESSAGE TO OTHER MEMBERS OF A CONVOY ENGAGED IN PROTECTING BRITISH MERCHANT SHIPS AGAINST U-BOAT ATTACKS. NEVERTHELESS, IN THE EARLY YEARS OF THE WAR LOSSES WERE GREAT, AND THE FUTURE OF BRITAIN HUNG ON A KNIFE EDGE.

MERCHANT SHIPPING LOSSES

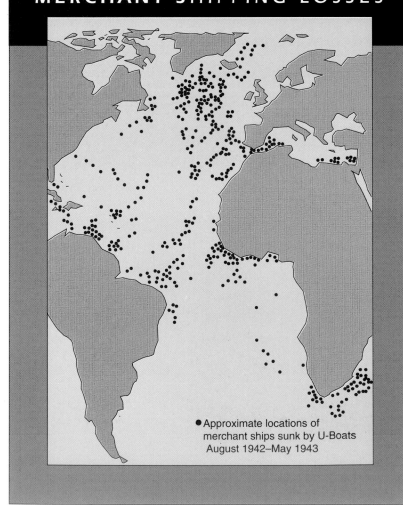

• Approximate locations of merchant ships sunk by U-Boats August 1942–May 1943

fact that at this point in the war, their campaign was largely ignored by the German High Command. Dönitz had asked for 30 new submarines to be manufactured every month. Instead, he got two at most. In such conditions, the success of Dönitz's private war was all the more spectacular.

The only answer to the U-boat menace was to escort merchant shipping across the Atlantic in huge convoys, often containing more than 50 ships each, guarded by Royal Navy warships. Arranged in columns to shorten their vulnerable flanks, the convoys zigzagged across the ocean, changing course when the warships engaged attacking submarines. In the early months of the war, the convoy system had some success, so much so that Dönitz's U-boats avoided them and, instead, concentrated their attacks on unescorted shipping. By the beginning of 1940, fewer than 10 escorted ships had been lost. However, as the submarines increased their range, losses soon began to rise. Initially, the convoy system could operate only between Britain and the mid-Atlantic, due to a shortage of available escort ships, many of which had been seconded into largely fruitless submarine hunts. Beyond the mid-Atlantic, ships once again became easy prey for German submarine commanders. A further blow came when the Fall of France in June 1940 allowed Dönitz to establish a U-boat base at Lorient, on the French Atlantic coast. This increased the range of the German submarines by almost 500 miles. Hitler now declared a complete blockade of Britain, and announced that all shipping sailing to or from the British isles, whether neutral or not, would be sunk. Aided by long-range Focke-Wulf FW200 bombers taking off from French runways, the U-boats began to wreak havoc on merchant shipping.

Dönitz organised his submarines into patrols that haunted the Atlantic shipping lanes, waiting to radio for support upon sighting a British convoy. Submarines from the surrounding area would then gather together into a 'wolfpack' and attack the convoy under cover of night. Sometimes, they would even surface inside the convoy itself, steering among the unsuspecting ships before launching their tor-pedoes at close range. Retreating or diving during daylight, they would repeat these attacks over subsequent nights until they ran out of torpedoes. This strategy was hugely effective. Escort captains whose job it was to defend the convoys could not risk chasing individual U-boats away without leaving the ships under their charge in even greater danger. Not only were the U-boats difficult to spot at night, but attacking on the surface made them almost invisible to the rudimentary radar defence systems with which British ships were equipped. During the sum-

ABOVE: THE OIL TANKER
SS DIXIE ARROW IN FLAMES
OFF CAPE HATTERAS IN
MARCH 1942.

mer of 1940, 240 merchant vessels were sunk. Only two U-boats were lost.

Conditions were terrible for the merchant seamen who kept the British supply lines going during this time. As losses mounted, every available ship was pressed into service, many of them old and ill-equipped. The relentless north Atlantic weather left sailors almost permanently soaked to the skin and freezing cold, and grabbing sleep where and when they could. Captains battling high seas and heaving ocean rollers struggled to keep their ships from colliding with others in the convoy. Visibility was so poor they had to communicate by flashing lights. And always there was the unseen, unsuspected danger of a U-boat lurking beneath the surface, waiting to strike. The tell-tale trail of torpedoes tearing through the water might be seen only when it was too late. Next, there was a mighty explosion, an upsurge of fire and smoke and a heavily laden merchant ship would slide all too fast beneath the waves. The crew, if they survived, had to take their chances.

Until the introduction of rescue ships, escort crews would often have to choose between going to the aid of the men struggling in the water and engaging the attacking U-boat. The convoy had to be kept moving at all costs. For tanker crews, with their highly flammable cargo, the danger was even greater. Captain T.D. Finch was on board one such tanker, the *San Emiliano*, when it was torpedoed by a U-boat in the Atlantic on the night

CAPTAIN F.J. 'JOHNNY' WALKER

Captain F.J. 'Johnny' Walker, a specialist in anti-submarine warfare, was put in charge of the Royal Navy's 36th escort group in 1941. To prepare his men for combat, Walker used a special simulator to put them through a rigorous and often ingenious training course in submarine hunting. Walker also devised a series of defensive 'set pieces', collectively known as Operation Buttercup, which were constantly rehearsed by his ships. Walker believed that only by carefully planning exactly how different escort ships and aircraft would work together, could they hope to defeat a U-boat attack. His preparations paid off on his first convoy mission, when his ships sank four U-boats during a running battle lasting six days. Walker himself described how he pursued an enemy submarine at such close range that his gun crew were 'reduced to shaking fists and roaring curses'. As Commodore Raymond Fitzmaurice reported, rather laconically, 'the convoy had few dull moments'.

VETERAN SUB HUNTER CAPTAIN 'JOHNNY' WALKER ON
BOARD THE BRITISH WARSHIP HMS STARLING.

of 9 August 1942. Within minutes, Finch later recalled, 'the ship was ablaze from bridge to stern, the whole sky being lit up by flames which must have been hundreds of feet high.' Sailors on fire threw themselves overboard, only to find that the sea was also a mass of flames. The *San Emiliano* had been carrying 12,000 tons of gasoline. Only seven of the ship's 48-man crew survived the night.

Overall, the loss of life among men of the merchant navy throughout the war was as high as it was in some sections of the armed forces. Over 30,000 merchant seamen were

LEFT: MORE THAN 30,000 MERCHANT SEAMEN LOST THEIR LIVES BEFORE THE WAR ENDED IN 1945. FOR THE TIME BEING AT LEAST THIS MAN HAS SURVIVED, BUT THE STRAIN AND EXHAUSTION IS UNMISTAKABLE.

BOTTOM LEFT: INSIDE THE CRAMPED GUN TURRET OF AN ALLIED WARSHIP EXHAUSTED CREW MEMBERS TRY TO GRAB SOME SLEEP BETWEEN ATTACKS. THROUGHOUT THE FIVE-YEAR BATTLE OF THE ATLANTIC, ALLIED MERCHANT SAILORS AND FIGHTING MEN ALIKE WERE STRETCHED TO THE VERY LIMITS OF ENDURANCE.

U-BOATS

During the six years of the war at sea, a total of 785 German U-boats were sunk by Allied ships and aircraft. But the damage done by the U-boats to Allied shipping was almost incalculable. Carrying a crew of 40, each U-boat was equipped with up to five torpedo tubes, stationed both forward and aft of the ship, from which self-steering torpedoes were fired after a complex targeting procedure had been carried out. The torpedoes themselves were usually set to pass 1 to 2 metres underneath their target rather than hit a ship directly. At that point, magnetic triggers would cause them to explode.

Life on board a submarine was always difficult. The crew's surroundings were cramped and claustrophobic, and their work required intense concentration. When submerged, U-boats could move at no more than a slow 3 knots, and their huge electric batteries had to be charged by diesel engines that could be operated only after the submarine had surfaced. At such times, the U-boat and its crew were especially vulnerable to attack from the air, and although they were armed with heavy machine-guns that could fire over 6000 rounds a minute, they had to be prepared at all times for an emergency 'crash' dive. If this manoeuvre failed to throw off pursuing planes or warships, decoy devices would be launched to try and fool the enemy's radar system. This was a desperate situation, because just one direct hit from a depth charge could shatter a submarine's hull.

The crew's last line of defence was to submerge, then sit and wait under the water. All the while, though, they were slowly exhausting their supplies of compressed air. Crews were under strict instructions not to surrender their ships – an act that could hand the enemy vital information for use in future submarine hunts. At such times, the crew would wait quietly, try to conserve oxygen and listen for the tell-tale sounds of Allied radar signals. They also had to prepare to surface and do battle once more when their air ran out and there was no option but to confront the enemy again. Life aboard a U-boat always required tremendous discipline and very strong nerves.

A U-BOAT CAPTAIN USES HIS SUBMARINE'S PERISCOPE TO SEARCH FOR PREY.

killed before the end of the war in 1945. It was a horrifying figure for non-combatants. Even so, there was never a shortage of men willing to sign up for the Atlantic convoys. When, in 1941, Britain began running convoys to aid the Soviet Union in its own battle with Germany, the merchant navy acquitted itself with equal bravery in the Arctic. If anything, the voyage, to ports like Murmansk on the Barents Sea in north-west Russia, was even more hazardous than it was in the Atlantic. Vital cargoes had to make their way through dangerous frozen seas, and were almost constantly exposed to German air attack.

Throughout 1940 and 1941, the Germans went on scoring successes against British shipping. During a lull in U-boat activity in the winter, two German battle cruisers, the *Scharnhorst* and the *Gneisenau*, sank over 20 merchant ships between them. Two others, the pocket battleship *Admiral Scheer* and the heavy cruiser *Admiral Hippe*r, accounted for a further 23, the *Scheer* venturing as far as the Indian Ocean to prey on supply lines from Britain's colonies in the East. On 23 May 1941, two of the Royal Navy's premier ships, the *Hood* and the *Prince of Wales* engaged the cruiser *Prinz Eugen* and the *Bismarck*, the Kriegsmarine's largest battleship, in the Straits of Denmark. In the ensuing battle, the *Hood* blew up and sank after her aft magazine was hit. Only three of the 1418 crew survived.

However, the Germans bought their victory at a high price. Two days later, attacked by torpedo-carrying Swordfish biplanes from the aircraft carrier *HMS Ark Royal*, the *Bismarck* was crippled. Her steering gear wrecked and her rudders jammed, *Bismarck* was unable to manoeuvre and became a sitting target for three torpedoes from the cruiser *Dorsetshire*, which sank her at 10.30 a.m. on Sunday, 25 May. Two thousand German sailors went down with their ship.

Elsewhere, British successes were rare. One notable exception took place on 8 March 1941, when the British convoy OB293 was set upon by a U-boat wolfpack led by Günther Prien and the crew of *U-47*, which had sunk the *Royal Oak* in 1939. Although Prien's U-boat was accompanied by the submarines of veteran captain Otto Kretschmer and a number of other experienced commanders, the British managed on this occasion to mount a powerful challenge. Two of the U-boats were crippled by depth charges from British escorts and one was forced to surrender. While attempting to pursue the fleeing convoy, Prien was obliged to crash-dive to avoid being rammed by the destroyer *Wolverine*. His damaged ship was chased until the *Wolverine* managed to destroy it with more depth charges. There were no survivors and within days, two more U-boats had followed *U-47* to the Atlantic seabed. They included Otto Kretschmer's vessel, although Kretschmer himself survived to spend the rest of the war in a prison camp. In Prien and Kretschmer, Dönitz had lost two of his best commanders.

By this time, there were almost 100 German submarines operating in the Atlantic. This gave vital importance to the 'lend lease' arrangement between Britain and the USA. Following his historic second re-election in 1939, President Roosevelt had convinced the US Congress that it must give Britain 'all aid short of war'. The 'cash and carry' system had outlived its usefulness and was abandoned. Although not yet prepared to enter the war, America, Roosevelt declared, was ready to become 'the arsenal of democracy'. Nearly 50 US warships were lent to Britain, US troops were garrisoned in Iceland, and the US Navy declared that it would escort shipping of 'all nationalities' between Iceland and the USA. In practice, this meant escorting British merchant ships for half their journey across the Atlantic. After a confrontation between the US destroyer *Greer* and a German U-boat on 4 September 1941, Roosevelt announced that 'from now on, if German or Italian vessels of war enter these waters, they do so at their own peril'. Unofficially, it was a declaration of war.

With the Atlantic convoys reinforced by US patrols, and the British gradually making improvements to their anti-submarine strategy, losses were substantially reduced in the second half of 1941. In November,

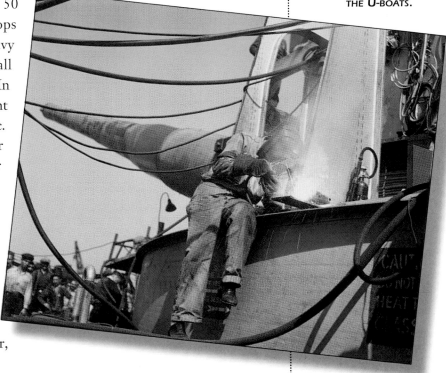

BELOW: A WELDER WORKS ON ONE OF THE USS IOWA'S GUN TURRETS AT THE NEW YORK NAVY YARDS. WITH THE USA'S ENTRY INTO THE WAR, THE TIDE WOULD BEGIN TO TURN AGAINST THE U-BOATS.

Dönitz was ordered to transfer U-boat operations to the Mediterranean for two months, to support the supply lines to the Afrika Corps. He later described this relaxation of pressure on British Atlantic shipping as 'unjustifiable'. However, with the USA's entry into the war in 1941, after the Japanese attack on Pearl Harbor, the situation was to change. Forced to send its best warships to the Pacific to counter the new Japanese threat, the USA soon found its own, unescorted merchant shipping in danger. By now, Dönitz had almost 200 submarines at his disposal, and he shifted his operations accordingly. In the first six months of 1942, the U-boats sank over 300 ships in US waters, the Gulf of Mexico and off the coast of Brazil. Over the whole year, more than 1000 Allied ships were lost to U-boat attacks. Britain, having endured almost three years of the German blockade, was now suffering severe shortages. The need for fuel oil in particular had become intense, and the strain upon the British Navy was becoming intolerable.

Yet, gradually, it was the Germans who were on the defensive. Ultimately, Britain was saved by a combination of scientific ingenuity, new tactics, and a massive shipbuilding programme. With the industrial might of the USA now behind it, the British merchant fleet was able to acquire ships as fast as they were being sunk. The number of escort ships was also increasing. By 1944, the US and British navies were able to assign up to 30 warships to each convoy – about four times as many as in 1942.

They were organised into submarine-hunting support groups, co-ordinated for the first time by British Coastal Command, and supported by new long-range Liberator bombers, whose pilots had been trained at Coastal Command's Tactical School. Their efforts were also helped enormously by a number of highly successful British submarine hunters like Captain F.J. 'Johnny' Walker. At home, new anti-submarine depth charges were being developed, as well as methods of intercepting German radio transmissions, which would warn convoys of nearby U-boat wolfpacks. Most decisive of all, the discovery of short-wave 'centimetric' radar finally gave the Allied submarine hunters a weapon against which the U-boats had no defence. Warships and aircraft armed with this extremely accurate system could track submarines day and night, whether they were on the surface or submerged.

The ball game was quite different now. Dönitz's U-boat commanders found themselves on the run. Throughout the second half of 1942 and into 1943, U-boat losses rose steadily, despite the fact that Dönitz now had over 400 submarines operational. Although British losses also continued to climb, the Allies were hitting back hard. The turning point finally came in May 1943, the month in which Dönitz lost 41 submarines and suffered a personal

RIGHT: ONE OF THE
BRITISH MIDGET SUBMARINES
THAT DAMAGED THE
GERMAN BATTLESHIP TIRPITZ,
WHICH WAS MOORED IN A
STRONGLY PROTECTED
ANCHORAGE IN NORTH
NORWAY.

LEFT: THE GERMAN CRUISER
ADMIRAL HIPPER UNDER
CAMOUFLAGE IN DRY DOCK
AT KIEL, WHERE IT WAS
CAPTURED BY ALLIED
SOLDIERS. AFTER 1943
THE GERMAN NAVY
WOULD NEVER AGAIN
RULE THE SEAS.

loss: his son had been serving on one of them. 'These losses are too high,' Dönitz informed Hitler, and suspended submarine operations in the north Atlantic. Between May and September 1943, no Allied ships were sunk by German submarines in the area. Instead, two British midget submarines scored a famous victory that September, sailing unobserved into Altenfjord, Norway, where the 42,000-ton German battleship *Tirpitz* was moored, and putting the giant ship out of action with explosive charges. By the time Dönitz resumed U-boat operations in the north Atlantic in the autumn of 1943, the tide had already turned. Despite technical improvements, including homing torpedoes and a 'schnorkel' tube that allowed U-boats to charge their batteries without surfacing, the German submarine fleet never again held the upper hand. In the first three months of 1944, only three Allied merchant ships were sunk. During the same period, Dönitz lost 29 submarines. Although Dönitz's operations would continue until the end of the war, for British shipping, the major crisis was over.

CHAPTER 10

The Desert War

AUSTRALIAN TROOPS ADVANCE TOWARDS ENEMY
LINES AS DAWN BREAKS OVER THE DESERT. GENERAL
LESLIE MORSHEAD OF THE AUSTRALIAN 9TH ARMY
ANNOUNCED TO HIS MEN BEFORE THE DEFENCE OF
TOBRUK: 'THERE'LL BE NO DUNKIRK HERE.'

ROMMEL

The war fought for North Africa between 1941 and 1943 was a conflict no one had ever planned to undertake. Yet, before it was finished, it would turn into a campaign neither side could afford to lose. What began as a minor territorial dispute between the British and Italian empires in Africa eventually dragged into combat hundreds of thousands of tanks, guns and men from countries as far apart as Poland, India, New Zealand, Australia and South Africa, as well as France, Italy, Britain and the USA.

Adolf Hitler was not, at first, particularly interested in a North African war, but partly because of the hero status acquired by his commander in the area, General Erwin Rommel, even he was forced to commit Germany to the fighting. The Desert War, where the battleground was large, featureless wastes of rock and sand, had its own character and its own rules, and made unique demands on the men who fought it.

When General Rommel arrived in North Africa with two German armoured divisions on 9 February 1941, his orders were simply to sustain the Italian Army. The Italians had already proved incompetent in Greece and Albania in 1940, and had been kicked out of Egypt by the British eight weeks before. They were, in fact, in danger of being forced out of Africa altogether. Weighing up the situation, Rommel almost immediately

BELOW: BRITISH TROOPS GET TO GRIPS WITH A TANK IN THE WORKSHOP IN PREPARATION FOR THE DEFENCE OF TOBRUK.

RIGHT: FRESH BRITISH TROOPS ARRIVE AT ALEXANDRIA IN 1940. DESPITE THEIR EARLY SUCCESS AGAINST THE ITALIANS, THEY WERE SOON TO FACE A MUCH TOUGHER FOE.

decided that attack was the best form of defence and on 31 March 1941 he launched an offensive on the British positions facing him without even waiting until his Afrika Korps was up to strength. The British, seriously depleted by the recent Greek campaign, were both overstretched and unprepared for the speed and ferocity of Rommel's attack. His men swept through the British lines in days, capturing the British Commander General O'Connor and pushing the enemy out of Italian

ABOVE: THE HARSH CONDITIONS OF LIFE IN THE NORTH AFRICAN DESERT LED TO A RELAXATION OF NORMAL MILITARY RULES FOR THE MEN WHO FOUGHT THERE.

LEFT: EXHAUSTED ARMY GUNNERS GRAB SOME MUCH-NEEDED REST IN THEIR DUGOUT. THEIR NUMBERS ALREADY DEPLETED BY THE DISASTROUS CAMPAIGN IN GREECE, THEY HAD LITTLE HEAVY EQUIPMENT OR AMMUNITION WITH WHICH TO COUNTER THE GERMAN THREAT.

Cyrenaica and eastwards towards Egypt. Rommel was held up only by the courage of the 9th Australian division, whose leader, General Leslie Morshead, announced to his men as they prepared to defend the port of Tobruk in Libya: 'There'll be no Dunkirk here.'

The speed of Rommel's advance took both sides by surprise. Originally ordered to carry out nothing more than a 'blocking action', he was now in a position to attempt an advance on Egypt and the vital Suez Canal, an indispensable lifeline, without which British supply routes to the Middle East and India would be severed, and Britain might be starved out of the war. The British fleet at Alexandria would be crippled, leaving Axis troops free to march across the Middle East and attack the Soviet Union from the south. In order to stop this happening, the British had to be reinforced and reorganised, and it had to be done fast.

First, General Archibald Wavell, Commander-in-Chief of the British forces in the area, was replaced by General Claude Auchinleck. This was perhaps unfair. Wavell had warned against weakening his forces by sending men to Greece just when they were starting to get

ABOVE: DESPITE BEING ASKED TO FIGHT A CAMPAIGN FOR WHICH HITLER HAD NEVER PLANNED, THE MEN OF THE AFRIKA KORPS ENJOYED A SERIES OF SPECTACULAR SUCCESSES IN THE EARLY DAYS OF THE NORTH AFRICAN CAMPAIGN.

ABOVE RIGHT: A GERMAN SOLDIER SURVEYS THE VAST WASTES OF EMPTY SAND THAT WERE TO MAKE UP THE DESERT BATTLEGROUND. IN SUCH CONDITIONS, SUPPLIES OF FOOD AND FRESH WATER WERE TO BECOME VITAL.

the better of the Italians. It was obvious, too, that the Germans would be considerably harder to beat. Auchinleck had at his disposal British, Indian, Australian, New Zealand and South African divisions, which he reorganised into a single 8th Army. But they were still poorly equipped. A huge offensive, Operation Battleaxe, was launched in June 1941 to relieve the siege of Tobruk, which had begun two months earlier, but here 200 new British tanks met disaster. Rommel had made his name as a panzer tank commander in France, and his highly trained and mobile fighting force had proved themselves perfectly suited to war in the desert. The British, by contrast, were still beginners in these stakes. Not only were the German panzer Mark IV tanks tougher than anything the British had, but they were supported by the huge 88mm anti-tank guns. At Tobruk, half the British tanks were destroyed in a single day, and Battleaxe was called off.

It was not until November 1941 that Auchinleck was ready to move again. He had planned his next move carefully, and this time, the siege of Tobruk was successfully raised by Operation Crusader, which also retrieved Cyrenaica from the Italians. In addition, the Libyan town of Benghazi was retaken on Christmas Eve, 1941, and the Afrika Korps was forced to retreat after five days of fighting. Though these locations would be contested again, both these victories had as much to do with the state of British and Axis supply lines as with military prowess, and for the next two years, the issue of supplies would dominate the North African campaign.

No army can operate without food, fuel and ammunition, and the Desert War was characterised by shortages of all three. Rommel's troops could be supplied only by convoy across the Mediterranean, and the RAF and Royal Navy were doing their utmost to ensure they did not get through. An Afrika Korps counter-attack on Benghazi, a valuable petrol and ammunition dump, failed due to lack of tank fuel – a telling illustration of how high the stakes were for both sides. Tobruk, though strategically worthless, was stocked full of food and supplies. When Rommel eventually captured the town on 21 June 1942, the surrender of 35,000 men paled beside German joy at finding thousands of tins of fruit, potatoes, cigarettes and canned beer.

Between January and May 1942, as Rommel sought to secure his supply lines, the British attempted to consolidate their position along the Gazala Line, which ran from the coastal plain up the Libyan escarpment. The British troops were becoming accustomed to the day-to-day problems of life in the desert – the perennial lack of water, the extremes of temperature that meant roasting by day and freezing by night, and the depressing effect of staring out at what the soldiers called 'miles and miles of eff all'. Uniform rules were relaxed and a uniquely casual working relationship was built up between officers and their men that, elsewhere, would have been regarded as contrary to discipline. Nevertheless, the British in the desert, nicknamed the 'Desert Rats', took justified pride in their abilities. They also had a great deal of respect for the skill of their opponents, and especially for the brilliance of Erwin Rommel, who became known, admiringly, as the 'Desert Fox'. The general opinion among the Rats was that the Afrika Korps contained men of considerable honour, which was more than had ever been said of the Italians.

In May 1942, Rommel was on the move again. The Free French troops, who held the southern end of the Gazala Line, managed to repulse a major attack, but when the German armour swung south, the British began to retreat. With less than 60 operational tanks at his disposal, Rommel nevertheless pressed on for Egypt. Tobruk fell again, and in Italy, with typically arrogant panache, Fascist dictator Benito Mussolini ordered a white horse to be prepared on which he planned to ride into Alexandria behind the triumphant German tanks. In Cairo, staff at British Middle East headquarters burned all their files in advance of the expected invasion, and the British fleet was moved from Alexandria to the Red Sea. It was then, on 23

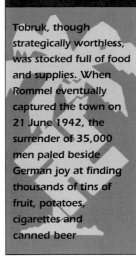

Tobruk, though strategically worthless, was stocked full of food and supplies. When Rommel eventually captured the town on 21 June 1942, the surrender of 35,000 men paled beside German joy at finding thousands of tins of fruit, potatoes, cigarettes and canned beer

AFRIKA KORPS V DESERT RATS

Throughout the Desert War, the British 8th Army and the soldiers of the Afrika Korps retained a unique respect for each other. Although in part this was due to the absence of any units of the German SS, who were responsible for atrocious crimes against soldiers and civilians alike in other theatres of war, there was also a genuine sense of chivalry between the two sides. This was reflected in the relationship between Rommel and Montgomery, who held each other in high regard. As one Desert Rat later remembered, he and his comrades felt their adversaries were 'a fine body of men, good clean fighters and well led'.

BRITISH INFANTRY MEN ADVANCE TOWARD A KNOCKED-OUT GERMAN TANK.

MALTA

The position of Malta in the central Mediterranean was of huge strategic importance as a base for Allied attacks on enemy supply lines to North Africa. Throughout 1940 and 1941 these raids, carried out by RAF planes and Royal Navy submarines, were so successful that 25 German U-boats were eventually recalled from the Atlantic to deal with the threat. As British successes against enemy shipping increased, Hitler decided to commit the full might of the Luftwaffe to subduing the island's population, and from 1941 onwards, Malta came under one of the heaviest and most sustained bombing campaigns of the war, as German planes attempted to 'neutralise' the island as a prelude to invasion.

Conditions for the Maltese were appalling. RAF fighter pilots and anti-aircraft gunners did their best to keep the island's vital runways open, but by the spring of 1942, Malta was under almost constant bombardment day and night. Most of the island's 300,000 inhabitants were reduced to living in a vast network of caves under the capital city, Valletta. British convoys of food and supplies from Gibraltar, unable to get through the U-boat blockade, were suspended. Morale was kept up only by the people's Roman Catholic faith and regular inspirational radio broadcasts from the island's governor, Sir William Dobie. At the end of April 1942, 47 RAF Spitfires were flown in to defend the island and reopen the convoy route, but most were destroyed in a surprise Luftwaffe attack while refuelling. Another 60 Spitfires flown in to replace them only narrowly avoided the same fate.

In June 1942, two supply ships got through from Gibraltar and disaster was averted. More supplies followed in August, by which time Hitler had begun to reconsider his invasion plans. Altogether, nearly 1500 Maltese civilians had been killed during the siege, and 1000 RAF planes had been lost, but their role in the war had been crucial. By stopping supplies of ammunition, fuel and food from reaching the Germans and Italians in North Africa, Malta ensured their eventual defeat, a fact that was recognised by both sides. The entire population of Malta was awarded the George Cross, the highest civilian award for bravery, by King George VI 'to bear witness to a heroism and devotion that will long be famous in history'. The George Cross has been an official symbol of Malta ever since

AN ANTI-AIRCRAFT CREW MAN THEIR POSITION DURING AN AIR RAID ON MALTA.

October 1942, that the 8th Army mounted its make-or-break, do-or-die defence at the town of El Alamein, in northern Egypt, only 65 miles from Alexandria.

'MONTY'

Pinned down between the Mediterranean and the vast, impassable Qattara depression, the two sides faced each other along a narrow strip of land, the only corridor into or out of Egypt. Arranged in four defensive 'boxes', the 8th Army held off wave after wave of German tanks for four days until Rommel, his troops exhausted and far from their supply lines, pulled back. At the same time, Winston Churchill once again shuffled his North African pack, replacing Auchinleck with General Sir Harold Alexander and appointing General Bernard Montgomery, 'Monty', head of the 8th Army.

Montgomery's arrival immediately galvanised those around him. He reportedly introduced himself to one brigadier with the words: 'Well, Freddie, you chaps seem to have been making a bit of a mess of things. Now what's the form?' What distinguished Montgomery most of all was his meticulous and patient approach. He was known for refusing to move unless his men had every piece of equipment it was possible to provide. He had studied Rommel's previous successes, and was confident that he knew how to defeat the Desert Fox. Noting that 'what Rommel liked to do was to get our armour to attack him', Montgomery planned to do precisely the opposite. Instead of throwing British armour forward and into the range of Rommel's anti-tank guns, he would dig in, and wait for Rommel to come to him. All Montgomery needed to ensure victory was the time to prepare. As he later wrote: 'Give us two weeks and Rommel could do what he liked. He would be seen off and then it would be our turn.'

Montgomery was right. Rommel's next attack, at Alam Halfa on 31 August 1942, was a failure, and his offensive was called off. After that, he was in no position to retreat. Nevertheless, Montgomery waited for two months before launching his counter-attack. Where Rommel was impulsive and brilliant, Montgomery was careful and methodical. Though total opposites, the two men were nevertheless almost perfectly matched. It was not until the pitch black desert night of 23 October 1942 that the 8th Army began a massive artillery bombardment on the German positions. The film record, which showed men and guns revealed only by brilliant flashes of light as the guns fired, became a classic of the war. Montgomery had amassed a force of nearly 200,000 men, almost twice those ranged against them, and 1000 tanks, many of them the new heavy 'Grant' modified M3s, lent by the Americans. For the next three days and nights, the 8th Army gradually battered down the enemy defences, until Operation Supercharge, led by New Zealand troops, smashed through the German lines. It was a decisive victory and signalled the beginning of the end of the Afrika Korps. From then on, the initiative belonged to the British and their allies.

El Alamein represented a turning point, not only for British fortunes in North Africa, but for the course of the war itself. Churchill would later claim: 'Up to Alamein we survived. After Alamein, we conquered.' One British soldier who was present recalled events less cryptically: 'It was clear to us that this was to be the final battle and if we lost, it would

LEFT: THE CHARISMATIC AND BRILLIANT AFRIKA KORPS LEADER, ERWIN ROMMEL, GERMANY'S YOUNGEST FIELD MARSHALL. HIS TACTICAL GENIUS EARNED HIM THE ADMIRING NICKNAME OF 'THE DESERT FOX' AMONG HIS BRITISH ENEMIES.

ABOVE: GENERAL BERNARD MONTGOMERY ATTENDS MORNING PRAYER. A GREAT LEADER OF MEN AND A MASTER OF THE MILITARY SET PIECE, MONTY WAS A PERFECT FOIL FOR ROMMEL. HIS SUCCESS AT EL ALAMEIN MARKED THE TURNING POINT OF THE DESERT WAR.

the US war machine dwarfed that of Britain, although it had yet to be tested against the might and skill of Nazi Germany. As US General Joseph Stilwell explained: 'The Limeys want us in (even) with our hastily made plans and our half-trained and half-equipped troops'

be every man for himself.' The effect of the German defeat was felt around the world. For the first time in the war, German tanks and troops had been beaten in combat. The British Empire had been saved and Britain's ability to make war had been confirmed. For Rommel, it was the start of a long, though often brilliantly fought, withdrawal. He was also about to run into a new enemy.

The plan to mount a joint Anglo–American invasion of north-west Africa had already been formulated four months earlier, after much heated discussion between the two allies. Eager to open a second front against Germany to aid the beleaguered Soviet Union, the USA had originally called for a direct invasion of France, but the British, far from ready for an undertaking of this magnitude, had vetoed the idea. Instead, they agreed to a plan that, they hoped, would both relieve the pressure on the Russian front and aid British troops already fighting in the desert: a series of Allied landings along the coast of French Morocco and Algeria, which were controlled by the collaborationist Vichy regime under Marshal Petain. A task force had been quickly set up, headed by US General Dwight D. Eisenhower. Despite the USA's recent entry into a war Britain had been fighting for nearly three years, the US military was to have the much higher profile during the campaign. In terms of resources – men, guns and equipment – the US war machine dwarfed that of Britain, although it had yet to be tested against the might and skill of Nazi Germany. As US General Joseph Stilwell explained: 'The Limeys want us in (even) with our hastily made plans and our half-trained and half-equipped troops.' But the Americans, if green, were also fresh.

OPERATION TORCH

On 8 November 1942, Operation Torch was launched. A total of 650 British and US ships converged on the North African coast to land troops at Algiers and Oran in Algeria and Casablanca in Morocco. At the same time, Free French underground agents were supposed to be seizing local military installations and communications lines to aid the Allied advance. Unfortunately, this action was uniformly unsuccessful, and in a number of places the invasion force met with considerable resistance. At Oran, despite radio broadcasts from President Roosevelt informing the startled locals that 'We come among you as friends, not as conqueror', the French opened fire on the Allied troops as soon as they had cleared the beach. Around Casablanca, where 35,000 US troops were attempting to get ashore, things went even more badly wrong. Landing craft capsized in heavy seas, drowning a number of men before they even reached the shore. Many of those who gained the beach found their units had broken up, and so had to wait for new orders before they could advance. In Casablanca itself, heavy resistance from the local French military lasted for over three days. Only at Algiers did the landings go off without major setbacks, although, to many who took part, even that seemed to be more by luck than judgement. As one American soldier reported: 'We received no opposition whatsoever. If we had, those in the water would have been helpless against enemy fire.'

The French were quick to condemn the Torch landings. From Vichy, Marshal Petain announced that 'France and her honour are at stake' and promised 'we shall defend ourselves'. Now, it was Eisenhower's turn to try and offer the French a deal. He approached Admiral Darlan, Commander-in-Chief of the French Navy, even though neither the Allies

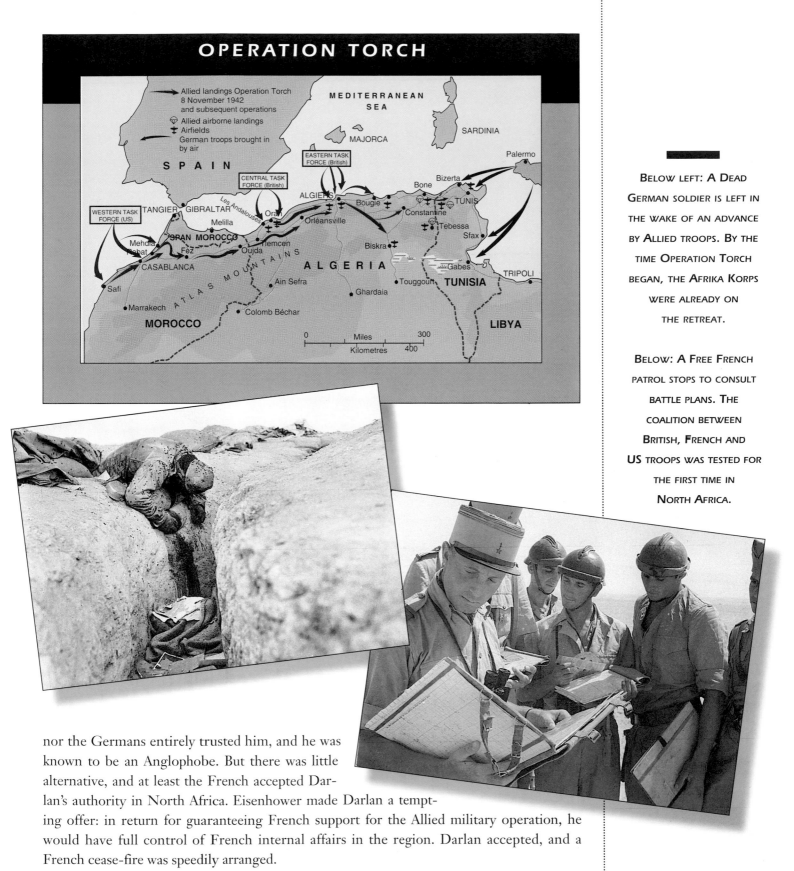

OPERATION TORCH

Allied landings Operation Torch 8 November 1942 and subsequent operations

Allied airborne landings

Airfields

German troops brought in by air

nor the Germans entirely trusted him, and he was known to be an Anglophobe. But there was little alternative, and at least the French accepted Darlan's authority in North Africa. Eisenhower made Darlan a tempting offer: in return for guaranteeing French support for the Allied military operation, he would have full control of French internal affairs in the region. Darlan accepted, and a French cease-fire was speedily arranged.

Nevertheless, the deal provoked considerable outrage in Britain, where Darlan had long been viewed as a Nazi sympathiser for his support of the Vichy regime. It had been Darlan's refusal to ally with the British that had led to the destruction or crippling by the

RIGHT: CONDITIONS AT AN
ALLIED HEADQUARTERS,
CONSTRUCTED INSIDE AN
ABANDONED WELL OUTSIDE
THE TOWN OF BARDIA.

ABOVE: MEMBERS OF THE
ROYAL CANADIAN AIR
FORCE ENJOY THEIR MEAGRE
RATIONS OUTSIDE THEIR
TENT. BY NOW THE MEN
HAD ADAPTED THEMSELVES
TO LIFE IN THE DESERT.

Royal Navy of almost all the French ships in port at Mers el Kebir on 3 July 1940. The Free French General de Gaulle was also angered, not least because he had not been informed of events in advance. De Gaulle warned the Allies: 'You don't get France by burglary.' French fury did not stop at words, though. On Christmas Eve, 1942, Darlan was assassinated by a Frenchman. As the political in-fighting continued, Germany was quick to react to the Allied landings and on 11 November invaded and occupied Vichy France. The Germans also attempted to seize what remained of the French fleet at the port of Toulon. Hitler planned to use the fleet to support his forces already in North Africa, but on 27 November French sailors scuttled their ships rather than let them fall into Nazi hands.

While the Allied High Command was busy negotiating, the Allied troops had already begun moving on. The British 1st Army advanced into Tunisia, hoping to beat German and Italian reinforcements who were already arriving from Sicily at the port of Tunis.

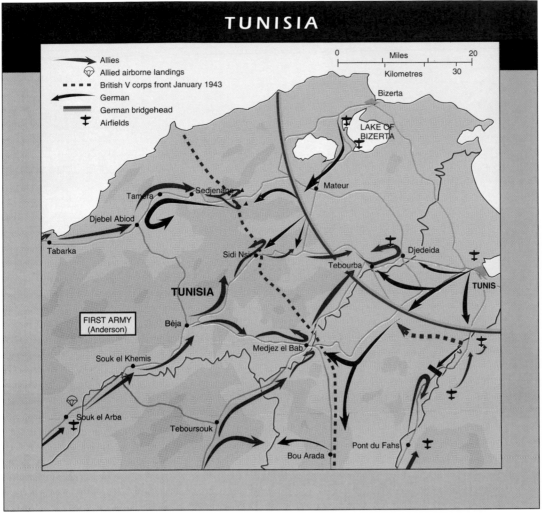

They were supported by US soldiers, who got their first taste of war in the battle for Longstop Hill, an attempt to take a heavily defended German position that ended in Allied defeat. Although poor supplies and bad weather were probably more responsible than American inexperience, this defeat did nothing to improve the low opinion the British had already formed of the US military. The British High Command was soon complaining about the 'poor fighting value of the Americans' and the tactical shortcomings of Eisenhower, a 'desk' general who never experienced the heat of battle in person. Montgomery himself summed up Eisenhower with the words: 'Nice chap, no General.' As far as the British were concerned, their US allies were untrained, undisciplined and unreliable in combat. For their part, the US military felt they were being forced to overextend themselves before they were up to strength. Their reputation was not enhanced when a unit of the US 1st Armoured Division was set upon by a surprise German assault through the pass they were supposed to be holding. General Omar Bradley, with the honesty typical of him, remarked: 'For the most part our soldiers abandoned their weapons and fled.'

The crunch for the US military came when Rommel's Afrika Korps, withdrawing westwards from Montgomery's 8th Army, broke through American lines at the Kasserine pass in Tunisia and threatened the Allied rear. Only the timely arrival of Montgomery himself forced Rommel to retreat, allowing US forces to reoccupy the pass. By that time, 3000 US

GENERAL MARK CLARK WITH GENERAL DWIGHT D. EISENHOWER,
LEADER OF THE JOINT ALLIED FORCES IN NORTH AFRICA.

GENERAL MARK CLARK

In order to secure support from the French Resistance forces in the weeks leading up to the Allied invasion of North Africa, US General Mark Clark was sent on a top secret mission to Algeria in October 1942. After travelling to Gibraltar in a US Liberator bomber, Clark was transported by British submarine to the North African coast, where, under cover of darkness, he was rowed ashore in a dinghy by two British commandos. In a small house not far from the beach, Clark met up with a group of French agents. In return for their support, he had been instructed to offer the overall leadership of Allied forces in the area, following the invasion, to the French General Henri Giraud, a war hero famous for twice escaping from German prison camps. The offer was actually a bluff, but Clark, as he later wrote, kept 'a poker face' throughout the negotiations. When the house was visited by suspicious police, Clark and his commando escort were forced to hide in the cellar, before making a dash back to the sea and returning to the submarine, unsure whether or not their mission had been successful.

soldiers had been taken prisoner and another 300 killed. Having learned the hard way that something had to change, Eisenhower took a number of important decisions after Kasserine. He handed over command of Allied military operations to his deputy, the British General Sir Harold Alexander, and then brought in the controversial General George S. Patton to take over and retrain the US II corps. Patton turned out to be the perfect man for the job. A flamboyant soldier famous for his habit of carrying two pearl-handled revolvers, he soon earned the nickname of 'Old Blood and Guts' from his men. His influence was soon apparent, too, as even Rommel reported himself astonished at 'the speed with which the Americans adapted'. Once better prepared and better supplied for the task in hand, US soldiers were ready to distinguish themselves. It was, Rommel later suggested, exactly the Americans' 'lack of regard for tradition and worthless theories' that enabled them to mend their ways so quickly.

For Rommel, the African campaign was now all but over. Denied permission to reorganise his forces, he returned to Germany in March 1943 after suffering a defeat along the heavily defended Mareth Line. The Allied victory there had been due to a brilliant combination of British, Free French, New Zealand and US armour, most of it advancing by night, and it signalled the end of Rommel's hopes for victory. In his absence, the Afrika Korps, now under the command of General Jurgen von Arnim, were finally trapped by British and US troops on the Cap Bon peninsula to the east of Tunis. With their backs to the sea, the Germans prepared for a siege. Instead, they were taken by surprise by a moonlight British tank charge, and had no choice but to surrender, despite Hitler's orders that they fight to the death. On 12 May 1943, nearly 250,000 German and Italian troops were taken prisoner, bringing the war in the desert to an end.

The success of the Allied campaign in North Africa would have great consequences for

Once better prepared and better supplied for the task in hand, US soldiers were ready to distinguish themselves. It was, Rommel later suggested, exactly the Americans' 'lack of regard for tradition and worthless theories' that enabled them to mend their ways so quickly

The success of the Allied campaign in North Africa would have great consequences for the course of the war…. over one million German and Italian troops had been lost… Combined with the losses they were suffering in Russia, this was a blow from which the Germans would never recover

ABOVE: 'OLD BLOOD AND GUTS', THE ABRASIVE GENERAL GEORGE S. PATTON, CAUGHT FOR ONCE WITHOUT HIS FAMOUS PEARL HANDLED REVOLVERS. HE WOULD CARRY HIS SUCCESSES IN NORTH AFRICA THROUGH TO THE INVASION OF EUROPE.

LEFT: A GERMAN SOLDIER DIGS A FOXHOLE IN THE WESTERN DESERT. DEMORALISED AND WITHOUT THEIR LEADER, THE AFRIKA KORPS WERE FINALLY DEFEATED BY THE COMBINED ALLIED FORCES IN THE SPRING OF 1943.

the course of the war. Altogether, over one million German and Italian troops had been lost trying to gain control of the region. Combined with the losses they were suffering in Russia, this was a blow from which the Germans would never recover. For the British, the campaign had lasted three years and had been hugely expensive in terms of both men and equipment. In Tunisia, there had been over 20,000 US casualties, but the US Army had proved itself in battle, and, for the first time, British and US troops had fought side by side, despite their continued misgivings about each other. The landings on the North African coast had also provided experience that would prove invaluable when the Allied High Command turned its attention to the invasion of France. Most importantly of all, the Allies were now poised to strike at Italy, the 'soft underbelly' of Hitler's 'Fortress Europe'.

CHAPTER 11

German Defeat in the East

GERMAN TROOPS STRUGGLE WITH THE ELEMENTS ON THE
EASTERN FRONT AS THE ONCE MIGHTY AND 'INVINCIBLE'
WEHRMACHT FACES DEFEAT AT THE HANDS OF THE
RUSSIANS – THE UNTERMENSCH WHOM HITLER
HAD ARROGANTLY PRESUMED TO VANQUISH WITHIN THREE
MONTHS OF THE COMMENCEMENT
OF OPERATION BARBAROSSA.

RIGHT: A SOVIET 'STORM GROUP' ADVANCES THROUGH THE SHATTERED REMAINS OF STALINGRAD. UNABLE TO BRING THEIR HEAVY WEAPONS TO BEAR INSIDE THE CITY, THE WEHRMACHT WERE FORCED TO ENGAGE THE RUSSIAN TROOPS AT CLOSE RANGE.

ABOVE: THE BATTLE FOR STALINGRAD SAW SOME OF THE FIERCEST FIGHTING OF THE SECOND WORLD WAR. ONE GERMAN OFFICER NOTED: 'STALINGRAD IS NO LONGER A TOWN. IT IS A FURNACE.'

THE BATTLE OF STALINGRAD

In the summer of 1942, Adolf Hitler, now leading the German Army from his Wolf's Lair in East Prussia, ordered his troops fighting in the Soviet Union to carry out a series of fresh offensives on the Soviet Union's most important centres. He had been thwarted in his attempts to take Moscow the previous winter, and decided that the Soviet capital could now wait. Instead, he would seize the city of Stalingrad, which stood on the River Volga near the junction of the Volga-Don canal. Hitler believed that Stalingrad, a major strategic and industrial centre, was also the defensive key to the valuable coal fields of the Don basin, which lay beyond. His plan was to hit at the industrial heart of the Soviet Union, rather than try to defeat outright its seemingly endless supplies of men and arms. Once he had shut down the country's industrial output, tanks would no longer be able to run, and guns would not fire. Then, the German armies would be able to take the Soviet capital at last.

The assault began on 23 August 1942. For the first two months, the German offensive rolled all before it, taking the towns of Kharkov and Kursk; by 4 September, it reached the outskirts of Stalingrad itself. The 6th Army under General Freidrich von Paulus was poised to overrun the city and secure a historic German victory. Back in Germany, Hitler was confident

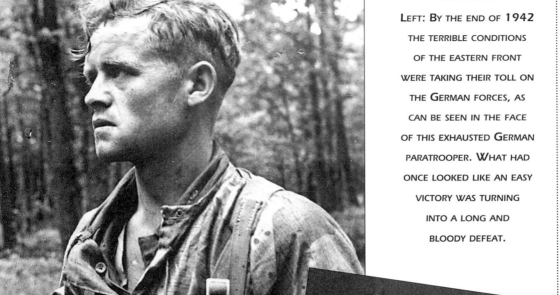

LEFT: BY THE END OF 1942 THE TERRIBLE CONDITIONS OF THE EASTERN FRONT WERE TAKING THEIR TOLL ON THE GERMAN FORCES, AS CAN BE SEEN IN THE FACE OF THIS EXHAUSTED GERMAN PARATROOPER. WHAT HAD ONCE LOOKED LIKE AN EASY VICTORY WAS TURNING INTO A LONG AND BLOODY DEFEAT.

Throughout the autumn and winter of 1942, Chuikov's 62nd Army forced the advancing Germans to fight for every single inch of Stalingrad. Street by street, house by house, even room by room, Soviet soldiers put up savage resistance, often engaging German troops hand to hand

enough to claim that the war had been won.

He had, however, once against counted without the Soviets' capacity for resistance. Hitler had also counted without General Vassili Chuikov, who had assumed the task of defending Stalingrad at this desperate time. Chuikov, a veteran of the Don front, had spent a great deal of time studying German military strategy and tactics. He had noted how the German infantry relied on air support from the Luftwaffe. Before any troops advanced, Chuikov had observed, the air force would always first bombard the enemy front lines to 'soften them up' for the tanks and men on the ground who would follow. Chuikov quickly realised that the best way to counter this strategy was to 'get as close to the enemy as possible' and lure the German infantry into fighting at such short range that the Luftwaffe would be unable to attack for fear of bombing their own men. But there was going to be a horrendous cost: it meant fighting the Wehrmacht in the streets and houses of Stalingrad itself.

Throughout the autumn and winter of 1942, Chuikov's 62nd Army forced the advancing Germans to fight for every single inch of Stalingrad. Street by street, house by house, even room by room, Soviet soldiers put up savage resistance, often engaging German

ABOVE LEFT: A RED ARMY SOLDIER BRANDISHES HIS TT33 SEMI-AUTOMATIC PISTOL. THE DESPERATE SOVIET DEFENCE OF THEIR MOTHERLAND ALLOWED NO QUARTER, AND RUSSIAN TROOPS USED EVERY WEAPON AT THEIR DISPOSAL.

Under the ruins of Stalingrad, the Soviet guerrilla army had turned cellars, sewers and even the caves in the banks of the River Volga into field hospitals, ammunition dumps and command posts. Their only supply line was across the river itself, from where reinforcements were ferried under cover of night

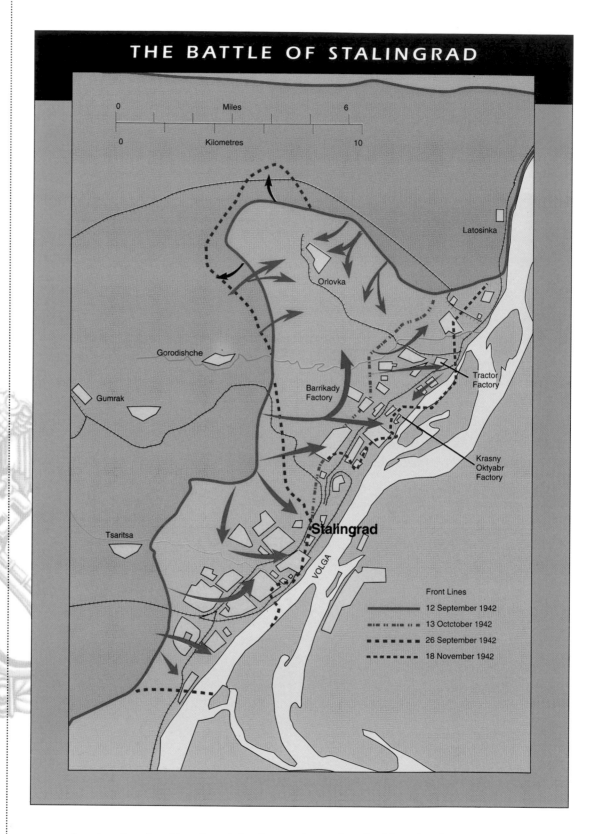

THE BATTLE OF STALINGRAD

Latosinka

Orlovka

Gorodishche

Gumrak

Barrikady Factory

Tractor Factory

Krasny Oktyabr Factory

Tsaritsa

Stalingrad

VOLGA

Front Lines

——— 12 September 1942
–·–·– 13 Octctober 1942
· · · · 26 September 1942
- - - - 18 November 1942

troops hand to hand, taking by night the territory they had lost by day. Most of the time, the two sides were close enough to throw insults at each other across the street. Sometimes, they were separated only by the rooms of a house. Chuikov had organised his soldiers into highly mobile 'storm groups', each containing a small number of men with a mixture of weapons – grenades, machine-guns and anti-tank rifles. They were able to carry out lightning attacks on German troops and then disappear back into the rubble of the city. By contrast, the German tanks were largely useless. In the narrow streets, they were unable to turn quickly when attacked from behind or from the side. Their guns lacked the elevation to fire on the upper floors of buildings from where Soviet troops aimed anti-tank guns at them. Meanwhile, hidden snipers, picking the enemy off without warning, struck terror into the hearts of the German infantry.

The charismatic Chuikov, an inspiration to the men under his command, soon gained a reputation among the Germans for being indestructible. Even so, his troops sustained huge losses as the enemy, supplied by over 3000 Luftwaffe flights a day, slowly took control of the south and central areas of the city. Under the ruins of Stalingrad, the Soviet guerrilla army had turned cellars, sewers and even the caves in the banks of the River Volga into field hospitals, ammunition dumps and command posts. Their only supply line was across the river itself, from where reinforcements were ferried under cover of night. But soon, even this was threatened. At the beginning of October 1942, as the front moved into the factory district in the north of the city, the fighting became even more intense. A German lieutenant reported that 'the street is no longer measured by metres, but by corpses'. Fighting raged for days around a strategically situated grain elevator, with the upper and lower levels changing hands a number of times. Inside the huge Barrikady and Krasny Oktyabr tractor factories, which dominated the area, gunfire blazed for three weeks.

BELOW: SOVIET T-34 AND T-26 TANKS (RIGHT AND LEFT) TOW RED ARMY SKI TROOPS TO THE FRONT. THE RUSSIANS WERE LEARNING FAST HOW TO BEAT THE GERMAN ENEMY, AND THEIR ADAPTABILITY AND VAST RESOURCES WOULD EVENTUALLY CARRY THEM ALL THE WAY TO THE BORDERS OF GERMANY.

ABOVE: THROUGHOUT
OCTOBER 1942 FIGHTING
BETWEEN RUSSIAN AND
GERMAN TROOPS
INTENSIFIED AROUND THE
INDUSTRIAL HEART OF
STALINGRAD. THE COMING
WINTER WAS ONCE AGAIN
TO PROVE LETHAL TO THE
WEHRMACHT, AS 90,000
MEN WERE LEFT TRAPPED
INSIDE THE CITY.

By the end of October, both sides seemed to have exhausted themselves. The rapid approach of another punishing Russian winter had restricted Luftwaffe flights into the city, severely cutting the 6th Army's supplies. But the Soviets had been preparing a nasty surprise. On 19 November, the Red Army launched a huge counter-attack on the enemy lines around Stalingrad. For months, General Georgi Zhukov had been building up a garrison of over one million men on the far bank of the River Volga. Now, they cut through the Romanian divisions stationed to the north and south and within three days surrounded the city. Von Paulus and his men were trapped inside Stalingrad. Predictably, Hitler ordered them to hold the city at all costs. Convinced that a German retreat at this stage would be psychologically devastating, the Führer denied his men even an attempt to fight their way out. Instead, he promised to mount a rescue mission, led by Field Marshal von Manstein. A column of panzers was sent to their aid, but was turned back by Soviet troops some 35 miles from Stalingrad. The few Luftwaffe flights that could get through the deteriorating weather became the beleaguered 6th Army's only lifeline.

Throughout December 1942 and January 1943, in the most appalling conditions, von Paulus's men held out, despite constant day and night bombardment from Soviet guns. Food and fuel were scarce. Men froze to death in their tanks as they slept. Others injured themselves as a ploy to be airlifted out of the city, even though they were committing an offence

LEFT: GERMAN TROOPS CONSTRUCT A MAKESHIFT FIRE TO WARM THEMSELVES IN THIS PROPAGANDA PHOTOGRAPH. IN REALITY, MEN WERE FREEZING TO DEATH IN THEIR TANKS AS THEIR FUEL AND SUPPLIES SLOWLY RAN OUT. NEVERTHELESS, THE FÜHRER HIMSELF HAD EXPRESSLY FORBIDDEN SURRENDER.

BELOW: A TRUER PICTURE OF LIFE INSIDE A GERMAN BUNKER ON THE EASTERN FRONT IN 1943 SHOWS CRAMPED CONDITIONS AND HOPELESSNESS ON THE FACES OF MANY OF THE MEN. MORALE WAS AT AN ALL-TIME LOW, AS SOLDIERS BROODED ON THEIR FATE.

punishable by death. Suicides were not uncommon. Then, on 24 January 1943, Soviet troops captured the two remaining German airfields in the city. Now, von Paulus and his men were totally cut off. It was the end. Seven days later, von Paulus and the 90,000 troops under his command surrendered to the Red Army. Eyewitnesses reported columns of German prisoners stretching for miles. Back in Germany, the government announced three days of national mourning. Hitler himself was devastated. The same day that von Paulus surrendered, Hitler had made him a Field Marshal, reminding him that no one of that rank in the German armed forces had ever capitulated. Hitler was unable to understand why von Paulus had not had the honour to die in battle or kill himself. He

complained that 'the heroism of so many soldiers is nullified by the actions of one single characterless weakling'.

The surrender of Stalingrad was the nadir of German fortunes and morale. To the German people, as well as to the rest of the world, it had suddenly been made clear that their armies were no longer invincible. Hitler himself, deep in his Wolf's Lair, was said to have brooded over Stalingrad for months afterwards, unable to come to terms with the magnitude of the failure. Once he had been convinced that history was on his side. Now, he was obsessed with the fact that his armies had been out-thought and outfought by supposedly inferior Slavs. At the same time, his armies in North Africa were being thrashed by the combined efforts of the British, and a powerful new enemy, the USA. With the USA's entry into the war, an almost unlimited new supply of men, tanks, aircraft and guns would soon be added to the forces now ranged against Germany. The heady days of early success, when Europe seemed to be at his mercy, had turned dark with defeat and despair.

General Zhukov's counter-attack on Stalingrad was followed by a quick and decisive victory over the Italian 8th Army on the Don river. Soon afterwards, the German forces in the Caucasus were forced to retreat through the town of Rostov in the face of overwhelming Soviet numbers. Almost all the territory the German forces had taken in the previous 12 months had now been lost. The Soviet advance continued in 1943, with Kharkov falling to the Soviet troops in mid-February. But there, a horrifying secret was revealed as the Russian troops discovered the atrocities of the Nazi occupation. They found a city that had lost half its 700,000 inhabitants in less than two years. Those who had not been transported to Germany or murdered by the SS had starved to death. It was a scenario that was to be repeated many times as the German retreat uncovered the full horrors that their occupation had inflicted on the Soviet people, and this hardened still further the Russians' resolve not to stop until the German war effort had been trampled into extinction.

With the coming of Spring in 1943, the rains once again halted all activity on the Russian front. This pause gave the German forces in the area a final chance to regroup and strengthen their lines around the panzer armies of Field Marshal von Manstein. German and Soviet troops were now facing each other across the River Donetz. To the north, the Red Army held the town of Kursk, as well as a large bulge of territory reaching some 100 miles forward of the Soviet lines. It was here that Hitler planned a final offensive. The success of the German counter-attack, which retook Kharkov on 14 March, convinced him that he could still win the war in the east. By launching an all-out attack on Kursk, Hitler believed his remaining forces – some one million men – would be able to cut off the 500,000 Soviet troops holding the area. New Tiger and Panzer tanks had been delivered to

To the German people, as well as to the rest of the world, it had suddenly been made clear that their armies were no longer invincible. Hitler himself, deep in his Wolf's Lair, was said to have brooded over Stalingrad for months afterwards, unable to come to terms with the magnitude of the failure

DEAD BODIES LIE IN THE STREETS OF LENINGRAD AFTER A HEAVY GERMAN ARTILLERY BOMBARDMENT.

city to organise its defences. Since the Leningrad Home Guard was formed from its workforce, Zhukov soon found himself sending people 'straight from the factory floor to meet the enemy'.

From the earliest days of Operation Barbarossa, Hitler had made the destruction of Leningrad into a personal quest. German artillery units were given specific orders to destroy historic buildings and sites of cultural interest such as the Hermitage museum and the Kirov theatre, which was famous for its ballet company. On 8 September 1941, 700,000 German and Finnish troops surrounded the city, but their attempts to storm it were defeated. Instead, as their numbers were gradually reduced to feed offensives elsewhere, they laid siege, bombarding Leningrad with shells day and night and hoping to demoralise and starve out the inhabitants. The stalemate was to last for two years, and cost the lives of nearly one million people.

Lake Lagoda, on which it stood, was crucial to Leningrad's survival. The southern shore of the lake was still held by Soviet forces, and this became the city's one and only lifeline. When the lake froze in the winter, the Russians built a road across it to ferry supplies into the city. Even then, what could get through was far from adequate. Inside Leningrad, there was never enough to eat, nor enough fuel to keep people warm. Bread made from sawdust, and soup from the bones of slaughtered horses, formed the staple diet. By the end of the siege, it was reported that no animals or birds could be found anywhere in the city. Between September 1941 and January 1944, over 600,000 people died in Leningrad from cold or starvation. Another 200,000 were killed by enemy shelling before the siege was finally lifted by the Red Army on 27 January.

THE SIEGE OF LENINGRAD

In the summer of 1941, as German troops approached Leningrad, this historic birthplace of the Russian Revolution of 1917 saw a desperate scramble to evacuate nearly two million people. Those who remained behind began the process of turning Leningrad into a fortress. Hundreds of gun emplacements and trenches were constructed, along with ammunition dumps and air raid shelters. Factories turned out tanks and guns as fast as they could go. On Stalin's orders, General Georgi Zhukov had flown to the

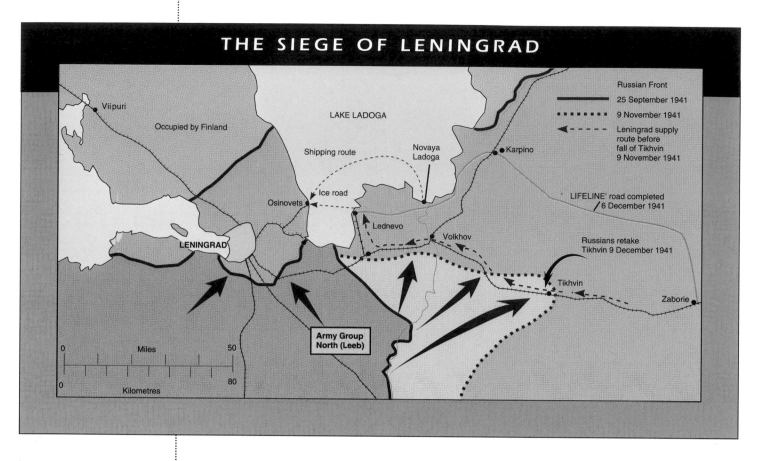

THE SIEGE OF LENINGRAD

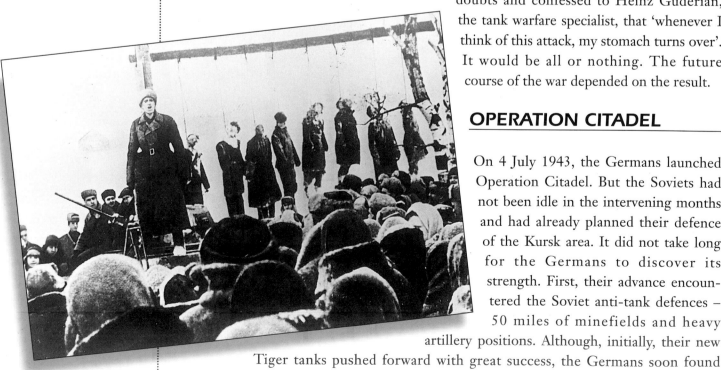

the front, and, to the north and south, the 9th and 17th Armies had regrouped. Hitler told his generals that victory at Kursk would 'shine like a beacon to the world' and would inspire his armies to a new assault on Moscow. But despite this bravado, even he had doubts and confessed to Heinz Guderian, the tank warfare specialist, that 'whenever I think of this attack, my stomach turns over'. It would be all or nothing. The future course of the war depended on the result.

OPERATION CITADEL

On 4 July 1943, the Germans launched Operation Citadel. But the Soviets had not been idle in the intervening months and had already planned their defence of the Kursk area. It did not take long for the Germans to discover its strength. First, their advance encountered the Soviet anti-tank defences – 50 miles of minefields and heavy artillery positions. Although, initially, their new Tiger tanks pushed forward with great success, the Germans soon found themselves stranded. Without machine-gun support, they were unable to defend them-

selves at close range, and fell victim to Soviet infantry armed with anti-tank rifles. Within a single day, the Soviets reported the destruction of nearly 500 enemy tanks.

Then, Zhukov unleashed the Red Army's counter-attack. On 12 July, the 600 tanks of the 4th Panzer Army met the Soviet 5th Tank Army. The result was reputed to be the largest tank battle in history, fought over an area of less than 12 square miles. This was the first time the German Army had ever faced such a concentrated Soviet force, and the losses on both sides were enormous. On 13 July, Hitler called off Operation Citadel, but the fighting continued. And on 17 August, after a day's continuous exchange of fire, victory went to the Russians. The 4th Panzer Army, which lost over 300 tanks, was routed. Hitler's final offensive on the Russian front had ended in failure. There could be no doubt now that the German Army was on the verge of defeat in Russia.

Inspired by the overwhelming success at Kursk, the Red Army resumed its advance westwards. Kharkov was liberated again on 23 August. On 6 November, Kiev was also reclaimed. There, the troops discovered yet more atrocities. In a city of nearly 500,000 people, less than 100,000 had survived the German occupation. Now, Hitler issued his 'Directive 51' to the German forces in the east, making the German retreat from the Russian front all but official. He announced that despite 'the hard and costly struggle against Bolshevism', which his men had waged for over two years, 'a greater danger now appears in the west'. Troops and guns, Hitler explained, were needed in western Europe to shore up defences against the 'Anglo-Saxon landing', which now seemed inevitable. However true the threat of an Allied landing

ABOVE: THE LEADERS OF THE SOVIET WAR EFFORT, WITH MARSHALL GEORGI ZHUKOV, THE MASTERMIND BEHIND COUNTLESS SOVIET VICTORIES, IN THE CENTRE.

OPPOSITE PAGE: A MEETING IS HELD IN A LIBERATED RUSSIAN VILLAGE TO HONOUR THE DEATH OF EIGHT PARTISANS WHO HAD BEEN TORTURED AND KILLED BY THE NAZIS DURING THE GERMAN OCCUPATION.

RIGHT: SOVIET SOLDIERS ON THE ROAD TO LENINGRAD STOP TO WARM THEIR HANDS ON A BURNING ROAD SIGN THAT BEARS THE GERMAN NAME FOR THE CITY. THE RAISING OF THE SIEGE OF LENINGRAD SENT A MESSAGE OF HOPE FLASHING AROUND THE WORLD.

may have been, it could do little to disguise the fact that the German Army had been beaten, and that Hitler was ordering its retreat.

Early in 1944, the Soviet advance reached Leningrad and the raising, on 27 January, of a siege which had lasted almost 900 days was celebrated right across the Soviet Union. It was quickly followed by further Soviet gains. In March, at Korsun on the River Dneiper,

THE SOVIET T-34 – THE TANK THAT DEMOLISHED GERMAN 'INVINCIBILITY'.

THE SOVIET T-34 TANK

The huge tank battle at Kursk in July and August 1943 was proof that, with the T-34, the Soviet military had come up with the answer to the feared German panzer tank. Faster, more manoeuvrable and better armoured than its German counterpart, the T-34 was also put to better use than the outdated BT tanks that it replaced. As the T-34s rolled off the Russian production lines, Soviet commanders were observing and learning from the Germans how to use tanks to attack the enemy's flanks rather than assaulting them head on. The defeat of Operation Citadel, like the Soviet victory at Stalingrad, showed that the Germans could be outfought and out-thought, and by an army that, in their arrogance, they had once presumed was easy prey.

upwards of 20,000 German and Belgian troops were massacred trying to escape encirclement. In the south, the drive to take back the Crimea from the German 17th Army began in April. Sevastopol was freed on 9 May, as its German occupiers attempted to flee by boat across the Black Sea to Romania. Much like the British at Dunkirk in 1940, they found themselves easy prey for the attacking air force. The local Tatar population fared little better. Thousands were deported by the Soviet Government, who suspected them of collaborating with the Germans. In Belarus, partisan groups aided the Red Army offensive by sabotaging railways and German communications. Here, Hitler had ordered his troops to hold their positions, but they could do little when confronted by the 1,500,000 men and 5000 tanks now ranged against them. Thirty-two German divisions were routed, and on 1 July 1944, the city of Minsk fell, with over 100,000 German casualties. By the end of the month, on 28 July, the town of Brest Litovsk was back in Soviet hands and the German invasion of the Soviet Union was over. The Red Army was preparing to advance into Poland and all points west towards Germany itself.

Overall, upwards of 20 million Soviet citizens died during the German occupation. In Belarus alone, nearly one million lost their lives. To judge by the characteristically meticulous SS records, over two million Russians died in prisoner of war camps or during 'transportation'. Millions of others simply disappeared. Many were kidnapped children who had looked sufficiently Aryan enough to be taken to Germany. One million Soviet Jews were either murdered, or died in concentration camps. More than any other single nation, the Soviet Union suffered the most appalling losses as a result of Hitler's ambitions.

BELOW: GERMAN POWS ARE MARCHED THROUGH THE STREETS OF MOSCOW. TWO MILLION OF THEM WOULD NEVER SEE THEIR HOMELAND AGAIN, AS THE RUSSIANS EXTRACTED A BLOODY VENGEANCE FOR THEIR OWN COUNTRY'S SUFFERING.

CHAPTER 12

The Second Front

An American soldier takes directions from an Italian civilian, Italy 1943–4. The mountainous terrain of northern Italy would take an enormous toll on both sides as the war on the Second Front raged into the bitter winter of 1944.

THE 'SOFT UNDERBELLY'

In April 1943, the Royal Navy submarine *Seraph* dropped a dead body in Spanish waters carrying fake papers referring to an imminent Allied invasion of Greece. The body floated ashore on the Spanish coast on 30 April. 'Major Martin', later known as the 'Man Who Never Was', was an invention of British Naval Intelligence. He had been given an entirely bogus identity, including a bank manager, a tailor and a fiancée called Pam. The ruse was good enough to convince the German High Command, which soon received news of the find from their old allies, the government of General Franco. As a result, they were busy preparing for an Allied assault from the Aegean Sea while across the Mediterranean the British 8th and US 7th Armies began landing troops on the south coast of Sicily on 10 July 1943.

ABOVE: BRITISH SERVICEMEN DRY THEIR CLOTHES AFTER LANDING ON SICILY. HARDENED BY THEIR EXPERIENCES IN THE AFRICAN DESERT, THEY WERE NOW READY TO STRIKE AT GERMAN DEFENCES IN MAINLAND EUROPE.

RIGHT: US ORDNANCE AND EQUIPMENT ROLLS ASHORE ON SICILY. THE ISSUE OF WHETHER OR NOT TO BUILD ON THE VICTORY IN NORTH AFRICA BY INVADING ITALY HAD BEEN HOTLY CONTESTED AMONG THE ALLIED HIGH COMMAND.

JAPANESE-AMERICAN TROOPS ADVANCE THROUGH THE ITALIAN COUNTRYSIDE.

ALLIED FORCES IN ITALY

The Allied forces in Italy contained the most diverse collection of soldiers ever formed into a field force. As well as US, British and French troops, the fighting forces co-ordinated by General Alexander included men from India, New Zealand, South Africa and Canada. They were joined by Poles, French Moroccans, a Jewish unit from Palestine and a Brazilian Expeditionary Force. Although Italy itself declared war on Germany on 13 October 1943, Italians were never granted the status of 'allies'. Instead, Italian soldiers were invited to fight alongside Allied troops as 'co-combatants'. In the event, their limited actions against German troops were totally overshadowed by the activities of the 100,000 Italian civilians who became partisan guerrillas.

A joint British and US invasion of Sicily had always been the long-term aim of the Allied campaign in North Africa, despite arguments between them over whether or not an assault on the Italian mainland should ensue. The Soviet Union was urgently requesting that a 'second front' be opened against German forces in Europe to relieve the pressure on the beleaguered Russian troops, and Churchill favoured a strike against what he called Europe's 'soft underbelly'. The USA preferred the idea of a single, massive assault on northern France across the English Channel, and felt that an Italian campaign would be a waste of men and resources. Although an early Italian surrender was likely, the Allies still expected stiff opposition from the strong, disciplined and well-led German forces already stationed in Italy. For the next two years, that is exactly what they got.

Defended by 10 Italian and two German divisions, the mountainous island of Sicily was not easy territory to conquer. It took General Montgomery and General Patton, who led the joint Allied forces, 38 days to achieve victory. In that time, the German Field Marshal Alfred Kesselring, Commander-in-Chief of the German forces in Italy, managed to evacuate over 100,000 German and Italian soldiers to the mainland.

The question for the Allies now was what to do next. Two weeks after the landings, Benito Mussolini had been called before the Italian Fascist Grand Council and removed from power by King Victor Emanuel III. The stunned dictator was then bundled into an ambulance and taken to a disused mountain hotel, where, it was intended, he would be imprisoned for the rest of the war. He was replaced as head of the Italian Government by Field Marshal Pietro Badoglio, the former commander-in-chief of the Italian armed forces, who had himself been sacked by Mussolini during Italy's ill-fated invasion of Greece in 1940. The Italians, however, had never been wholehearted about the war. Now, three years later, with an Allied invasion looming, the Italian Government seemed only too glad of a chance to surrender and get out. But the Allies were not to come by this 'whitewash' all that easily.

Negotiations between the new government and the Allied High Command began almost immediately after the end of the Sicilian campaign on 19 August, but for 45 days the Italian leadership stalled over announcing a cease-fire. Not only was Badoglio hoping

> The Italians, however, had never been wholehearted about the war. Now, three years later, with an Allied invasion looming, the Italian Government seemed only too glad of a chance to surrender and get out. But the Allies were not to come by this 'whitewash' all that easily

for better terms than the unconditional surrender demanded by the Allies, but he was also aware that the German Army was preparing to occupy and defend Italy.

Throughout July and August 1943, Allied planes mounted almost continuous bombing of the Italian mainland in an effort to persuade the government to make up its mind. During the same period, a wave of strikes protesting at Italy's continued involvement in the war threatened to cripple the industrial north of the country. In the end, the Allies decided to force the Italians' hand by invading the mainland on 3 September 1943. After covering the short distance

ABOVE: US FORCES LANDING AT SALERNO IN MAINLAND ITALY FACED STIFF RESISTANCE FROM THE HEAVILY DEFENDED GERMAN POSITIONS. SOON, EVERY MAN WHO COULD CARRY A RIFLE WOULD BE PUSHED INTO THE FRONT LINE, AS GENERAL MARK CLARK'S RESERVES WERE RAPIDLY EXHAUSTED.

RIGHT: FOLLOWING THE ITALIAN SURRENDER, GERMAN TROOPS QUICKLY OCCUPIED TOWNS AND VILLAGES ACROSS THE COUNTRY. THESE PARATROOPERS ATTEMPT TO HOLD MONTE CASSINO AGAINST THE ALLIED ADVANCE.

ABOVE: DON LUIGI PIAZZA,
AN ITALIAN PRIEST AND
LEADER OF A PARTISAN
BAND, SHARES A JOKE WITH
A FELLOW PATRIOT.
EQUIPPED WITH SUPPLIES
DROPPED BY ALLIED PLANES,
THESE MEMBERS OF 'THE
ARMY OF NATIONAL
LIBERATION' ORGANISED IN
SECRET HIDEOUTS IN THE
ITALIAN MOUNTAINS.

ABOVE LEFT: THE ITALIAN
PEOPLE FINALLY TOOK
UP ARMS AGAINST THE
GERMANS. THIS SCHOOL
TEACHER FOUGHT IN A PAR-
TISAN UNIT IN NORTHERN
ITALY, COMMITTED, LIKE
THOUSANDS OF OTHERS,
TO FREEING HER COUNTRY
FROM THE NAZI YOKE.

across the Straits of Messina, which was between two and eight miles wide, the British 8th Army carried out a series of landings near the town of Reggio di Calabria. They encountered little resistance and, by the end of the day, the Allied presence in Italy was established. The Italian surrender was made official five days later, the day before US troops began landing at Salerno, 30 miles from Naples, in south-western Italy. The American GIs ran into considerably more difficulty than the British. Within hours of the cease-fire, German troops had occupied Rome and other major towns and cities across Italy. At Salerno, they had already established well-defended artillery positions in the hills surrounding the town, and the US 5th Army met fierce resistance. It took General Mark Clark's troops five days to fight their way inland. Despite this setback, by 1 October the Allies had succeeded in their initial military objectives: the capture of the port of Naples and the airfields at Foggia. From there, they could then land a complete invasion force supported by air cover.

As he had already done in Sicily, Field Marshal Kesselring once again made a series of tactical retreats, pulling the German troops back towards the Apennine mountains, the central 'spine' of Italy, which ran 800 miles from the north down to the Straits of Messina. Kesselring knew he would have the rugged mountain terrain on his side and planned to exploit it to the full in order to prevent the Allied troops reaching their next target: Rome.

Kesselring's 'Gustav Line' was dominated by Monte Cassino, a 1703-ft-high peak capped by a beautiful 1300-year-old Benedictine monastery that stood at the entrance to

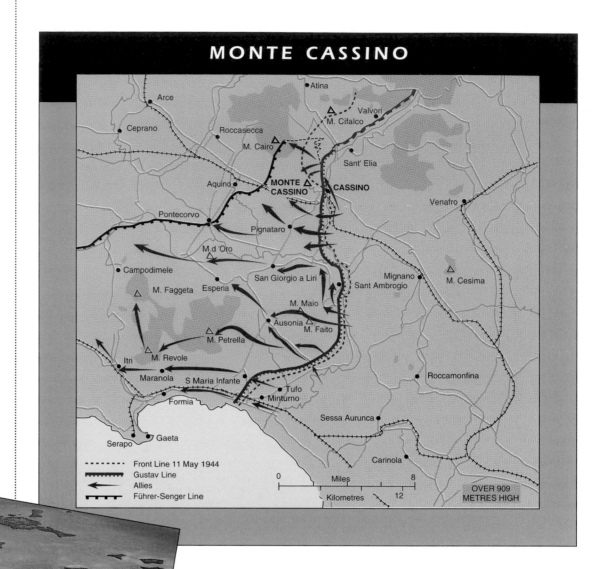

MONTE CASSINO

- - - - Front Line 11 May 1944
━━━━━ Gustav Line
◄━━━ Allies
━━━━━ Führer-Senger Line

0 ⎓ Miles ⎓ 8
⎓ Kilometres ⎓ 12

OVER 909 METRES HIGH

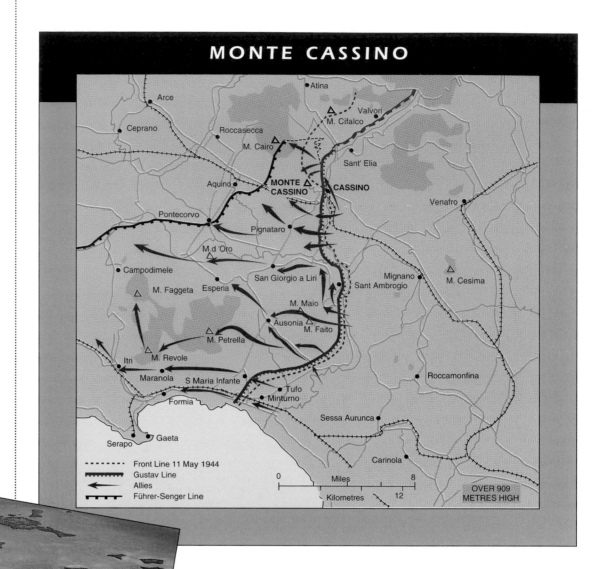

BELOW: AMERICAN B17 BOMBERS WERE USED IN THE ATTACK ON THE HEAVILY ENTRENCHED GERMAN POSITIONS AT MONTE CASSINO, BUT THEIR BOMBARDMENT ONLY SERVED TO GIVE THE ENEMY BETTER COVER.

BOTTOM: THE HISTORIC MONASTERY AT MONTE CASSINO EXPLODES UNDER THE WEIGHT OF THE ALLIED BOMBING. AS THE FIGHT FOR THE PEAK DRAGGED ON, CONDITIONS FOR THE MEN ON BOTH SIDES OF THE CONFLICT SOON BECAME INTOLERABLE.

the Liri valley, blocking the only road north to the Italian capital 75 miles to the northeast. To clear the path, the Allies would have to flush the Germans out of the mountains. What followed were six months of some of the most bitter fighting of the war as US, British and New Zealand troops made repeated attempts to capture the heavily defended German positions. The conditions were atrocious. Not only did fighting along exposed mountain roads leave troops almost permanently open to attack from above, they were also vulnerable to the elements. The freezing mountain cold took a heavy toll of Allied troops who had spent the last year in the simmering deserts of

The conditions were atrocious...The freezing mountain cold took a heavy toll of Allied troops who had spent the last year in the simmering deserts of North Africa. One GI later remembered: 'For years afterwards, my toes were numb from frostbite.' Losses on both sides were severe

LEFT: AN ALLIED SOLDIER SURVEYS THE UTTER DEVASTATION WREAKED ON THE AREA AROUND MONTE CASSINO. THE BATTLE FOR THE MOUNTAIN WOULD EVENTUALLY COST THE LIVES OF OVER 100,000 MEN.

North Africa. One GI later remembered: 'For years afterwards, my toes were numb from frostbite.' Losses on both sides were severe. Over 80,000 Allied troops lost their lives in the campaign, as did 50,000 German soldiers. Gurkhas from Nepal, who had fought for the British ever since the early days of the Raj in India, were particularly hard hit as their phenomenal valour and experience of mountain warfare made them natural front-line troops.

The key to Monte Cassino was the ancient monastery on top of the mountain, which over-looked the entire area. Determined that it should

ANZIO

The landings behind German lines at Anzio, 30 miles south of Rome, on 22 January 1944 were carried out to try to relieve pressure on Allied troops fighting in the Apennine mountains. However, after coming ashore and spending a week digging into defensive positions, the 50,000 men of the US 6th Army were pinned down by a German counter-attack, and for the next four months suffered almost constant bombardment from inland. During the fighting, the town of Carrocetto changed hands no less than eight times as the Allied troops repeatedly tried, but failed, to break out of their beachhead. Churchill referred to the operation as 'a stranded whale' and US General John Lucas was roundly criticised for not having advanced when he had the opportunity. After suffering considerable losses, the Allied forces eventually broke through the German defences on 23 May 1944.

ALLIED LANDING SHIPS UNLOAD SUPPLIES AS THE FIGHT FOR ANZIO RAGES ON.

not fall into German hands, the British General Bernard Freyberg requested, with reluctance, that it be destroyed by Allied bombers, despite the fact that it was still inhabited by the Benedictines. On 15 February 1944, having gained permission from Pope Pius XII, Allied aircraft dropped some 600 tons of bombs on the historic monastery, levelling it to a mass of smashed stone and smoking ruin. The destruction of this historic building was for nothing, however. Its ruins presented even better defensive opportunities and German troops soon dug themselves into the rubble. When the German positions were finally taken three months later, it was due to the combined efforts of Polish and French Moroccan troops. The Moroccans, known as 'Goums', dressed in traditional native costume and, armed with long knives, broke through the German lines by

ABOVE: A FRENCH MOROCCAN GOUM OF THE FRENCH EXPIDITIONARY FORCE IN ITALY TAKES ADVANTAGE OF A PAUSE IN THE FIGHTING TO SHARPEN HIS KNIFE. RENOWNED FOR THEIR BRAVERY AND SAVAGERY, THE GOUM TROOPS WHO ATTACKED MONTE CASSINO GAVE THE GERMAN ENEMY NO QUARTER.

RIGHT: TANKS OF THE ALLIED 5TH ARMY ROLL PAST THE ANCIENT COLISEUM AFTER THE LIBERATION OF ROME IN JUNE 1944. THE FIRST AXIS CAPITAL HAD FALLEN.

LEFT: ITALIAN PARTISANS
FILL A COMMANDEERED BUS.
ALTHOUGH FEW ITALIAN
SOLDIERS OFFICIALLY
FOUGHT ALONGSIDE THE
ALLIES, THE ITALIAN PEOPLE
THEMSELVES PLAYED A
MAJOR PART IN ALLIED
VICTORIES ACROSS ITALY.

climbing the 'impassable' Petrella Peak and attacking from the rear. Their spectacular advance was so successful that it soon gave rise among Allied troops to the phrase 'Goumed right off the map'. On 18 May, the Polish troops, who had suffered appalling casualties, finally entered the ruins, by which time Kesselring had already begun another long retreat.

    Meanwhile, in an attempt to relieve the pressure on Monte Cassino, US troops had landed at Anzio, 20 miles south of Rome, on 22 January 1944, but were pinned down on a critically exposed beachhead for the next four months. The breakout did not come until 23 May. The link-up with forces moving up from the south took place on 25 May, and 10 days later, amid scenes of joy, tears and cheers, US troops entered Rome on 4 June. Emotional scenes like this were soon to take place elsewhere in Europe as the Allied saviours liberated

ABOVE: ITALIAN REFUGEES
ON THE MOVE WITH THE
FEW POSSESSIONS THAT
THEY MANAGED TO
CLING ON TO.

FLORENCE AND THE PONTE VECCHIO

Birthplace of the 15th-century Italian Renaissance and home of countless art treasures, the city of Florence was occupied by German troops as part of the defensive Gothic Line until August 1944, when it was liberated by the combined efforts of Italian partisans and Allied troops. Although many of the city's magnificent statues had been covered or removed to prevent damage from Allied bombs, the retreating Germans attempted to buy themselves time as Allied forces entered the city by blowing up the series of historic bridges that crossed the River Arno. Only the famous, and historic, Ponte Vecchio was saved, after locals pleaded with the German forces to spare it.

MANY OF FLORENCE'S HISTORIC BRIDGES DID NOT SURVIVE THE WAR. THE
PONTE VECCHIO WAS A LUCKY EXCEPTION.

towns and cities from their Nazi bondage, but, for the moment, it was enough that President Roosevelt could proudly announce: 'The first Axis capital is in our hands. One up and two to go!'

In his eagerness to reach the Italian capital before the British, General Mark Clark had failed to encircle Rome and, as a result, most of the German 10th Army, of almost 30,000 men, escaped. German headquarters presented the retreat rather differently, issuing a report explaining that 'as there was a danger that Rome, one of the oldest cultural centres in the world, would be directly involved in the present fighting, Hitler has ordered the withdrawal of German troops in order to prevent its destruction.' This, though, did little to disguise the fact that an eventual Allied victory in Italy was starting to look more and more likely, despite Kesselring's considerable defensive skills.

In the meantime, though, the Allies had found themselves with other pressing problems. As the Allied forces liberated more and more territory, they faced great difficulty in providing for the Italian population. Millions had been rendered homeless and hungry by the war, which had also destroyed most of the country's infrastructure. An Allied Military Government of Occupation (AMGOT) was set up to feed the starving Italians, keep the streets clean, issue money and carry out the other essential duties of government. However, as Roosevelt warned, its work would be 'gradual' at best. The port of Naples, occupied by the Allies between October 1943 and December 1944, illustrated the problems they faced. A city of over one million inhabitants, most of them living in dire poverty, Naples had first been occupied by German troops who attempted to impose forced labour on the population. The Neapolitans would have none of it. There was a widespread public uprising and four days of open warfare in the city streets. By the time the Allies took control, starvation and disease were rife, largely as a result of the massive Allied bombing campaign that led to the city's liberation on 1 October 1943. US soldiers reported that hundreds of thousands of children who had been orphaned by the war were turning to crime and prostitution to survive. There was little that could be done. Attempts to remedy the situation were already hampered by arguments between the British and US governments over how much Italy should be punished for its role in the war. The British favoured a much tougher line than the USA.

The British were now also becoming increasingly concerned about growing support among the poor and dispossessed for the numerous Italian communist organisations that had sprung up since the surrender. They feared an eventual communist takeover. This, though, was an over-anxious attitude. The communists were only a few among many groups of Italians intent on resisting the German forces. For instance, following the cease-fire declaration, 10,000 Italian soldiers on the Greek island of Cephalonia had been executed for refusing to surrender to their former

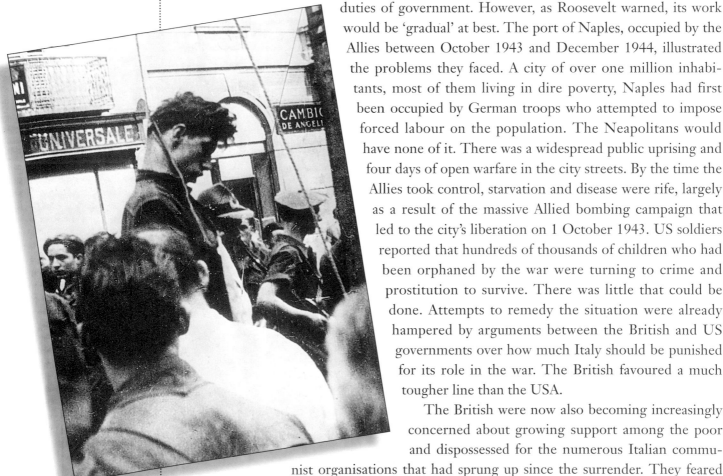

BELOW: A PUBLIC HANGING OF A SUSPECTED ITALIAN PARTISAN MEMBER IS CARRIED OUT BY GERMAN TROOPS AS A WARNING TO OTHERS. GERMAN RETRIBUTION FOR PARTISAN ACTIVITIES WAS CHARACTERISTICALLY BRUTAL.

German comrades. The German occupation of Rome on 11 September 1943 had been met by fierce local resistance, and 600 Romans had been killed. Later, as the retreating German Army established new defensive positions at the Gothic Line along the River Arno, Italian partisan organisations took up the fight. As in the rest of occupied Europe, an underground resistance movement had quickly sprung up in Italy and, by 1944, there were almost 100,000 partisans operating in the north alone. In many places, they set up their own local governments, as well as engaging in savage fighting with German and fascist soldiers. Made up largely of local peasants, who lived off the land and operated from hide-aways in the hills, partisan units sabotaged German supply lines

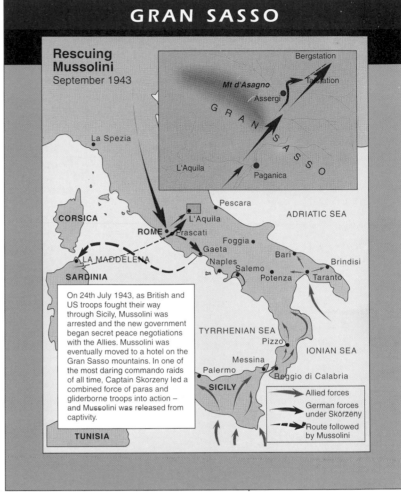

GRAN SASSO

Rescuing Mussolini
September 1943

On 24th July 1943, as British and US troops fought their way through Sicily, Mussolini was arrested and the new government began secret peace negotiations with the Allies. Mussolini was eventually moved to a hotel on the Gran Sasso mountains. In one of the most daring commando raids of all time, Captain Skorzeny led a combined force of paras and gliderborne troops into action – and Mussolini was released from captivity.

→ Allied forces
→ German forces under Skorzeny
⇢ Route followed by Mussolini

MUSSOLINI IS RESCUED FROM HIS MOUNTAIN PRISON (TOP) IN AN AUDACIOUS COMMANDO RAID.

THE RESCUE OF MUSSOLINI

After being removed from power in July 1943, the former fascist dictator of Italy, 'Il Duce' Benito Mussolini, was imprisoned by what was left of his own government. Three months later, at Hitler's personal request, a daring mission was mounted to rescue him by Colonel Otto Skorzeny, a dashing 6ft 6ins tall German commando with a scar across his cheek. Skorzeny, once known as 'the most dangerous man in Europe', together with a team of crack parachute troops landed at the mountain resort where Mussolini was held, subdued the guards and quickly removed Hitler's old ally. Later, Mussolini was installed as head of the Republic of Salo, with a 'capital' at Gargagnano on Lake Garda. From there, Il Duce was supposed to lead fascist operations, but his most noteworthy action was the trial and execution of five politicians who had voted for his removal when the Allies invaded. One of them was Mussolini's own son-in-law, Count Galeazzo Ciano, who was shot on 11 January 1944.

RIGHT: US TROOPS ON
PATROL IN NORTHERN ITALY
DURING THE HARSH WINTER
OF 1944, WHICH STALLED
THE ALLIED OFFENSIVE
UNTIL THE FOLLOWING
SPRING.

During August 1944, one SS battalion, commanded by Major Walter Reder, embarked on a 'march of death' across Tuscany, executing every man, woman and child in each of the villages they entered. The situation grew even worse during the harsh winter of 1944

and communications and ambushed their troops, as well as preventing the seizure of grain for transportation back to Germany. Partisan organisations even took control of the northern half of Florence after assisting in the liberation of the historic city on 5 August 1944.

German reprisals against partisan activities were extremely retributive. As in occupied Russia, SS units were unleashed on the Italian countryside to use brutality and terror in an effort to subdue the civilian population. In September 1943, the town of Boves in Piedmont had been burned to the ground in response to partisan activities in the area. During August 1944, one SS battalion, commanded by Major Walter Reder, embarked on a 'march of death' across Tuscany, executing every man, woman and child in each of the villages they entered. The situation grew even worse during the harsh winter of 1944 as Kesselring's troops launched their own campaign to destroy the Italian resistance once and for all. Trapped in the hills and poorly equipped, many partisans were hunted to their deaths. At the Marzabotto commune in Emilia, almost 2000 of them were killed by German soldiers.

Meanwhile, the Allied advance had stalled and General Alexander announced that there would be no fresh Allied offensive until the following spring. He suggested that partisan groups in northern Italy cease activity and 'go to ground' for their own safety. This was taken as an insult by many partisans. It also encouraged Mussolini's remaining fascists to begin their own campaign against peasant villages 'suspected' of harbouring the resistance fighters.

The effects of the winter were also felt in the industrial cities of northern Italy, the more affluent part of the country. There, people were living without food or fuel in homes shattered by Allied bombs. In cities like Turin, sabotage and lack of raw materials for factories administered by the occupying Germans had led to mass unemployment. The SS had begun rounding up workers for transportation back to Germany to aid the ailing Nazi war effort. Resistance took the form of a series of widespread strikes organised by communist groups and trade unions throughout the winter and into the spring of 1945, accompanied by equally widespread industrial sabotage and the occupation of factories by their workers. As in the countryside, the urban resistance paid a high price for these activities. In Milan, 15 'political prisoners' were shot in public for the destruction of one German lorry. Nevertheless, in the last week of April 1945, as Allied troops once again began to advance northwards, a combined force of workers and partisans finally rose up en masse against the German occupation. This 'National Insurrection' spread through the cities of northern Italy within hours. In Genoa, the resistance cut off supplies and communications to the local German barracks and seized the city after two days of fighting. In Turin, armed factory workers battled German soldiers until partisans arrived to relieve them. In Milan, where fighting centred around the Pirelli tyre plant, the German forces surrendered on 26 April as Allied soldiers approached.

By then, the struggle for Italy and, in fact, the war in Europe itself were almost at an end. At midday on 2 May 1945, Kesselring, who had already been negotiating with the Allies for some days, announced the total surrender of the German forces. On hearing the news, Mussolini immediately attempted to escape to Switzerland with his mistress, Claretta Petacci, and a large amount of gold bullion. Mussolini and Claretta were captured by partisans outside the village of Dongo near Lake Como. They were executed on the spot. Afterwards, their bodies were hung upside down from a girder in a filling station at Milan's Piazza Loreto. There, a large crowd massed to abuse, spit upon, curse and otherwise excoriate them. The scene was so brutal that even the Allies protested.

The Italian campaign had cost the Allies over 300,000 casualties and the Germans over 500,000. In addition, 30,000 resistance fighters had lost their lives struggling to free their country. Later, there was considerable debate over whether the campaign in Italy should have taken place at all. However, the fact remained that by allowing Italy to surrender and then tying down considerable German resources, those who fought and died on the 'second front' made a major contribution to the eventual defeat of Nazi Germany.

> Mussolini and Claretta were...executed on the spot. Afterwards, their bodies were hung upside down from a girder in a filling station at Milan's Piazza Loreto. There, a large crowd massed to abuse, spit upon, curse and otherwise excoriate them. The scene was so brutal that even the Allies protested

LEFT: MUSSOLINI AND HIS MISTRESS, CLARETTA PETTACI, LIE DEAD IN A MILANESE SQUARE, THE ITALIAN PUBLIC HAVING ENACTED A GRUESOME REVENGE ON THEIR CORPSES. ONE OF THE ITALIAN DICTATOR'S FAVOURITE SAYINGS HAD BEEN: 'EVERYONE GETS THE DEATH HE DESERVES.'

CHAPTER 13

Operation Overlord

US TROOPS PREPARE TO GO ASHORE,
JUNE 6, 1944 AS PART OF OPERATION OVERLORD.
THE ALLIED LIBERATION OF EUROPE HAD BEGUN.

D-DAY

Just after dawn on 6 June 1944, German soldiers manning the French coastal defences of Adolf Hitler's 'Fortress Europe' looked out across the English Channel to see one of the most incredible sights of the Second World War. A huge fleet of 5000 Allied ships and 154,000 men was heading straight for them. Operation Overlord, the largest amphibious invasion in history, was under way. The Allied liberation of Europe had begun.

Preparations for the invasion had been proceeding on both sides of the Channel for over two years. In Britain, the Supreme Headquarters Allied Expeditionary Force (SHAEF) had been set up in 1943, with US General Dwight D. Eisenhower at its head. For months, the British and US governments had been promising the Soviet Union that they would mount a joint assault on western Europe to relieve the pressure on Soviet troops fighting the German Army in the east. The question was how and where to strike. The fjord-slashed coastline of Norway and rugged shores of northern Europe were considered impractical for a large-scale invasion, although this had not stopped

BELOW: ALLIED HURRICANE AIRCRAFT GO INTO ROUND-THE-CLOCK PRODUCTION IN THE MONTHS LEADING UP TO OPERATION OVERLORD. ALLIED AIR SUPERIORITY OVER NORTHERN FRANCE WAS TO PLAY A VITAL ROLE IN THE D-DAY LANDINGS.

ABOVE: GENERAL DWIGHT D. EISENHOWER, SUPREME COMMANDER OF THE ALLIED EXPEDITIONARY FORCE, WHO DECIDED TO CONCENTRATE THE ALLIED ATTACK ON THE BEACHES OF NORMANDY, DESPITE OTHERS' MISGIVINGS.

CENTRE: SPRING 1944. A US NAVY BOAT REHEARSES FOR THE NORMANDY LANDINGS IN THE ENGLISH CHANNEL.

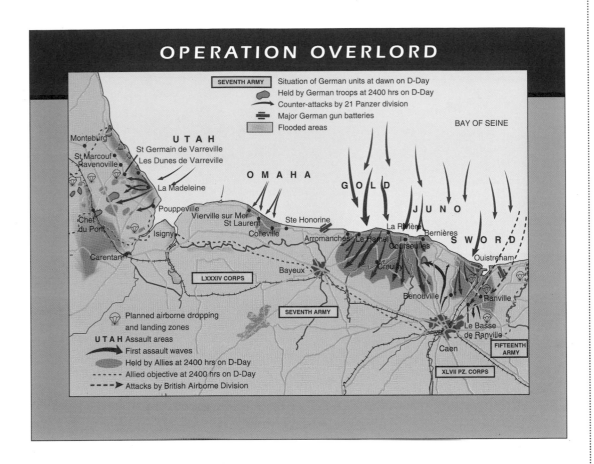

OPERATION OVERLORD

SEVENTH ARMY	Situation of German units at dawn on D-Day
	Held by German troops at 2400 hrs on D-Day
	Counter-attacks by 21 Panzer division
	Major German gun batteries
	Flooded areas

BAY OF SEINE

UTAH
Monteburg
St Germain de Varreville
St Marcouf
Ravenoville
Les Dunes de Varreville

OMAHA

GOLD

JUNO

La Madeleine
Pouppeville
Vierville sur Mer
St Laurent
Ste Honorine
La Rivière
Bernières
SWORD
Chef du Pont
Isigny
Colleville
Arromanches
Le Hamel
Courseulles
Ouistreham
Carentan
Bayeux
Creully
Benouville
Ranville

Planned airborne dropping
and landing zones
UTAH Assault areas
First assault waves
Held by Allies at 2400 hrs on D-Day
Allied objective at 2400 hrs on D-Day
Attacks by British Airborne Division

LXXXIV CORPS
SEVENTH ARMY
Le Basse de Ranville
Caen
FIFTEENTH ARMY
XLVII PZ. CORPS

BELOW: 'OVERPAID, OVER-
SEXED AND OVER HERE' –
US TROOPS STATIONED IN
BRITAIN GATHER FOR A
PHOTOGRAPH IN JUNE
1944. THE PRESENCE OF
20 DIVISIONS OF US
SERVICEMEN THROUGHOUT
THE BRITISH MAINLAND
CAUSED A MAJOR UPHEAVAL
IN THE BRITISH WAY OF LIFE
IN THE RUN UP TO
THE INVASION.

Germany from maintaining a large standing army in Norway in case of Allied attack. The flatlands of Belgium and the Netherlands were also dismissed. The choice had eventually come down to either Calais or Normandy in northern France as the only two areas suitable for landing the huge invasion force that Eisenhower and his command believed necessary to ensure success.

Most of the German High Command, including Hitler himself, had long been convinced that the Allies would eventually strike at Calais. Not only was Calais a major port, it was also only 20 miles across the Channel from the English coast. Normandy, on the other hand, was some 65 miles from the coast of southern England. For this reason, throughout 1943 and 1944, a huge German defensive force was built up in the Pas de Calais, made up of men and equipment recalled from the Russian front. It was only on D-Day, the day of the invasion itself, that the Germans discovered they were in the wrong place.

SUBTERFUGE

Throughout 1944, the German High Command was well aware that an Allied attack on western Europe was being planned, but thanks to a number of ingenious British deceptions, they were kept from discovering where it was to take place.

The main thrust of the British programme of subterfuge was to keep the Germans believing that the invasion was to come via the region around the port of Calais. Allied air superiority meant that Luftwaffe reconnaissance missions could reach only as far as the south-eastern tip of England. In order to exploit this weakness, hundreds of artificial gliders were parked on dummy runways in the area, giving German pilots the impression that a huge airborne assault was being prepared. To compound the illusion, extra ships and landing craft were harboured around the port of Dover and a bogus invasion division, 'Army Group Patton', was invented and discussed in transmissions that were known to be monitored by German spies. This, too, was said to be bound for the assault on Calais. In the days leading up to invasion, extra bombing missions were laid on over the Calais region to give the impression that the German defences were being ' softened up' ready for an assault.

On the morning of D-Day itself, hundreds of Allied aircraft flew over Calais dropping millions of small squares of silver foil called 'window'. This was designed to confuse the enemy radar into thinking that a huge attack was being mounted. At the same time, a fleet of warships in

US SHERMAN TANKS ARE LOADED ABOARD A LANDING CRAFT IN READINESS FOR LANDING ON THE FRENCH COAST.

the Straits of Dover trailed radar-reflecting balloons and broadcast false radio transmissions to make it seem as if a huge armada was sailing on Calais. Their efforts were so successful that even after it became clear that an attack was being carried out on Normandy, Hitler remained convinced that this was merely a feint, and that the real assault was still to come in the north.

The British, Canadian and US soldiers in those craft had been preparing for this moment for many months. Throughout the spring of 1944, the joke had been that southern England was liable to sink under the weight of men and equipment being gathered there

By that time, the first wave of the Allied invasion had already gone in under cover of darkness. Overnight, British and US aircraft had dropped over 5000 tons of bombs on the Normandy coast in an effort to knock out the German defences and communications. They were followed by three divisions of paratroopers, 12,000 men whose job it was to secure the French villages and bridges along the flanks of the invasion force to prevent German tanks from the surrounding areas mounting a counter-attack. Their costs were high. Hundreds were shot down by the surprised German gunners before they reached the ground, and many more were forced to bail out early and land in the sea. In the dark, many men were scattered across the French countryside, miles from their target. Another 11,000 men came in by glider, but many gliders carrying equipment crashed on landing. Nevertheless, there were many successes, and in a number of places the paratroopers found themselves being welcomed with open arms into the houses of the startled but ecstatic locals. Even those who missed their targets helped by confusing German reports about where the attacks were being concentrated. Dummy parachutists, part of a huge programme of subterfuge operations, were being dropped all over northern France to achieve the same effect.

The Allied naval bombardment of the Normandy coast began at 5.30 a.m. on 6 June. Although not as heavily defended as those around Calais, the beaches of Normandy were still protected by a formidable combination of German artillery, machine-gun emplacements, mines and barbed wire. Since taking charge of the defence of France in January 1944, Field Marshal Erwin Rommel, the 'Desert Fox', who formerly led the Afrika Korps, had also ordered that thousands of new obstacles be constructed on the beaches, many of them mined with explosives and hidden by the water at high tide. In fact, Rommel had been one of the few who suggested that an attack on Normandy was likely, and had requested that tanks be diverted from Calais to aid its defence. Fortunately for the Allies, Rommel was overruled by Field Marshal von Rundstedt, the German Commander-in-Chief.

ABOVE: GERMAN OFFICERS IN NORTHERN FRANCE STOP FOR A BRIEFING. AWARE THAT AN ALLIED ATTACK WOULD SOON TAKE PLACE, THE GERMAN HIGH COMMAND WAS SPLIT BY ARGUMENTS OVER HOW THE ATLANTIC FRONT SHOULD BEST BE DEFENDED. ONLY ROMMEL INSISTED THAT FRENCH BEACHES SHOULD BE BETTER FORTIFIED.

LEFT: US ARMY ORDINANCE MEN SHARE A LAST CUP OF COFFEE WITH TWO BRITISH WOMEN WHILE WAITING FOR THE ORDER TO CROSS THE CHANNEL. MANY OF THEM WOULD NOT RETURN.

Trapped in their bunkers and pillboxes, the German troops were amazed by the ferocity of the Allied attack. They were being pounded from miles out to sea by the massive naval guns of seven Allied battleships. Altogether, there were more than 130 other warships bearing down upon them. Even more incredibly to German eyes, they were accompanied by wave after wave of thousands of landing craft carrying men and tanks towards the Normandy beaches.

The British, Canadian and US soldiers in those craft had been preparing for this moment for many months. Throughout the spring of 1944, the joke had been that southern England was liable to sink under the weight of men and equipment being gathered there. Twenty divisions of American GIs had been stationed throughout Britain, along with thousands of tons of tanks, trucks and artillery. Training operations for the landings had been regularly carried out along the English coastline, leading on one occasion to the deaths of hundreds of troops whose exercise was attacked by German motor-torpedo boats in the Channel. During the same period, British commandos in midget submarines were carrying out their own secret night-time landings on the Normandy beaches to examine the German defences and collect samples of sand and clay. Their reports had led to the construction of a series of specially adapted amphibious tanks and other machines – 'Funnies' – which were to wade ashore with the first wave of men. Some 'Funnies' would be used to lay track across the beaches or blow up mines hidden in the sand with rotating flails. Packed into their flat-bottomed landing craft and buffeted by the heavy seas, the men and machines of the invasion force now raced towards the German guns.

Their targets were five separate beaches, code-named Omaha, Utah, Gold, Juno and Sword. Omaha and Utah were the responsibility of two divisions of US troops led by General Omar Bradley, while three divisions of British and Canadian soldiers led by General Sir Miles Dempsey had been assigned to take Gold, Juno and Sword. Their route in was not an easy one. Although they were supported by rocket-firing motor boats, the Allied landing craft were vulnerable in the face of the shells and machine-gun bullets being thrown at them by the defenders of Hitler's 'Atlantic Wall'. Hundreds were killed before they even reached the beaches. Those who did manage to get ashore were faced with battling their way through mines, floating defences and barbed wire. If they survived, they had to make for the German positions firing at them across open, unprotected sands.

At Utah beach, this was achieved with minimal casualties: 197 men were killed for 23,000 eventually put ashore. But at Omaha, the landing party almost met with disaster. Not only had the German defences survived the Allied bombardment almost intact, but

BELOW: EXHAUSTED US SOLDIERS AT UTAH BEACH ARE DRAGGED ASHORE FROM A CAPSIZED LANDING CRAFT. AT OMAHA BEACH HUNDREDS MORE MEN WERE DROWNED AT SEA OR CUT TO PIECES BY THE GERMAN GUNS.

GERMAN TROOPS INSPECT BRITISH CASUALTIES FOLLOWING THE ILL-FATED 1942 RAID ON DIEPPE.

DIEPPE 1942

Preparations for the invasion of France had begun well in advance of D-Day. Two years earlier, in 1942, an Allied commando raid was carried out on the French port of Dieppe to test the German coastal defences. On the morning of 19 August, a force of 5000 Canadian troops and British commandos was put ashore by landing craft to try to knock out German gun batteries and seize the port itself. They were supported by a massive naval bombardment and the biggest RAF operation mounted since the Battle of Britain in 1940. The result, however, was catastrophe. Almost 1000 Canadian soldiers were killed by the German guns and a further 2000 were captured. Subsequently, the Allied High Command gave up the idea of attempting to capture such heavily defended ports, and instead ordered artificial 'Mulberry' harbours to be used to land ships and equipment for Operation Overlord.

the assault on the beach itself was launched too far out to sea. As the amphibious tanks disembarked from their landing craft, they immediately sank. The same thing happened to many of the men, who were dragged under the water by their heavy equipment and drowned. The engineers who swam ashore to try to clear the path by blowing up the mines and obstacles took huge losses. Most of the division's commanding officers were killed by German shells or gunfire within the first few minutes.

The men who managed to land on the beach at Omaha were completely disorganised and terrified. The mangled bodies of their fallen comrades filled the surf around them, soon to be joined by those of the wounded who were drowned by the rising tide. Only

ABOVE: BRITISH INFANTRYMEN PREPARE TO BREAK OUT OF THE NORMANDY BEACHHEAD. IN CONTRAST TO THE AMERICANS, THEIR LANDINGS HAD BEEN REMARKABLY SUCCESSFUL, WITH VERY FEW CASUALTIES.

LEFT: ONCE INLAND THE ALLIES SOON DISCOVERED THAT THE ENEMY INTENDED TO DEFEND FIERCELY EVERY INCH OF TERRITORY. HERE, A GROUP OF BRITISH TROOPS, TAKEN PRISONER DURING THE FIGHTING, IS LED AWAY FROM THE FRONT.

the efforts of men like Colonel George Taylor in getting the troops organised and moving again averted an even worse disaster. Taylor rallied his soldiers with the words: 'Two kinds of people are staying on this beach – the dead and those who are about to die. Now, let's get the hell out of here!'

They had to keep going. Behind them, more troops and tanks were already streaming towards the beach, threatening a gigantic traffic jam. By the end of the first day, despite having suffered over 4000 casualties, the troops on Omaha had secured their beach. Elsewhere, the landings had met with much less difficulty. At Gold beach, British frogmen had

landed before dawn to start dismantling the German mines and obstacles under cover of darkness. By the time the first wave of British and Canadian troops hit the beach at 7.25 a.m., the demoralised German defenders had been under naval bombardment for almost two hours. At Juno beach, the story was similar, and the Canadian troops and Royal Marine commandos who were landed there quickly moved inland to take the villages of Courseulles and Bernieres. At Sword beach, a number of tanks were lost after being launched too far from the shore, but the British 3rd Infantry, supported by Free French commandos, landed with minimal casualties and soon secured the area.

By nightfall on D-Day, 150,000 Allied troops were ashore in France. Despite the carnage on Omaha beach, fewer than 3000 men had been killed, an incredible success for such a hazardous operation. Eisenhower and Churchill had feared that over 10,000 men would be lost even if the landings were successful. Already, many of the injured were back in England, and huge Mulberry artificial harbours were being towed towards Normandy to land even more equipment. The danger now was that the Germans would counter-attack while Allied equipment was still pouring onto the Normandy beaches, and Allied troops were still confined to the narrow beach-heads they had established. However, with German mobility severely restricted during daytime by total Allied air superiority, and with General Bernard Montgomery, the hero of El Alamein, now in charge of the ground forces, the German Army had lost its chance to push the invasion force back into the Channel.

ABOVE: A GERMAN ARMOURED CAR WAITS FOR ACTION IN THE TOWN OF CAEN. THE GERMAN DEFENDERS STATIONED THERE HELD THE TOWN FOR A MONTH, DESPITE THE HUGE ALLIED FORCE RANGED AGAINST THEM.

RIGHT: THE FREE FRENCH LEADER CHARLES DE GAULLE MARCHES THROUGH THE ARC DE TRIOMPHE IN PARIS DURING CELEBRATIONS TO MARK THE CITY'S LIBERATION. BY NOW THE DEMORALISED GERMAN FORCES HAD BEGUN THE RETREAT BACK TO THEIR FATHERLAND.

What the Germans could do was defend their territory, making the Allies pay a high price for each and every advance. At Caen, three Panzer divisions led a determined German counter-attack that prevented Montgomery's forces from taking the town for over a month. Thousands of US soldiers – more than died during the landings – were lost trying to take the town of St Lo. In the Cotentin peninsula, US tanks and troops were trapped behind the huge, ancient hedgerows that dominated the 'Bocage' countryside and which provided the defending Germans with natural cover. However, as Montgomery's attacks on Caen drew more and more of the enemy's forces towards his men, US troops, led by General George S. Patton, were eventually able to break through the German lines to the south. Supported by a savage aerial and artillery bombardment, the Americans trapped most of German Army Group B in the narrow country lanes around the town of Falaise. Upwards

THE FRENCH RESISTANCE

Throughout the four-year occupation of France, the German forces had been opposed by members of the French Resistance, who waged a guerrilla war against their enemy. After beginning as a series of isolated acts of violence and sabotage, the Resistance grew into a full-scale 'Secret Army' under the overall leadership of General de Gaulle. De Gaulle, the former French defence minister, had escaped to Britain when Germany invaded France in 1940, and led the Free French forces from London, co-ordinating a number of different groups that included the French Communist Party. The activities of the Resistance included spying for the Allies, sabotage of communications and equipment and aiding Jews, Allied airmen and prisoners of war to escape from France. They were also responsible for punishing French citizens accused of collaborating with the Germans. In the more mountainous regions towards the south of France, partisan groups known as Maquis waged their own guerrilla war against the German occupiers.

In the days leading up to Operation Overlord, the Resistance played their part by cutting telephone lines and destroying railways in order to disrupt the German defences. German reprisals were fierce. On 10 June, four days after the Allied invasion had begun, a German SS unit burned the town of Oradour to the ground, killing all 642 of its inhabitants. Altogether, an estimated 90,000 Resistance workers were killed or sent to concentration camps for their activities.

A FRENCH RESISTANCE UNIT RETURNS FROM A PATROL, PROCLAIMING 'V FOR VICTORY'.

of 50,000 German soldiers were killed in the fighting, and a further 200,000 were taken prisoner. Those who escaped began the long retreat towards Germany.

Meanwhile, General Leclerc of the Free French was leading the 2nd Armoured Division towards Paris, where the largely communist underground, inspired by the Allied victories, was staging a widespread uprising against the enemy occupation. Although wary of getting involved in a bloody street fight for the city, the Allied High Command sent US troops who had recently landed in the south of France to aid in the liberation of the French capital. Fears that Paris would become another Stalingrad proved unfounded. Despite Hitler's calls for the city to be turned into 'a field of ruins', the demoralised German soldiers were soon overwhelmed and surrendered en masse.

On 26 August, Charles de Gaulle led a victory parade down the Champs Elysees. Paris was free and the liberation of France all but complete. The next target was Germany itself.

ABOVE: CHEERING FRENCH WOMEN WELCOME THE ALLIED TROOPS AS THE OCCUPATION OF THEIR COUNTRY NEARS ITS END.

THE ROAD TO SURRENDER

On 1 July 1944, Field Marshal Karl von Rundstedt, Commander-in-Chief of German forces in western Europe was asked by his fellow Field Marshal, Wilhelm Keitel, what the German response to the recent Allied invasion of France should be. Von Rundstedt reportedly replied: 'Make peace, you fools!'

Within hours, news of the remark reached Hitler, and von Rundstedt was replaced by Field Marshal Günther von Kluge. This did not, however, change the situation that the Führer and his people faced as the consequences of the D-Day invasion became clear. The Germans had just scored a success at Arnhem in the Netherlands, where 10,000 British troops were lost trying to capture a key bridge in an assault launched on 17 September 1944. Even so, in the three weeks following the Normandy invasion, Allied troops elsewhere had liberated most of France and the Low Countries. In Italy, German forces were steadily retreating northwards, despite fighting a brilliant defensive campaign. On the eastern front, Soviet troops had smashed the remnants of the German Army in the Soviet Union and were now overrunning Poland, Bulgaria and Romania. In Yugoslavia, Marshal Tito's partisans were on the verge of liberating Belgrade from Nazi occupation.

The German people, many so far untouched by the direct effects of war, were at last beginning to feel the results of their Führer's actions. Since 1942, the Nazi architect Albert Speer had been head of German war production. During that time, and in spite of the damage done to the country's infrastructure by Allied bombing, Speer had actually managed to increase Germany's industrial output by a wholesale reorganisation of its workers and resources. This had included using a large amount of slave labour. In 1944, with defeat looming, Speer went a step further, and ordered the 'total mobilisation' of Germany and its citizens in support of the war effort. For the first time, all women under 50 were forced to sign up for compulsory labour. They might find themselves with responsibilities as diverse as producing ball-bearings for tanks, or operating anti-aircraft guns. The schools

RIGHT: ALBERT SPEER (RIGHT), HITLER'S ARCHITECT AND GERMAN MINISTER FOR ARMAMENTS AND MUNITIONS. RESPONSIBLE FOR THE GERMAN WAR ECONOMY, HE WOULD LATER SERVE 20 YEARS IN PRISON FOR HIS USE OF SLAVE LABOUR.

were closed, and the children put to work on farms gathering in the harvest or working on production lines in armaments factories. Older children were called up into the *Volksturm*, the People's Militia. This last line of defence against the Allies was made up of poorly trained and ill-equipped old men and young boys. Later, Allied soldiers were shocked to

find themselves fighting against 'soldiers' as young as 12, and old men the age of their grandfathers.

However, it was those civilians living in large towns and cities who were the first to experience directly the horrors of war. At the Casablanca Conference of 1943, the British and US air forces had agreed to begin a joint, round-the-clock bomber offensive on industrial targets throughout Germany, aiming for the 'systematic obliteration, one by one, of the centres of German war production'. But despite scoring notable successes like the famous raid by RAF 617 Squadron on the Mohne and Eder dams along the River Ruhr, it was soon realised that a large number of bombing missions were missing their targets. Speer had cunningly split up the workings of a number of vital factories into individual operations, separated and spread throughout Germany, so that no single attack could entirely cripple production. In response to this situation, RAF Bomber Command, under the leadership of Air Marshal Arthur Harris, switched to a policy of 'saturation bombing'. As well as carrying out raids on communications and industrial installations, bomber crews were ordered to start targeting large towns and cities, with the specific aim of causing as much loss of civilian life as possible. Not only was it hoped that this would eventually destroy German morale, but it presented the RAF with targets that were considerably easier to hit.

LEFT: THE FACE OF A SHELL-SHOCKED GERMAN WOMAN TELLS THE STORY OF ANOTHER ALLIED AIR RAID. FOR THE FIRST TIME THE GERMAN PEOPLE WERE BEGINNING TO SUFFER EN MASSE THE EFFECTS OF THE WAR THEIR FÜHRER HAD UNLEASHED.

FAR LEFT: THE CONTROVERSIAL AIR CHIEF MARSHALL SIR ARTHUR 'BOMBER' HARRIS, COMMANDER-IN-CHIEF OF ALLIED BOMBER COMMAND, ATTENDS THE DEBRIEFING OF 'DAM BUSTER' PILOT GUY GIBSON'S CREW.

This last line of defence against the Allies was made up of poorly trained and ill-equipped old men and young boys. Allied soldiers were shocked to find themselves fighting against 'soldiers' as young as 12, and old men the age of their grandfathers

Armed with incendiaries, high explosives and huge 4000lb 'blockbuster' bombs, RAF Lancasters and Halifaxes began flying night missions over German cities in huge numbers. The destructive power of these 'thousand bomber' raids was immense. In July 1943, over 30,000 people were killed in Hamburg by a firestorm started by four nights of continuous bombing. By the time the fire died down, 80 per cent of the city had been destroyed. Further firebombing raids followed on Cologne and Berlin, as well as smaller towns in the industrial Ruhr valley, and each time the death toll was in thousands. The campaign reached a climax with the firebombing of Dresden, a historic and beautiful city of little military consequence, on 14 February 1945. Over 35,000 lives were lost. Witnesses reported that in the aftermath, what was left of the city looked like the surface of the Moon.

If the intention of the strategic bombing campaign was to speed the capitulation of the German people, then it was a failure. Like Londoners during the Blitz, ordinary Germans simply carried on with their lives as best they could in defiance of the death and destruction raining down on them.

Altogether, over 500,000 died during the Allied bombing campaign, including more than 100,000 children. The ethics of this strategy became the subject of heated debate among the British High Command. At one point, questions were even raised in parliament about the 'moral danger' of continuing the deliberate bombing of civilians on such a scale. Such sentiments were not universal, but when, in the House of Lords, the Marquis of Salisbury was reminded that the Nazi Luftwaffe had ushered in the era of strategic bombing, he replied: 'Of

course the Germans began it, but we do not take the devil as our example.'

As it happened, the devil had not yet run out of tricks. Germany was about to begin a new bombing campaign of its own. Suffering a chronic shortage of resources, Hitler turned in desperation to his scientists to come up with new, more economic 'miracle weapons' that might alter the course of the war. Working at the isolated Peenemunde research complex on Germany's Baltic coast, a team led by a brilliant young engineer, Wernher von Braun, first developed the V-1, a remote-controlled, pulse jet-powered flying bomb with a one-ton warhead. The 'V' stood for *Vegeltungswaffe*, or reprisal. From

FAR LEFT: THE BODIES OF A GERMAN MAN, WOMAN AND CHILD LIE SIDE BY SIDE FOLLOWING THE ALLIED AIR ATTACK ON COLOGNE.

LEFT: MOURNERS AT A COLOGNE CEMETERY GATHER TO SAY A FINAL FAREWELL TO LOVED ONES LOST IN THE BOMBING. HITLER WOULD SOON LAUNCH HIS OWN REVENGE ON THE BRITISH PUBLIC IN THE SHAPE OF THE NEW 'V' WEAPONS.

THE WHITE ROSE UNDERGROUND

The White Rose Underground began its activities by distributing anti-Nazi literature in 1939. It was organised by a 17-year-old German Catholic, Sophie Scholl, and her elder brother, Hans, 20, a former member of the Hitler Youth. Together with friends, the Scholls printed anonymous leaflets protesting against the war and the Nazi Party, and distributed them all over Germany. On 18 February 1943, they were spotted handing out leaflets around Munich University by a janitor who promptly arrested them and reported them to the Gestapo. When the secret police searched the Scholls' apartment, they found 'subversive' literature and hundreds of stamps and envelopes. Four days later, Sophie and Hans Scholl were tried, tortured, found guilty of subversion and sentenced to death. Both were beheaded. Before she died, Sophie told her friends: 'So many people have died for this regime that it's time someone died against it.'

LEFT TO RIGHT: HANS SCHOLL, SOPHIE SCHOLL AND CHRISTOPH PROBST.

RIGHT: A V2 ROCKET – THE WORLD'S FIRST BALLISTIC MISSILE – TAKES OFF FROM ITS LAUNCH PAD SOMEWHERE IN NORTHERN EUROPE. BETWEEN SEPTEMBER 1944 AND MARCH 1945 THE 517 V2 ROCKETS THAT FELL ON LONDON KILLED 2,700 PEOPLE.

THE ALLIED FRONT

US attacks
British attacks
French attacks
German pockets
Occupied by Allied forces 28 March 1945
Occupied by Russian forces 16 April 1945

13 June 1944 onwards, thousands of these unmanned 'Buzz Bombs', 'Doodlebugs' or 'Flying Bombs', as they were variously called, were launched indiscriminately at London and southern England. On 8 September, V-2s – giant liquid-fuel rockets packed with explosive and capable of reaching Mach 1, the speed of sound, in under half a minute – were also added to the campaign. The V-1, V-2 and others in the pipeline were undoubtedly intended as terror weapons. The hard, rasping roar of the V-1's engine was a fearful sound that no one who heard it ever forgot, all the more so when the engine cut out and the missile started its dive earthwards. The V-2, on which space rocket technology was later based, was more insidious. Flying through the atmosphere, between 50 and 60 miles high and more, it fell on its targets quite literally out of the blue, and completely without warning. Altogether, more than 9000 British civilians were killed by the V weapons in 1944 and 1945. After the war, Werner von Braun was spirited out of Germany by US military intelligence and later worked on the US space programme.

Despite the destruction and loss of life caused by the V weapons and other technical developments such as the new Messerschmitt Me-163 'jet' fighter, which was powered by rockets and could reach speeds of up to 596mph, there was a growing tide of panic in Germany throughout 1944 as the enemies of the Reich seemed to be advancing from all sides. In Germany itself, rationing had been introduced, and living conditions steadily deteriorated as the war effort sucked in all available resources. A flourishing black market had quickly sprung up as a result. To a great many Germans who had shown absolute faith in their Führer, the reversal of Germany's fortunes seemed like a betrayal of everything they had been promised. In such circumstances, dissent was inevitable, and it has often been asked why the German people did not rise up and rid themselves of Hitler in the way the Italians had done with Mussolini. That, though, was easier said than done.

There was, in fact, a German resistance movement that had encouragement from inside the

Wehrmacht, but it was given little chance to act. During the final year of the Third Reich, as discontent spread, SS activities against 'enemies of the state' increased rapidly. The Nazi regime protected itself by turning on its own people, striving to keep them in line by using surveillance, the concentration camps, midnight arrests and summary public executions of suspected 'traitors'. Among those to be executed were the youthful founders of the White Rose Underground.

Within the German military itself, resistance to Hitler had been growing ever since the defeat at Stalingrad in 1943 had made it clear that the Nazi machine was not invincible after all. After D-Day, figures as high up in the German chain of command as Erwin Rommel were being openly critical of Hitler's policies. There had already been a number of failed attempts on the Führer's life before 20 July 1944 when the last bid was made to kill him. That day, Colonel Claus Schenk, Count von Stauffenberg, a well-respected soldier who in 1943 had lost an eye, his right hand and forearm and the third and fourth fingers of his left hand when his staff car was attacked by low-flying aircraft in North Africa, left a briefcase full of dynamite under a table at Hitler's headquarters at Rastenburg in east Prussia. The resulting explosion all but destroyed the room in which Hitler and a number of his generals were discussing the course of the war. However, possibly saved by the thickness of the table, the Führer survived with nothing more than a few bruises, though physically and mentally he never fully recovered. Von Stauffenberg was afterwards shot. So were his fellow conspirators, a group of high-ranking officers who had realised too late that Germany was being led to disaster. Their deaths were followed by a savage purge of the German military High Command, during which thousands, however remote their connection, were tried and executed for plotting to overthrow the Führer. Rommel, one of Hitler's greatest commanders, was not directly involved in the plot. He was, nevertheless, forced to commit suicide for his suggestion that Hitler should be removed from power. Hitler, meanwhile, entertained himself by watching film of the conspirators hanging from meat hooks.

Fear of the enemy also kept the German people from surrendering en masse. They had always been taught that the Russians were subhuman barbarians, and were now hearing horrifying tales of rape and torture as the Red Army advanced from the east. Joseph Göbbels, Hitler's chief of propaganda, whipped up these fears to the point of hysteria in a

ABOVE: THE NEWS OF THE ATTEMPT ON HITLER'S LIFE RAPIDLY SPREAD TO THE ALLIES, PROVIDING FURTHER EVIDENCE OF COLLAPSING GERMAN MORALE.

ABOVE LEFT: COLONEL CLAUS SCHENK (FAR RIGHT) WAITS TO GREET HITLER SHORTLY BEFORE HIS FAILED ASSASSINATION ATTEMPT.

RIGHT: DR JOSEF GÖBBELS, THE THIRD REICH'S CHIEF OF PROPAGANDA, MEETS THE PEOPLE OF BERLIN DURING A MORALE DRIVE. ALTHOUGH A DEEPLY CYNICAL AND EMBITTERED MAN, GÖBBELS WAS A BRILLIANT SPEAKER WHO GALVANISED THE GERMAN PEOPLE WITH HUGELY POP-ULAR RADIO BROADCASTS.

series of radio broadcasts that also made much of the Allies' demand that Germany surren-der 'unconditionally'. This, Göbbels told the German people, would mean the total destruction of their nation. Had not Stalin called for the 'laying waste' of all German fac-tories and property, and the 'battering to death' of the entire German people? With these

THE SOVIET ADVANCE INTO BERLIN

Just as they had already done at Stalingrad, the Red Army took Berlin street by street. They had travelled halfway across Europe to get there, and were wary of losing more men than was absolutely necessary in the final days of the war. The Russians were faced by some 60,000 German troops, a great many of them old men and boys of the Volksturm. In the confusion that descended on Berlin in the last weeks of the Third Reich, one Russian officer actu-ally managed to get a German switchboard operator to connect him to Dr Göbbels at the Ministry of Propaganda across town. When he asked how long Berlin could be expected to hold out, the officer was told that Göbbels expected the defence of the city to carry on for months. However, when the officer queried Göbbels about how he planned to escape, he was told that his question did not deserve an answer. After a couple more minutes of polite conversation, Göbbels hung up. Göbbels, in fact, never escaped. On 30 April 1945, he and his wife Magda poisoned their children and committed suicide.

On 3 May, a delegation of high-ranking German offi-cers met General Bernard Montgomery to request that they be allowed to surrender their forces in Berlin to him rather than to the Red Army, from whom they expected precious little mercy. Many of the Soviet troops in the city

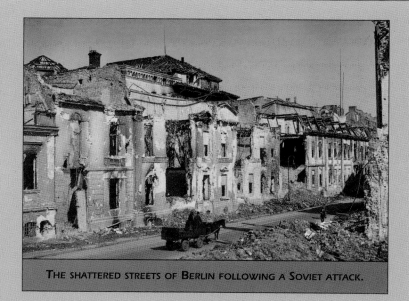

THE SHATTERED STREETS OF BERLIN FOLLOWING A SOVIET ATTACK.

had already begun to extract their own bloody revenge for German atrocities committed in the Soviet Union. Montgomery, however, was in no position to accede to such a request, as it had already been agreed among the Allies that the Russians would take Berlin. Three days later, another delegation, this time to the US military, made the same request. It was again denied.

grim reminders in their ears, it was not surprising that the closer the Allies came to victory, the more fiercely the Germans fought to defend themselves.

Most of all, though, the Germans hung on because their leader, although by now addicted to drugs, half paralysed and isolated from them in his Wolf's Lair at Rastenburg, still had absolute control over both the country and the vast majority of his people. Hitler was sufficiently in command of the military situation to order an audacious counter-attack on the advancing Allies in December 1944.

THE BATTLE OF THE BULGE

After amassing a force of over 250,000 men and more than 1000 tanks in the Ardennes forest, Hitler's troops swept through US forces in Belgium in an attempt to reach the port of Antwerp and divide the Allied lines. They got as far as the town of Bastogne before they were beaten by a brave American fight-back and were halted by lack of fuel. This last desperate stand, known as the Battle of the Bulge, cost the German Army over 100,000 men killed or taken prisoner.

At the beginning of 1945, as the Allied noose tightened around the remains of his forces, Hitler returned to Berlin to take up residence in a bunker under the Reichschancellery. The Ardennes campaign had managed to hold up the Allied armies in the west for six weeks, but that was all. As Hermann Göring observed, Hitler seemed to have aged 15 years since 1942. He spoke to the German people for the last time on 30 January, ironically

Rommel...was not directly involved in the plot. He was, nevertheless, forced to commit suicide for his suggestion that Hitler should be removed from power. Hitler, meanwhile, entertained himself by watching film of the conspirators hanging from meat hooks

LEFT: AFTER THE SUDDEN DEATH OF PRESIDENT ROOSEVELT, FORMER US VICE-PRESIDENT HARRY TRUMAN TOOK HIS PLACE. HERE (CENTRE) HE MEETS WITH STALIN AND THE BRITISH DEPUTY PRIME MINISTER CLEMENT ATTLEE. BEHIND TRUMAN IS ERNEST BEVIN, BRITAIN'S INDOMITABLE MINISTER FOR LABOUR.

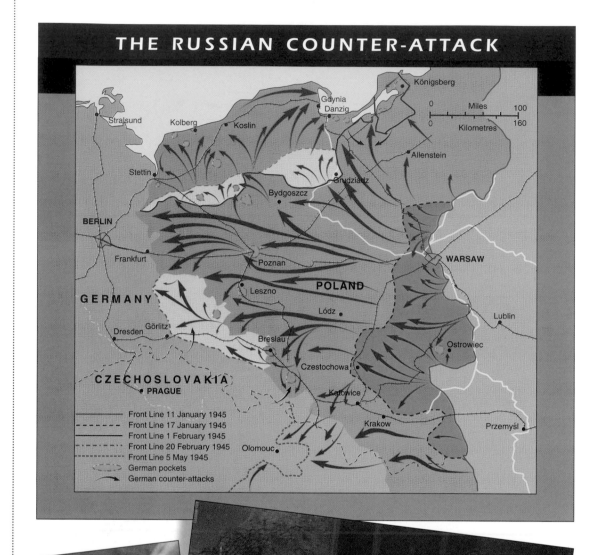

THE RUSSIAN COUNTER-ATTACK

BELOW RIGHT: GENERAL JODL, HITLER'S CHIEF MILITARY ADVISOR, SIGNS THE TOTAL, UNCONDITIONAL SURRENDER OF ALL GERMAN FORCES AT GENERAL EISENHOWER'S HEADQUARTERS IN RHEIMS, FRANCE.

BELOW: FIELD MARSHALL BERNARD MONTGOMERY WITNESSES THE SIGNING OF THE OFFICIAL SURRENDER OF GERMAN FORCES IN HOLLAND, DENMARK AND NORTHERN GERMANY BY ADMIRAL HANS VON FRIEDENBURG, LUNEBERG HEATH, 6.25 P.M.

the twelfth anniversary of his appointment as chancellor, urging them to fight to the end against the approaching Russian 'hordes', reminding them that God was on their side. He then instructed Speer to begin a 'scorched earth' policy that amounted to the destruction of Germany as a 'punishment' for the people who had 'betrayed' their Führer. Speer, realising at

LEFT: RELIEVED GERMAN SOLDIERS – MOST OF THEM YOUNG BOYS – SURRENDER TO THE US 7TH AND 24 ARMIES ON THE AUSTRIAN BORDER. THEY COULD EXPECT FAR BETTER TREATMENT FROM THE AMERICANS THAN THEY MIGHT HAVE RECEIVED AT THE HANDS OF THE RUSSIANS.

last that Hitler no longer cared what happened to the German people, pretended to obey but in fact did nothing.

By now, the Soviet forces were rolling all before them in the east. Czechoslovakia, Hungary and Austria were occupied in turn, and by the beginning of February 1945, the Red Army was less than 40 miles from Berlin. Across Germany, a mass exodus began, as people crammed the roads in an attempt to escape the Soviet advance, carrying whatever possessions they could on carts, horses and on their own backs. Those who could not or did not get away in time faced an uncertain future at the hands of the oncoming Russian soldiers, many of whom were now embarking on their own private campaigns of looting and rape in revenge for their country's sufferings. Meanwhile, at the Yalta conference, which had convened on 4 February 1945, the 'Big Three' – Churchill, an ailing President Roosevelt and Josef Stalin – had already carved up Europe between them. With the exception of Austria, the Soviet Union would 'administer' all the countries its troops now occupied. Despite the misgivings of both Britain and the USA, it was also agreed that Soviet forces were better placed to take Berlin. This strategy had been aided by Eisenhower's refusal to make a direct drive for the German capital instead of advancing on the Reich from France along a broad front.

On 7 March 1945, 8000 Allied troops became the first to break into Germany from the west when they crossed the River Rhine by way of the Ludendorff bridge at Remagen, which a retreating German unit had failed to destroy behind them. Germany's greatest natural

ABOVE: EAST EMBRACES WEST, AS AN AMERICAN GI HUGS A SOVIET COMRADE IN ARMS, SOUTHERN GERMANY, MAY 1945.

CANNON FIRE FROM A MESSERSCHMITT CHOPPED OFF THE WING OF THIS
B-17 FLYING FORTRESS JUST 18 MILES NORTH OF BERLIN.

US AIR LOSSES

In the summer of 1942 US bombers stationed at air bases in Britain began flying missions over Germany. While the RAF concentrated its efforts on night bombing as its part of the Allied 'combined bomber offensive', the giant B-17 Flying Fortresses of US 8th. Air Force operated during the day. This meant that USAAF air crews could target specific military and industrial installations that were impossible to attack by night, but it also denied the US bombers the protection of darkness. The consequences of this were illustrated by the August 1943 raid on the ball-bearing factory at Schweinfurt. Flying in huge formations without fighter cover, the US bombers were easy prey for the Luftwaffe and German anti-aircraft crews on the ground, despite themselves being heavily armed with a number of guns. Of the 229 B-17s that set out on the mission, 36 were shot down, an attrition rate of over 15 per cent.

This was unacceptable to US Bomber Command, and as a result of the disaster daylight missions over Germany were suspended for a full five months, only to be resumed after the development of new long-range Mustang fighters, which, equipped with extra fuel drop tanks, were able to provide escort for the bomber crews all the way to Germany and back. Heavily armed and capable of flying at over 400 miles per hour, the Mustangs soon achieved Allied air superiority over Europe. Nevertheless, German defences, and what was left of the Luftwaffe, continued to take a huge toll. During 1944 alone the 8th Air Force lost 2400 bombers over western Europe. Final figures released in October 1945 stated that in total more than 18,000 USAAF aircraft had been lost in air raids over Germany. The lives of 79,265 US airmen were lost with them.

OPPOSITE PAGE TOP LEFT: TWO JUBILANT LONDONERS CELEBRATE THE END OF THE WAR IN EUROPE. THE HEADLINE OF THE SUN NEWSPAPER SAYS IT ALL.

OPPOSITE PAGE TOP RIGHT: THE COVER OF THE DAILY MAIL SHOWS THE SCENE IN PICADILLY CIRCUS, LONDON, AS WORD SPREADS ABOUT THE IMPENDING DECLARATION OF PEACE.

defence had been breached. Field Marshal Kesselring was recalled from the fighting in Italy to shore up the German defences. He introduced himself to his troops with the sardonic words 'Gentlemen, I am the new V-3', but could do little to stop the rest of the Allied forces crossing the Rhine after a series of massive airborne landings. Almost 500,000 German soldiers of Army Group B surrendered as the Ruhr was overrun by the US 1st and 9th Armies. At the same time, the Russian 8th Army, which, led by General Vasili Chuikov, had defeated the Germans at Stalingrad, moved towards Berlin and began bombarding the city with rockets.

On 21 April 1945, the first Soviet tanks entered Berlin. By now, most of the inhabitants were living in cellars to escape the constant bombardment, equally afraid of the Russians and of the remorseless SS units that patrolled Berlin summarily executing suspected 'deserters'. Food and water were scarce. Electricity and gas supplies had been cut off or destroyed. Almost 500,000 Soviet troops ringed the city. Meanwhile, in his chancellery, beneath the rubble and the ruin, Hitler was living in delusion. In this last week of his life, he still believed that Germany could triumph. Following the sudden death of President Roosevelt on 12 April, he was convinced that the moment had finally come for a 'turn in the fortunes of war'.

Hitler told his troops on the eastern front that 'countless new units are replacing our losses', when in fact there were none. As the Red Army advanced through the ravaged streets of Berlin, German soldiers were deserting in their thousands. When the news reached him that SS chief Heinrich Himmler, too, was preparing to surrender, Hitler became enraged. He announced to those still left in his command bunker: 'Nothing now remains! Nothing is spared me! There is no bitterness, no betrayal that has not been heaped upon me!'

Finally, on 29 April, after marrying his mistress Eva Braun and naming Admiral Dönitz as his successor, Hitler shot himself, and his wife took poison. Afterwards, their bodies were burned in what was left of the garden of the Reichschancellery. A week later, on 7 May, Germany officially surrendered. A quarter of a million Berliners had been killed during the siege of the city. Eight million Germans were now refugees. An estimated 30 millions had died in Europe as a result of Nazi policies. The fate of six million Jews, hounded, brutalised, starved, beaten, worked to death or murdered was yet to come to light.

ABOVE: THE FRONT COVER OF THE BRITISH RADIO TIMES, AS THE BBC CELEBRATES THE VICTORY.

CHAPTER 15

Midway

to

Hiroshima

DEVASTATION ON THE BEACHES OF TARAWA IN THE GILBERT
ISLANDS AS DAZED SURVIVORS SEARCH FOR THEIR FALLEN
COMRADES. JAPANESE MACHINE-GUN POSITIONS HAD MADE SHORT
WORK OF THE MARINES AS THEY EMPTIED
FROM THEIR LANDING CRAFTS.

MIDWAY

Buoyed up by their whirlwind successes of the previous six months, the Japanese decided to extend their outer defensive perimeter to the extreme west. Admiral Isoroku Yamamoto, architect of the attack on Pearl Harbor, intended to invade the easternmost island of the Hawaiian chain, Midway. In the north, he planned to take possession of the Aleutian islands of Attu and Kiska, off Alaska. After the conquest of these islands, Yamamoto intended to invade Hawaii itself. Then, he believed, the USA would be forced to surrender, leaving the Japanese masters of the entire Pacific area.

To carry out his intricate battle plan, Yamamoto gathered together over 140 ships, including the four powerful aircraft carriers, *Akagi*, *Kaga*, *Hiryu* and *Soryu*, and placed them under the command of the Pearl Harbor veteran, Vice-Admiral Nagumo. By splitting his forces in two, sending one force to the Aleutians, and concentrating the other on Midway, Yamamoto hoped to divide the already weakened US fleet. However, it was a plan that failed disastrously, as the surprise on which Yamamoto depended for success was blown wide open by US codebreakers, who had discovered that the Japanese attack was scheduled for 4 June 1942.

The battle opened with a Japanese raid by 35 dive-bombers, 36 torpedo bombers and 36 fighters on Midway Island. US planes stationed on Midway suffered heavy losses, but the resistance put up by the island's defenders,

who continued to raid the Japanese fleet, convinced Nagumo that a second raid was necessary before the invasion could take place. It was while his planes were refuelling and rearming on the carrier flight decks that disaster struck. The US carrier force, which Admiral Nimitz, Commander of the Pacific fleet, had been able to concentrate on Midway, now came into action with stunning effect. Within five minutes, the whole direction of the war in the Pacific was changed. Planes from the US carriers *Yorktown*, *Hornet* and *Enterprise* plunged down on the Japanese fleet with little warning and, soon after, a suicidal raid by US torpedo-bombers wreaked confusion on board the Japanese ships. These carriers were sunk, forcing Nagumo to call off the invasion.

In total, the Japanese lost four carriers, half their entire carrier fleet, hundreds of aircraft and over 3500 expertly trained pilots and seamen. These were losses the Japanese were never able to make up, and their relentless advance across the Pacific had been delivered its first and most decisive blow. The US success was achieved despite their being heavily outnumbered by the Japanese in both planes and ships. Even more surprising was the fact that the pilots of the *Enterprise* and *Hornet* had never experienced carrier-to-carrier warfare before. Though the Americans lost the *Yorktown*, they had turned the tide of the war in the Pacific and seized an initiative they were never to relinquish.

BELOW: LOADING A DEMOLITION BOMB ON BOARD THE USS ENTERPRISE DURING THE FIRST FEW DAYS OF THE ATTACK ON GUADALCANAL, WHICH COMMENCED 7 AUGUST 1942.

GUADALCANAL

BELOW: THE VAIN BUT
BRILLIANT US GENERAL
DOUGLAS MACARTHUR IN A
CHARACTERISTIC POSE, WITH
PIPE IN MOUTH.

In spite of the disaster suffered at Midway, and the previous failure to take the Papua New Guinea capital, Port Moresby, the Japanese attempted to continue their advance in the south-western Pacific. If they could succeed in capturing Port Moresby, they would be only 300 miles north of Australia, and that would enable them to disrupt at will the supply lines between Australia and the USA.

General MacArthur, however, was determined to move onto the offensive. He launched two operations designed finally to stem the Japanese advance and begin the massive task of driving them back across thousands of miles of Pacific Ocean, where they had already begun to form their 'South-East Asia Co-Prosperity Sphere'. To start with, MacArthur sought to lift the threat from Australia by clearing the Japanese from Papua New Guinea and the Solomon Islands. Both tasks were made extremely difficult due to limited resources and the fanatical ferocity of the Japanese defence.

The Japanese had other ideas. A base was established at Buna, on the north coast of New Guinea, from which Japanese soldiers aimed to trek over the perilous Kokoda Trail, which ran across the Owen Stanley mountains, before dropping down to attack Port Moresby. With Australian troops, aided by local natives, resisting the Japanese advance, the USA began its assault on the Solomon Islands. On 8 August 1942, the US Marine Corps went ashore on Guadalcanal, so signalling the start of some of the most fearsome fighting of the entire Pacific campaign.

GENERAL TOJO WITH CHILDREN WHO LOST THEIR FATHERS IN THE WAR, JULY 1943.

TOJO

General Hideki Tojo was the man directly responsible for Japan's decision to go to war against the British and the USA. By the time he became prime minister in 1941, after serving as army minister since 1940, Tojo had already gained a well-deserved reputation as a military hard-liner. He was Chief of Staff of the Kwantung Army in Manchuria, which, quasi-independently, entered into full-scale war with China in 1937. Tojo was a committed nationalist who believed Japan's army should play a leading role in the country's government. The decision to attack Pearl Harbor was largely Tojo's. The successes of the other Axis powers, Germany and Italy, in Europe during 1940 had convinced him that Japan should take advantage of the weakened state of the European imperialists to extend her own empire in the Pacific. In 1944, however, Japan's spectacular victories began to turn into equally spectacular defeats. After the US capture of Saipan put Allied bombers within range of Japan, Tojo was forced to step down as prime minister. In 1948, after failing to commit suicide, he was hanged for war crimes and for planning to wage aggressive war.

US troops came ashore quickly, meeting little resistance, and proceeded to capture a half-constructed Japanese airfield. Renaming it Henderson Field, the Marines held on to it for dear life, as the US Navy on its own was hard pressed to supply them. Even without the airfield, the Japanese could reinforce their garrison on Guadalcanal. But the Japanese realised the importance of the airfield, and launched a huge offensive against it on 23–6 November. The Marines defended the airfield by every means at their disposal, from machine-guns and rifles to fists and boots.

While the fighting continued on Guadalcanal, General MacArthur had become concerned at the lack of progress being made against the Japanese in New Guinea. In order to get results, he sacked commanders whom he believed showed insufficient fighting spirit. MacArthur's judgement was harsh. He had little knowledge of the conditions his US and Australian troops were fighting under, but his quest for results could not be denied. He told General Robert Eichelberger, the new man in charge, to take New Guinea or 'not come back alive'. By December 1942, Eichelberger had taken Buna, providing the Allies with their first land victory in the Pacific campaign.

Meanwhile, Guadalcanal was proving a magnet for both the Japanese and the US forces. The Japanese military had no doubts about the island's importance, describing the battle to hold it as 'the fork in the road that leads to victory for them or us'. Groups of fast Japanese destroyers, dubbed the 'Tokyo Express' by US sailors, brought reinforcements in at night, while the US Navy did its utmost to stop them. By the end of the year, sufficient losses had been sustained by both sides to name the waters closest to the island 'iron-bottomed sound', but in the battle of attrition, the Japanese were slowly, but surely, coming off worse. By January 1943, they conceded the inevitable, as attempts to reinforce the island met with unacceptable casualties. Troop withdrawals began that same month, and the island was successfully evacuated by February.

These Allied victories on Guadalcanal and New Guinea proved decisive. Now, the Allies could begin advancing up the Solomon Islands chain, towards Bougainville and the

ABOVE: US MARINES OFFERED FIERCE RESISTANCE TO THE JAPANESE IN ORDER TO DEFEND THE AIRFIELD ON GUADALCANAL. THE MEN ABOVE WERE AMONG THOSE WHO LOST THEIR LIVES IN THE EFFORT.

MacArthur's judgement was harsh. He had little knowledge of the conditions his US and Australian troops were fighting under, but his quest for results could not be denied. He told General Robert Eichelberger, the new man in charge, to take New Guinea or 'not come back alive'

Bismarck Archipelago, where the Japanese had a massive naval base at Rabaul. Once these outposts of the Japanese Empire had been neutralised, the Allies could press on towards the Philippines and, eventually, to the Japanese home islands themselves.

TARAWA

In addition to the push towards Rabaul, moves were also under way to open up the central Pacific, and the Marshall Islands. On 20 November 1943, the Marines landed at Tarawa in the Gilbert Islands. They quickly captured the 2.5-mile-long island, which was defended by 4500 Japanese. They fought for it, literally, to the last man, but at the cost of over 1000 US soldiers. Although US casualties were insignificant compared to those borne by the Japanese, the numbers of those killed and wounded shocked American public opinion. What they had to realise, though, was that the USA had to expect these levels of casualties every time they attempted to eject the Japanese from one of their hundreds of island strongholds. Japanese soldiers refused to surrender as a matter of routine, even when faced with overwhelming firepower, numbers, resources and certain death. Their determination to fight to the finish made the war in the Pacific especially bitter and particularly bloody.

US soldiers had to use flame-throwers and dynamite to bring the Japanese out of their coconut log pillboxes. An American war reporter on Tarawa described a typical scene: 'As soon as (the flame-thrower) touched him, the Jap flared up like a piece of celluloid. He was dead instantly, but the bullets in his cartridge belt exploded for a full 60 seconds after he had been charred to almost nothingness.'

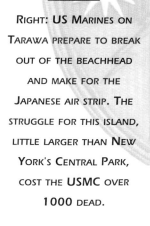

An American war reporter on Tarawa described a typical scene: 'As soon as (the flame-thrower) touched him, the Jap flared up like a piece of celluloid. He was dead instantly, but the bullets in his cartridge belt exploded for a full 60 seconds after he had been charred to almost nothingness'

RIGHT: US MARINES ON TARAWA PREPARE TO BREAK OUT OF THE BEACHHEAD AND MAKE FOR THE JAPANESE AIR STRIP. THE STRUGGLE FOR THIS ISLAND, LITTLE LARGER THAN NEW YORK'S CENTRAL PARK, COST THE USMC OVER 1000 DEAD.

ISLAND-HOPPING

The Japanese Prime Minister, Hideki Tojo, hoped that this fanatical resistance would enable the Japanese Empire to make up the massive gap in wealth and military resources that existed between the USA and Japan. He believed that the US troops, whom the Japanese had considered 'soft', would tire of receiving this kind of punishment as they pushed across the Pacific Ocean towards the Japanese home islands. Tojo, however, was sadly mistaken if he thought the Allies lacked the resolve to pursue the war to total victory.

President Roosevelt and his commanders were both impressed and horrified by resistance shown by the Japanese and they developed strategies to deal with it. One was the new military technique that became known as 'island-hopping'. The other was the invention of a super weapon that would change the shape of warfare for ever.

'Island-hopping' was a process whereby the USA could use its superiority at sea and in the air to capture the smaller and weaker Japanese-held islands, then use the occupied territory to establish new bases that would isolate and neutralise the larger Japanese concentrations in the area. One such base to be indirectly assaulted in this way was Rabaul. Once islands surrounding Rabaul had been seized, in 1944, the base was isolated and left to 'wither on the vine'. This technique saved money, time and, most vitally, lives. By 1944, using the 'island-hopping' strategy, the USA was ready to begin the liberation of the Philippines.

ABOVE: AS THE ISLAND-HOPPING STRATEGY BEGINS TO PAY OFF, ALLOWING THE USA TO COMMENCE THE LIBERATION OF THE PHILIPPINES, THESE US MARINES TAKE A MOMENT TO LEND A MORE PERSONAL HELPING HAND.

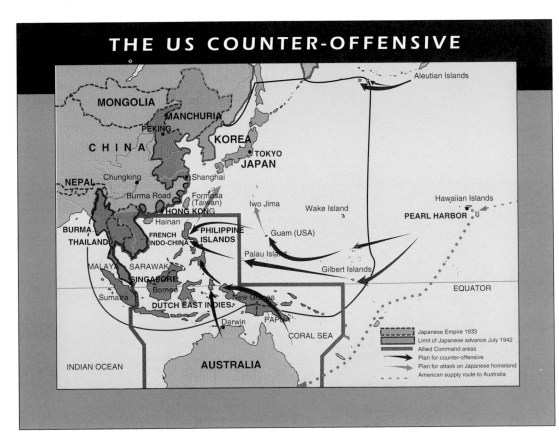

THE US COUNTER-OFFENSIVE

THE ATOMIC BOMB

As the island-hopping proceeded, so did the work on a super weapon designed to bring about a speedy Japanese surrender. The atomic bomb was also designed to make sure that the Allies beat the Germans to the making of this most deadly of weapons. Most of the early work undertaken by the Allies on the bomb had been done in Britain, but the British lacked the resources to pursue the research to its conclusion. The project was therefore passed on to the USA soon after it joined the war in December 1941. President Roosevelt devoted the $2 billion necessary for the project, and US, British, Canadian and other scientists began a race against time to complete the bomb before their enemies got there first.

THE PHILIPPINES

Despite, or because of, the increasingly swift Allied advance across the Pacific, Japanese resistance, already dogged, became increasingly fanatical. The Japanese High Command decided that the Philippines must be defended at all costs and, accordingly, the war-scarred remnants of the Imperial Japanese Navy were committed to the destruction of the American invasion force. The confrontation on 24 and 25 October 1944 became known as the Battle of Leyte Gulf and remains to this day the biggest single naval battle ever fought. The Japanese plan was simple. The Imperial Navy's remaining aircraft carriers would be used as bait to draw off the US ships defending the invasion force, while Japanese battleships attacked the undefended troops coming ashore.

In the event, however, the Imperial Navy suffered yet another crushing blow, and one that was to end its days as an effective fighting force. US submarines, torpedo boats and

WOMEN IN THE WAR

Unlike any previous conflict, the Second World War affected soldiers and civilians, men and women in equal measure, and American women lost no time in answering the call to work for the war effort in factories as well as the newly established female branches of the armed services. Following the example of the tough 'can do' propaganda poster, 'Rosie the Riveter', American women poured into the munitions factories to ensure that manufacturing levels were not adversely affected by the industry's loss of men to the armed forces.

American women, unlike their British counterparts, were not conscripted to the war effort; high wages alone proved sufficient encouragement for more than six million to enter the workforce. Yet, even though their wages often increased, women found their average earnings were still only half that of men. By 1944 American women made up just one-third of a workforce dedicated to producing not only the munitions that the USA needed to take on the armed might of Japan and Germany, but also a quarter of Britain's needs and 10 per cent of the Soviet Union's.

REAL LIFE ROSIE THE RIVETERS GET TO WORK IN THE GRUMANN AIRCRAFT FACTORY.

RIGHT: JAPANESE KAMIKAZE SUICIDE PILOTS PRESENT THEIR EMPEROR WITH A FINAL BOW BEFORE CLIMBING ON BOARD THEIR EXPLOSIVE-FILLED PLANES, WHICH THEY HOPE TO CRASH LAND INTO THE US FLEET.

ABOVE: DURING THE BATTLE OF LEYTE GULF, DESTROYERS OF THE US FLEET LAID SMOKESCREENS TO PROTECT ALLIED SHIPS FROM ATTACK BY THE JAPANESE.

aircraft carriers proved more than equal to the challenge offered them by the world's two largest warships, the *Yamato* and the *Musashi*. Most of the Japanese fleet was sent to the bottom after they failed to realise that their plan was on the verge of success, and committed a tactical blunder that led to their total destruction. The USA destroyed 26 Japanese ships and damaged another 25, but their victory was not without loss. One US carrier was wiped out by a new Japanese weapon, the kamikaze pilot, a title that meant 'divine wind'. The kamikaze, on a one-way mission with his plane full of explosives, effectively committed suicide for his emperor. After performing sacred rituals, he left his base with the intention of crashing his aircraft into the nearest Allied target. As the war in the Pacific reached its final stage, the kamikaze pilot and others who were, likewise, prepared to kill themselves for the emperor, played an increasingly prominent role.

With the Japanese fleet destroyed, the Americans were able to secure Leyte, and then press on north to the largest island of the Philippines group, Luzon. MacArthur fulfilled his pledge to return, and by 3 March 1945 Manila was once more in US hands. Although it was not yet clear to all those involved, the war in the Pacific had entered its final phases. By the time US troops entered Manila, the Marine Corps was well on the way to capturing Iwo Jima, a small volcanic island whose airstrips put B-29 bombers within range of Japan, and were beginning preparations for the capture of Okinawa in the Ryukus, the southernmost group of the Japanese home islands.

OKINAWA

As had occurred many times before right across the Pacific, the Marines' initial landings on Okinawa met with little initial resistance. But the ferocity of the Japanese will to fight back against the massive military strength of the USA had lost none of its fury. If anything, this close to the heartland of Japan, it increased. By the time the Marines had taken Okinawa on 22 June, there had been nearly 2000 kamikaze attacks, 20 or 30 per day, causing appalling damage to the US landing fleet and the Marines themselves. Yet, for all the losses they caused, the kamikaze attacks could not change the course of the war. With the capture of Okinawa, the Allies not only had another airstrip from which to carry out air raids on Japan, they also had a base from which Japan itself could be invaded.

The invasion of Japan was not a prospect the USA contemplated with relish. The Imperial Japanese Army and Navy had, for the last four years, displayed a desperate and suicidal wish to defeat them

RIGHT: A RARE SIGHT. JAPANESE TROOPS SURRENDER ON OKINAWA. MANY JAPANESE PREFERRED SUICIDE TO CAPTURE, YET THESE NAVAL TROOPS HAVE GIVEN THEMSELVES UP UNDER THE COVER OF THE WHITE FLAG TO A MEMBER OF THE US MARINE CORPS.

DROPPING THE BOMB

The invasion of Japan was not a prospect the USA contemplated with relish. The Imperial Japanese Army and Navy had, for the last four years, displayed a desperate and suicidal wish to defeat them. They had refused to surrender time and time again, and when resistance could no longer change the final outcome, Japanese forces had displayed a desire simply to kill as many Americans as possible before they themselves died. US Army chiefs estimated that the invasion of Japan might take until 1946 or 1947 to complete and could cost upwards of one million American dead. To lessen these expected casualties, the Americans were keen to have Stalin's Red Army help in the invasion.

BELOW: THE CREW OF THE ENOLA GAY, THE B-29 THAT DROPPED THE ATOMIC BOMB OVER HIROSHIMA, POSE FOR A SNAPSHOT SHORTLY BEFORE TAKE-OFF, AUGUST 1945.

TOP LEFT: SURVIVORS OF THE BLAST. WELL OVER ONE HUNDRED THOUSAND PEOPLE WERE KILLED BY THE EXPLOSION AND THE AFTER-EFFECTS OF THE RADIATION IT RELEASED.

LEFT: THE RUINS OF HIROSHIMA, AUGUST 1945. THE ATOMIC BOMB UNLEASHED UNBELIEVABLE DEVASTATION ON WHAT WAS A THRIVING JAPANESE CITY.

Harry S. Truman (had to) decide whether or not to drop the new atomic bomb on Japan. Truman believed he had little choice but to use the bomb.

ABOVE: THE OFFICERS AND MEN OF THE USS MISSOURI GATHER TO WATCH THE JAPANESE DELEGATION ARRIVE TO SIGN THE OFFICIAL DOCUMENT OF SURRENDER, TOKYO BAY, 1945.

ABOVE RIGHT: THE JAPANESE DELEGATION ARRIVES.

The Soviet dictator, welcoming the chance to extend his influence into Manchuria and Japan itself, agreed, though he did not declare war on Japan until 8 August 1945.

Air strikes were the inevitable prelude to the invasion, but while they were in progress, an extremely difficult choice had to be made. President Roosevelt had died suddenly on 12 April, and it fell to his Vice-President, Harry S. Truman, who succeeded him, to decide whether or not to drop the new atomic bomb on Japan. Truman believed he had little choice but to use the bomb. No matter how dreadful it was, it could shorten the war and save American lives.

On 6 August 1945, the first atomic bomb was dropped on Hiroshima. This new device unleashed an explosive force equivalent to 20,000 tons of high explosive, killing some 78,000 people and injuring another 78,000. Hiroshima itself was virtually vapourised, blasted out of existence by the awesome power harnessed inside a single bomb. On 9 August after Hiroshima failed to prompt a Japanese surrender, a second atomic bomb was dropped on Nagasaki. This time, 26,000 died and over 40,000 were injured. The dead, however, were the lucky ones, for the wounded suffered in ways never seen before as radiation burned and slowly poisoned them. Decades later, the victims of Hiroshima and Nagasaki were still dying. The Americans had ended a war with the most fearsome weapon ever devised and one that would cast its malignant shadow over generations yet unborn.

SURRENDER

Six days later, on 14 August, the Japanese Emperor, Hirohito, who was regarded as divine by his subjects, made his first-ever radio broadcast. Hirohito explained to his people, who were hearing his voice for the first time, that 'the war has developed, not necessarily to our advantage'. It was as close as the Emperor could get to admitting defeat. On

28 August, US troops began the occupation of Japan, and on 2 September General MacArthur accepted the official capitulation on board *USS Missouri*, moored off Tokyo Bay. With the end of the fighting in the Pacific, the Second World War reached its final conclusion, almost six years to the day after it had begun.

LEFT: IN HAWAII, WHERE IT ALL STARTED FOR THE USA, EARLY RISING WORKERS AND SERVICE MEN CELEBRATE THE JAPANESE SURRENDER AND THE ALLIED VICTORY IN THE PACIFIC, REPRESENTING THE CLOSING OF THE SECOND WORLD WAR'S FINAL CHAPTER.

FIRESTORMS OVER JAPAN

The prelude to the Allied invasion of Japan was an intensive bombing campaign designed to cripple Japan's war economy, communications, resources and will to fight. Unfortunately, such widespread strategic bombing inevitably led to horrific numbers of civilian casualties.

US raids over Japan proper began towards the end of 1944. The principal aircraft used was the B-29 'Superfortress'. As the offensive progressed, debate grew within the US Army Air Force about the most effective tactics. Eventually, after some heart-searching, precision bombing was abandoned in favour of the carpet bombing of Japan's cities, which often contained houses built of paper and wood as a defence against earthquakes. Consequently, the incendiaries delivered in low-level night-time attacks, using up to 500 bombers at a time, led to firestorms right across Japan. The authorities were helpless in the face of this gargantuan assault. Attempts by civilians to put out the flames were pathetic. All they had was the regulation sandbag and bucket of water to contend with a phenomenal 10 million incendiary bombs, many containing napalm, which rained down from the skies. Many Japanese families who attempted to escape the flames by hiding in water tanks were later found dead after being boiled alive. By July 1945, nearly one million Japanese civilians had been killed as firestorms ate their way through Tokyo, Osaka, Kobe, Kawasaki and Yokohama.

A US AIR FORCE SUPERFORTRESS RAINS FIRE ON JAPAN.

CHAPTER 16

The Empire in Crisis – Australia, India and Burma

US TROOPS ADVANCE ACROSS A BAMBOO FOOTBRIDGE
DURING THE ALLIED PUSH INTO BURMA, WHICH, ALONG WITH INDIA
AND AUSTRALIA, WAS UNDER THREAT FROM THE JAPANESE SINCE THE
FALL OF SINGAPORE IN 1942. THE FIGHT-BACK ON ALL FRONTS
WOULD EVENTUALLY LEAD TO THE SURRENDER OF THE JAPANESE
IN AUGUST 1945. THEREAFTER, HOWEVER, THE BRITISH EMPIRE –
ALONG WITH THOSE OF THE FRENCH AND THE DUTCH – WOULD
NEVER BE THE SAME.

THE FALL OF SINGAPORE AND RANGOON

In early 1942, as Japanese troops were marching through the British South-East Asian colonies of Burma and Malaya, a major diplomatic row erupted between Britain and Australia. Outraged at the British decision to evacuate the Malayan capital Singapore – a huge British outpost considered vital to the defence of the region – the Australian Prime Minister John Curtin ordered that a troopship full of Australian soldiers who were bound for the defence of the Burmese capital Rangoon should turn round and return home. As far as Curtin was concerned, Australia would now have to defend itself from a Japanese invasion, and could no longer spare men to prop up what he saw as British imperial interests elsewhere.

Curtin's actions directly contravened the orders of British Prime Minister Winston Churchill, who had already made it clear that he regarded 'keeping the Burma road open as more important than the retention of Singapore'. Not only did the Japanese advances in Burma threaten Allied supply lines to China, they also raised questions about the security of another neighbouring British possession – India. Curtin, however, saw Churchill's refusal to hold on to Singapore – and so too the corridor between the advancing Japanese and the Australian mainland – as an 'inexcusable' betrayal. As his predecessor Robert Menzies had put it: 'what Britain calls the Far East is to us the Near North'. Australia was in grave danger, and Britain, it seemed, was neither willing nor able to help, despite the fact that since 1941 some of Australia's best troops had been fighting to defend British interests in North Africa.

The fact was that Britain was by now almost exhausted by nearly three years of war with Germany. She had precious few resources to spare for defending any of her overseas territories, despite the fact that colonial supply lines and troops had been so important in keeping the British war effort alive. For Australia these were desperate times. On 19 February 1942, Darwin – the main supply base of the Australian Navy – was bombed by Japanese aircraft for the first time, and the following month it was announced that Japanese troops had invaded New Guinea, less than an hour's flight from the Australian mainland. The Australian government had no choice now but to look to the USA, the only other significant power in the Pacific, for its defence, rather than to Britain.

In April 1942, US troops began to arrive in Australia in great numbers and a US South-West Pacific Area general headquarters was installed at Brisbane. An Australian Imperial Force was set up and later fought alongside US troops, first in the liberation of New Guinea, where, despite being initially demoralised by disease and the terrible jungle conditions, they performed heroically, and then throughout the US 'island-hopping' campaign across the Pacific. Some of the 'fathers and sons' of the Australian Imperial Force were veterans of the First World War, while others were untrained, but as far as they were concerned, they were fighting for nothing less than the 'front line defence of Australia'. They played a major – though not always recognised – part in that defence. A total of over

Some of the 'fathers and sons' of the Australian Imperial Force were veterans of the First World War, while others were untrained, but as far as they were concerned, they were fighting for nothing less than the 'front line defence of Australia'

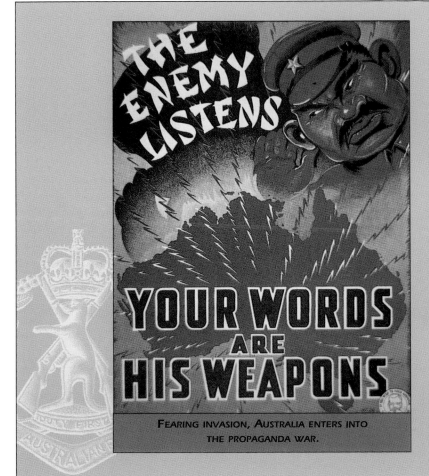

FEARING INVASION, AUSTRALIA ENTERS INTO THE PROPAGANDA WAR.

THE AUSTRALIAN HOME FRONT

As a territory of the British Empire, Australia was committed to the war against Germany from the outset, but it was not until after the Japanese attack on Pearl Harbor in 1941 that ordinary Australians began to feel the effects of war directly. With their overseas supply lines threatened and the realisation that their country might be invaded, the Australian people were forced to adapt – much as the British had – to life under siege. For the first time, civilian conscription was introduced. So was rationing of food, clothing and fuel. The production of beer and spirits was cut by over a third, and consumption of tea was restricted to less than two ounces per person per week. As in Britain a Women's Land Army was created, putting 2000 women to work in the countryside, while thousands of others were called up for civil and coastal defence duties. Even Italian prisoners of war were put to work, many of them on farms. The Japanese bombing of Darwin in February 1942 had a huge psychological impact on the Australians, who had never before been attacked on their own soil by a foreign power, and led to widespread panic and rioting. It was followed by the 'invasion' of Australia by thousands of US troops under the command of General MacArthur, as the Allied fight back in the Pacific began. This caused another kind of upheaval: more than 10,000 Australian women eventually emigrated to the USA with their new-found American husbands.

17,000 Australian servicemen eventually lost their lives in the fight against Japan. While Australian troops battled the Japanese to the south, the situation in Burma was growing worse. Japan's strategic aims for the invasion of Burma were ambitious. As well as removing the British from South-East Asia, the Japanese military command intended to close the Burma road by which the USA had been supplying China with Lend Lease aid since 1941. Both Britain and the USA had been supporting the Chinese nationalist leader Chiang Kai-Shek in his struggle against Japan ever since the Japanese invasion of China in 1937. In 1940 US President Roosevelt had lent Chiang almost 100 planes and their pilots – the famous ' Flying Tigers' – to fight alongside his own air force. By closing the only land route into China, the Japanese sought to cut off this flow of aid and starve the Chinese forces into sub-

ABOVE: GROUND CREW SERVICE A 'FLYING TIGER'; ABOVE LEFT: MAJOR GENERAL CLAIRE CHENNAULT; TOP: 'FLYING TIGER' LOGO.

THE FLYING TIGERS

Led by former stunt pilot General Claire Chennault, the 'American First Volunteer Group' was a small band of US pilots recruited in 1941 to aid Chinese nationalist forces who were fighting to free China from the Japanese. They soon became famous, both for their distinctively painted Warhawk fighter planes and for the daring and skill they showed in battles with Japanese planes in the skies over China. Chenault reportedly encouraged them by offering a bounty of $500 for every Japanese aircraft shot down. As more and more of the original Flying Tigers were themselves shot down, their places were eventually taken by more conventional Liberator bombers, which were used to fly missions over Tokyo and to attack Japanese shipping.

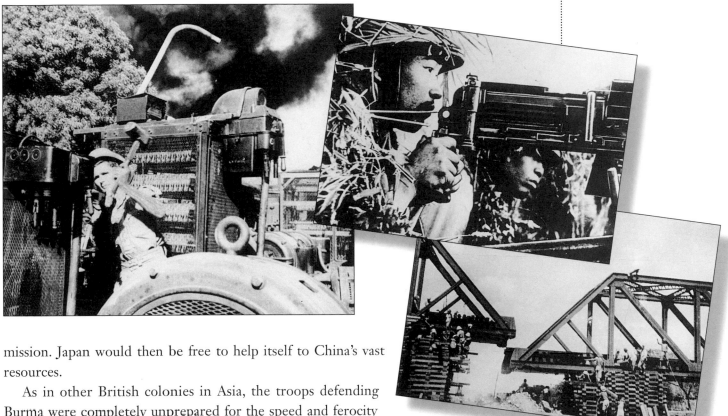

mission. Japan would then be free to help itself to China's vast resources.

As in other British colonies in Asia, the troops defending Burma were completely unprepared for the speed and ferocity of the Japanese advance. Instead of waiting for roads to be cut for tanks, the enemy exploited the vast jungle that covered most of the country, moving forward on foot or bicycle and repeatedly outflanking and 'hooking' the British defences from behind. By comparison, the troops of the 1st Burma and 17th Indian divisions were unskilled in the art of jungle warfare and were defending a country that for the most part did not seem to want them there. Burma had been gradually taken over by Britain in the 19th century, and made a province of India in 1886, since which time there had been an active and vigorous resistance to British rule.

On 9 March 1942, Rangoon, the Burmese capital, fell to the Japanese advance. The enemy had been stalled long enough for the retreating British to destroy most of the port's facilities before they fell into enemy hands but the cost had been high. The destruction of the Sittang bridge cut off the only escape route for an entire Indian division who were facing the Japanese, forcing them to attempt to swim across the river. Three thousand of them made it, but almost all the Gurkha brigade – who were brave fighters but had never learned to swim – drowned during the crossing. By this time General Sir Harold Alexander had arrived to co-ordinate troop movements in Burma, but there was little he could do other than to authorise a slow withdrawal along the Irawaddy river. On 21 April 'the longest retreat in British military history' had begun, as 30,000 troops set out to try to fight their way through the 600 miles of dense jungle and dangerous mountain passes that stood between them and the relative safety of India. Surviving on starvation rations and battling constant monsoon rains, it took them nine weeks and cost 4,000 lives. Meanwhile, the US-led Chinese 5th and 6th Armies who had crossed into Burma to engage Japanese troops in the north of the country were also being pushed back into China. On 30 April, the Burma road was closed and, by the end of May, Burma had fallen.

ABOVE LEFT: AS SMOKE RISES FROM BURNING OIL WELLS, A BRITISH SOLDIER DESTROYS MACHINERY AT YENANYUANG ON THE IRAWADDY RIVER TO PREVENT IT FALLING INTO ADVANCING JAPANESE HANDS.

ABOVE RIGHT: WORK BEGINS ON A RAILWAY BRIDGE IN NORTHERN BURMA, SABOTAGED BY ALLIED TROOPS.

ABOVE CENTRE: JAPANESE GUNNERS PREPARE TO OPEN FIRE ON CHINESE NATIONALIST TROOPS.

For the next year, as British and US forces regrouped in India and China, the Japanese attempted to consolidate their position in Burma. Although in private the Japanese Prime Minister, Hideki Tojo, envisaged a 'New Order' in which Japan would control the entire Asian region, publicly he spoke of creating a 'Greater East Asia Co-Prosperity Sphere' of sovereign nations free from European imperial interference. In this ambition Japan was supported by the leaders of nationalist movements in all the former Dutch, French and British colonies that had been 'liberated' by Japanese troops. In December 1943 the Tokyo 'Greater East Asian Conference' was attended by representatives from Manchuria, the Philippines, Thailand and Burma – where a Japanese puppet government and National Army had been set up under Prime Minister U Ba Maw. Unfortunately, Maw's tacit endorsement of Japanese rule did not prevent Japanese troops from using Burmese civilians alongside British POWs as slave labour on a number of military projects.

The most infamous of these was the building of the Burma railway, over which the Japanese planned to move troop reinforcements between Thailand and Rangoon. Between October 1942 and November 1943 tens of thousands of British and Australian POWs were put to work trying to cut the railway through almost impossible jungle terrain. Although using POWs in this manner was outlawed by the Hague Convention, the Japanese simply declared that those who did not work would not be fed. Conditions for the workers were terrible, and the combination of malaria and the brutal treatment meted out by the Japanese guards eventually led to the loss of over 100,000 lives. It has been calculated that 400 men lost their lives for every mile of track laid.

THE INSPIRATIONAL GENERAL WILLIAM SLIM. CHURCHILL DESCRIBED HIM AS HAVING 'A HELL OF A FACE'.

THE FORGOTTEN ARMY

The men of General Slim's 14th Army fought their campaign against the Japanese in some of the most hostile conditions that British soldiers faced in the Second World War. Permanently undermanned and undersupplied and often having to survive on little more than starvation rations, they were also frequently prey to malaria, dysentery, typhus, blood-sucking leeches, poisonous insects, deadly snakes and everything else the Burmese jungle could throw at them. Under these circumstances, their resounding success was remarkable, especially when most of the men felt they were receiving little recognition or support back home for their efforts. Ingenuity and adaptability played a large part in their victories, and they learned fast how to make the most of their surroundings. Improvements were made in medical treatment for men on the front line. An entire network of roads was built through the dense, muddy jungle, using little more than fallen trees. Troops were trained to hold their positions against an enemy that they often could not see through the thick forest. Patrols learned how to bypass enemy lines without being spotted themselves. Most of all, it was the extreme bravery, comradeship and discipline of the 14th's united Commonwealth troops that ensured their survival.

Also present at the Greater East Asian Conference was the Indian nationalist Subhas Chandra Bose, who arrived by German U-boat. Civil unrest in India at the British refusal to grant the colony its own government had been growing throughout the war. Around the world Indian soldiers were fighting and dying in defence of the British Empire, and Indian supplies were proving essential to the survival of Britain itself, yet the British Government would offer only to 'consider' the issue of self-rule for the Indian people once the war was over. The Indian nationalist cause, officially led by Mahatma Mohandas Gandhi, was exploited by Bose throughout the war in a series of anti-British propaganda broadcasts made from Japan. He was also responsible – with permission from the Japanese military – for raising the 'Indian National Army', which was made up of Indian POWs captured by the Japanese in Malaya. Bose saw himself as a future leader of an independent India, and between 1942 and 1944, he repeatedly called on Japan to 'march on Delhi' and kick the British out.

THE CHINDITS

In India, during this time, a new fighting force was being built from the survivors of the Indian 17th and Burmese 1st divisions. Commanded by General William Slim – 'Uncle Bill' to his troops – the 14th Army was made up of British, Indian, Gurkha and African troops who spent months training in jungle warfare in preparation for their eventual return to Burma. Slim had been appointed in the final days of the retreat from Burma and was aiming to hit back at the Japanese by 'going in where he took a licking coming out'. He would be aided in his campaign by the controversial and passionately religious Brigadier Orde Wingate, an expert on guerrilla warfare who had played a part in masterminding the 1941 defeat of Italian forces in Ethiopia. Wingate had convinced Prime

ABOVE LEFT: A JAPANESE LEAFLET DROPPED ON BURMA URGES INDIANS TO JOIN THE NATIONAL ARMY AND KICK THE BRITISH OUT OF THE SUB CONTINENT.

ABOVE RIGHT: MEMBERS OF THE INDIAN NATIONAL ARMY TRAIN IN BURMA, 1944.

ABOVE CENTRE: INDIAN TROOPS USE MULES TO CARRY BURMESE GUNS AT A MOUNTAIN BATTERY ON THE INDIA–BURMA BORDER.

ABOVE: CHINDIT TROOPS PREPARE TO DESTROY A RAILWAY BRIDGE.

RIGHT: A CHINDIT MULE IS LOADED, SOMEWHAT UNWILLINGLY, ONTO A DAKOTA TRANSPORT PLANE BOUND FOR THE BURMESE FRONT LINE. AIR SUPPORT PLAYED A HUGE PART IN THE ALLIED OPERATION TO RETAKE BURMA.

TOP RIGHT: A MEMBER OF THE 1ST PUNJAB REGIMENT OF THE BRITISH 14TH ARMY KEEPS LOOKOUT ON THE ARAKAN FRONT, WHERE THE 7TH INDIAN DIVISION HELD A 1000-YARD-SQUARE 'BOX' OF TERRITORY AGAINST A MASSIVE JAPANESE ATTACK.

Minister Churchill to let him start what amounted to a private war deep behind Japanese lines in Burma, destroying enemy bridges, railway lines and communications with his crack band of 'Chindit' troops. Taking their name from the stone lions said to guard Burmese tombs, the Chindits soon became experts at 'long-range penetration' and led Churchill to praise Wingate's 'genius and audacity'. However, the Chindits frequently paid a high price for their limited successes, and in March 1943 suffered heavy losses after pushing too deep into enemy territory. The scattered survivors were forced to trek back 1000 miles through the jungle, living off plants and what animals they could trap.

The first objective of the Allied South-East Asia Command, set up in August 1943 to co-ordinate the efforts of both the Chindits and the 14th Army, was to reopen the land route to China. Since the capture of the Burma road, US pilots based in India had been flying non-stop missions over the Himalayas to supply the joint US and Chinese forces with everything from men to mules. Working 12 hours a day, seven days a week, they pushed themselves and their ageing Dakota and Commando aircraft to the limit to get over the Himalayan mountain range – average height 20,000ft – more commonly known as 'the Hump'. The Allied plan was to advance into northern Burma and seize the airfields

at Myitkyina, cutting out the need to fly supplies over the Hump and securing a base for
the long-range bombing of Japan. At the
same time, a second force was to capture the
southern Arakan region in preparation for an
eventual seaborne invasion of Rangoon.

The US–Chinese Army was led by US
General Joseph Stilwell, who had been
appointed Chiang Kai-Shek's Chief of Staff in
1942. A great leader to his men but a poor
diplomat, Stilwell's abrasive style had earned
him the nickname 'Vinegar Joe', and he made
no secret of his distrust of both Chiang – whom
he called 'the Peanut' – and the British themselves. Serving under Stilwell were Colonel
Frank D. Merrill's 5307th division, better
known as 'Merrill's Marauders', a band of 3000
US fighting men who had volunteered for 'hazardous' service in China and who supported
Stilwell's 'New Chinese First Army' as they
pushed into northern Burma. Like the Chindits, the Marauders were accustomed to guerrilla warfare, and, also like the Chindits, they
endured huge losses in their trek through the
hazardous Kumon Pass in monsoon conditions
to reach Myitkyina. At one point, Merrill suffered a heart attack, but discharged himself
from hospital to rejoin his men.

The British thrust towards Arakan suffered its own setbacks in the shape of a determined Japanese counter-attack, but the real
crunch for Slim's forces came when three
divisions of Japanese troops crossed the
Chindwin river and invaded India in the third
week of March 1944. Their intention was to

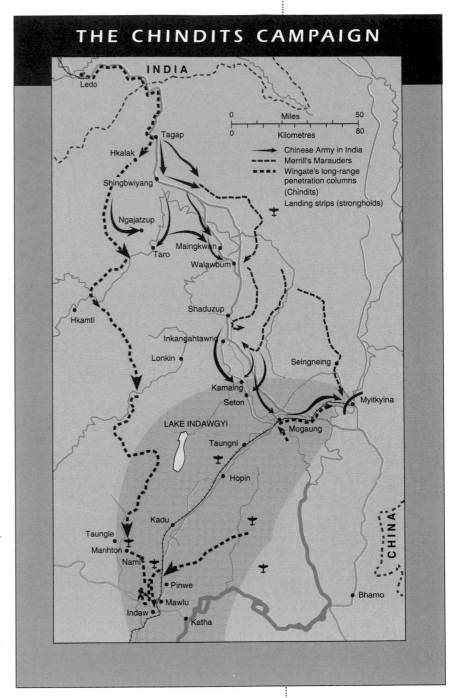

capture the US airfields and sever Stilwell's lifeline, but it seemed obvious that a full-scale
invasion of the subcontinent was going to follow. At the tiny outpost of Kohima in the
Assam mountains, 500 men of the West Kent Rifle Brigade had to hold out for almost a
month against a massive Japanese onslaught before 2000 Indian reinforcements arrived.
Even then they were still hugely outnumbered. Five thousand feet up in the mountains,
surrounded by thick jungle that reduced visibility to less than 50 feet and shelled from
above by day and night, they survived for three months – supported entirely by supplies
from the air – before the siege was lifted. By the end, no man's land was only as wide as the
tennis court that had once belonged to the region's district commissioner. The dead and
wounded were lying in shallow trenches out in the open.

RIGHT: MEN OF THE
US 5307TH DIVISION –
'MERRILL'S MARAUDERS'
– TAKE A WELL-EARNED
REST FROM THE FIGHTING
IN BURMA.

BELOW: BRIGADIER
GENERAL FRANK
D. MERRILL.

The bravery and discipline shown at Kohima was reflected at Imphal, where air support once again allowed Slim's troops to dig in and hold out against the Japanese. The Japanese lost over 50,000 men before starting to retreat. By contrast, the 14th Army had suffered slightly more than 16,000 casualties and now went onto the offensive, pursuing the retreating Japanese back into Burma, despite the monsoon rains. For the rest of 1944, they fought a bitter war of attrition with the retreating Japanese troops, and slowly advanced towards the Irawaddy river. Slim's leadership and training had transformed the men who had been forced out of Burma two years previously – and who were now as adept as the Japanese at waging jungle warfare. When, in December 1944, they crossed the Irawaddy at several locations on improvised rafts, they showed they had learned the lessons of the Japanese bicycle advance.

There were setbacks. On 24 March 1944 Wingate was killed in a plane crash, and a series of

WEST AFRICAN TROOPS PARACHUTE INTO THE BURMA JUNGLE FROM AN RAF SUPPLY PLANE.

AIR SUPPORT

One of the unique features of the campaign in Burma was the extent to which the troops relied on air support. An estimated 96 per cent of all the 14th Indian Army's supplies were flown in, most of it landing at scratch airstrips that the troops had carved out of the jungle. Over 300,000 reinforcements from India reached the front line in planes flown over the Himalayas by US pilots, and almost as many casualties were flown out over the same route. During the Japanese attacks on Kohima and Imphal in 1944 the entire 5th Indian division was airlifted 500 miles north to support the British lines in a spectacular operation.

disastrous glider operations resulted in the loss of a large number of men. Stilwell's US and Chinese troops took Myitkyina in early August 1944, but Stilwell himself was recalled to the US in October of the same year at Chiang's request. Nevertheless, Mandalay fell to the 14th Army on 20 March 1945, and was quickly followed by the vital communications centre of Meiktila. The Japanese, now exhausted and demoralised by US successes in the Pacific, tried to retreat en masse once more, but fell prey to repeated ambushes by Indian Keren guerrillas. On 3 May 1945, Rangoon was back in British hands.

The fact that Britain granted Burma its independence in 1948 led many in the 14th Army to complain that they had fought for nothing. In fact, they had fought to deliver not just the Burmese but British, Indian and Australian prisoners of war from brutal Japanese rule, and had probably saved India from a full-scale invasion in the process. The bravery of Indian troops themselves had also once again pressed the case for Indian independence from Britain, and that would soon be accepted. Their efforts also ensured that China stayed in the war, which in turn meant that Japan was never able to concentrate all its military strength in battles elsewhere with Britain, Australia and the USA.

LEFT: NEPALESE GURKHA TROOPS OF THE 14TH ARMY CLEAR A JAPANESE FOXHOLE AFTER A SUCCESSFUL ADVANCE.

BELOW CENTRE: BRITISH SOLDIERS REACH THE OUTSKIRTS OF MANDALAY IN MARCH 1945.

BELOW: ALLIED SHIPS UNLOAD SUPPLIES AT RANGOON DOCKS AFTER THE BRITISH ARRIVAL.

LEFT: WATCHED BY SOLDIERS OF THE 5TH INDIA DIVISION, JAPANESE TROOPS LEAVE BURMA THE WAY THEY CAME IN – BY BICYCLE. THE JAPANESE SURRENDER WAS SIGNED ON 28 AUGUST 1945.

CHAPTER 17

The Final Solution

THE HORROR REVEALED. US SOLDIERS ATTEND TO THE REMOVAL
OF CORPSES, BUCHENWALD DEATH CAMP, 1945. TRAGICALLY,
THEY REPRESENT ONLY ONE SMALL HANDFUL OF THE MILLIONS
WHO HAD BEEN CRUELLY AND SYSTEMATICALLY EXTERMINATED AS
PART OF THE ENDLOSUNG – THE FINAL SOLUTION. IT HAD ITS
ROOTS IN T4, A PROGRAMME OF EUTHANASIA AIMED PRIMARILY
AT THE MENTALLY AND PHYSICALLY HANDICAPPED – A GROTESQUE
REHEARSAL FOR ITS LATER AND PRINCIPAL PURPOSE: THE
GENOCIDE OF THE JEWS.

ENDLOSUNG

On 20 January 1942, a group of high-ranking Nazi officials gathered in the Berlin suburb of Wannsee. They had been given a task of the utmost secrecy, handed down by Hitler and passed on to them by Hitler's deputy, Hermann Göring. The task the Führer had placed in their hands was to arrange for the extermination of the entire Jewish population of Europe, a policy the Nazis termed *Endlosung*, the 'Final Solution' of the Jewish question.

Chairing the meeting was Reinhard Heydrich, second-in-command of the SS and head of the Reich Main Security Office. A fairly young man – he was 38 – Heydrich was so ruthless that even Hitler was said to be wary of him. Although the official minutes of the meeting contained thinly veiled euphemisms to describe the rounding up and transportation of Europe's Jewish population to death camps, Heydrich himself was in no doubt of their fate. As he said, the Final Solution would see Europe 'combed through from west to east', and no Jews would be left alive.

Although it was treated as a state secret, carrying out the Final Solution would require thousands of SS guards, scientists, doctors and administrators to see it through to completion. Many of them relished the task, including the man at the heart of the practical administration, Adolf Eichmann, head of the SS Race and Resettlement Office. Anti-Semitism had been present in Germany for centuries and German Jews had been cruelly persecuted, dispossessed and murdered in the early, pre-war years of Nazi power. Now, though, anti-semitism was to take its most evil and most diabolical form.

Even before Heydrich and his colleagues sat down to their meeting in Wannsee, SS units, with the co-operation of the German Army, had been systematically murdering Jews in the occupied territories of Poland since 1939 and the Soviet Union since 1941.

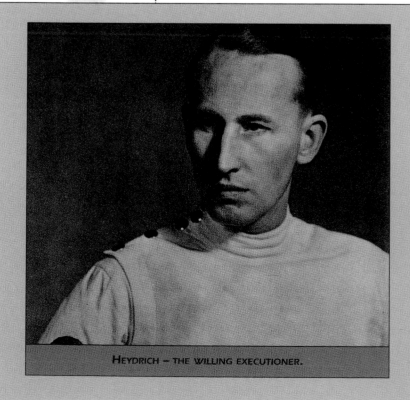

HEYDRICH – THE WILLING EXECUTIONER.

REINHARD HEYDRICH

Reinhard Heydrich, whose looks were those of the perfect Aryan, but who was rumoured to have Jewish blood, was Himmler's deputy and second-in-command of the SS. In 1933 he oversaw the setting up of Dachau, the original concentration camp, and the first to bear the supremely cynical slogan *Arbeit Macht Frei* – work makes you free. It was Heydrich who rounded up 25,000 wealthy Jews after *Kristallnacht* and sent them to the concentration camps. He was soon rewarded for his work by receiving control of the Reich Main Security Office, RSHA, and began setting up the first Einsatz groups – or action groups – for operations in Poland as well as organising the construction of the Jewish ghettos. It was these Einsatzgruppen SS troops who first began the systematic murder of European Jews. Heydrich was then given the task of organising the Final Solution, to which end he chaired the Wannsee conference at the beginning of 1942. He was also appointed Reich Protector of Bohemia and Moravia (Czechoslovakia) in September 1941. He was critically injured by Czech resistance fighters in Prague on 29 May the following year. It took him six days to die of his injuries, on 4 June.

Indeed, the Nazi desire to 'solve' the Jewish question had reached such a sophisticated level by this time that bullets were no longer considered a humane way of killing the millions of Jews who had come under German control as Hitler's war machine rolled further east. Humane that is, for the executioners. Many of them were buckling under the sheer strain of slaughtering thousands upon thousands of men, women and children by first stripping them naked, then shooting them in the back of the head, and afterwards tossing their corpses into mass graves. So, to preserve the sanity of his men, Heinrich Himmler, head of the SS, was keen for other methods of annihilation to be developed. In December 1941, the first use of gas on Jews took place at the Polish village of Chelmno. Jews from the surrounding area were placed in vans, ostensibly for transportation to work camps. The vans were specially designed so that the vehicles' exhaust fumes were fed back inside the hermetically sealed interiors, killing the Jews by carbon monoxide poisoning. After this, slaughtering Jews by gas was considered so successful that it was soon employed at death camps in German-occupied Poland. With this, the killing of Jews began to proceed on an industrial scale.

But how had it come about that Germany, apparently one of Europe's most cultured and civilised nations – albeit one with a strong militaristic tradition – had adopted as an official policy of state the genocide of Europe's Jews? And not only them, but also the mentally defective, homosexuals, freemasons and gypsies as well? Since he took over the Nationalist Socialist German Workers' Party, originally formed in 1918 to encourage

ABOVE: ADOLF EICHMANN, THE SUPREME BUREAUCRAT AND DRAUGHTSMAN OF THE FINAL SOLUTION. AFTER THE WAR HE EVADED CAPTURE BUT WAS HUNTED DOWN AND CAPTURED BY THE ISRAELI GOVERNMENT, WHICH TRIED AND EXECUTED HIM IN 1960.

ABOVE LEFT: GERMAN OFFICERS POSE PROUDLY FOR THE CAMERA AS THEY MURDER RUSSIAN VILLAGERS.

nationalism among the working classes, and which after 1920 he turned into the militaristic, vengeful Nazi Party, Adolf Hitler had made no secret of his paranoid hatred of the Jewish people. They were, he believed, a race, not a religion, and one that 'degraded' German life. In the twisted, racist, Nazi philosophy that saw life as a never-ending struggle between competing races, the Jews were dangerous enemies of the pure 'Aryan' or German people. As such, they had to be eradicated. Precisely how Hitler was to achieve this remained obscure until long after he came to power in 1933. Even then, the plans for mass extermination of the Jews were largely kept secret from the majority of Germans, and from the world.

In his political testament, *Mein Kampf*, Hitler described the moment when he first became fully aware of the Jewish 'peril'. He was living in Vienna before the First World War, and it was there that the revelation took place. He wrote:

BEFORE THE NAZIS MOVED TOWARDS THE EXTERMINATION OF JEWS, THE PHYSICALLY AND MENTALLY ILL WERE AMONG THEIR FIRST VICTIMS.

I suddenly encountered a phenomenon in a long kaftan and wearing black side-locks. My first thought was: is this a Jew? They certainly did not have this appearance in Linz [Hitler's home town]. I watched the man stealthily and cautiously, but the longer I gazed at this strange countenance and examined it section by section, the more the question shaped itself

that did not conform to the criteria laid down by Nazi ideology. Many of the methods of killing that were later used against the Jews were also used to exterminate people who fell into these 'categories'.

The euthanasia programme was known as T-4, short for the operations address Tiergartenstrasse 4, but despite Hitler's attempts to get it under way earlier, it did not come into force until late in 1939. The Nazis were more sensitive to, or wary of, public opinion than is often realised, and were careful to keep the 'mercy killings' secret. Relatives of the victims were given false reports of their deaths. By the time T-4 had run its course, over 70,000 people had been gassed by medical staff or killed by lethal injection. Despite Nazi attempts to keep the project under wraps, the Catholic bishop of Münster, Clemens August, Count von Galen, a courageous and outspoken opponent of the Nazis' racist policies, learned of the project and, on 3 August 1941, delivered a sermon in Münster Cathedral attacking euthanasia as 'plain murder'. The Nazi leadership was stunned at this condemnation. Together with a subsequent incident in which a crowd, apparently incensed by T-4, booed Hitler for the first time, this led to the shelving of the operation. By then, however, it had essentially run its course. Many of the staff who carried out T-4 were transferred to the operation of the Final Solution, where their expertise in murder by gassing was put to use in the extermination camps.

EUTHANASIA

The Nazi decision to rid Germany of what they called 'life unworthy of life', that is the mentally ill, homosexuals, those stricken with hereditary diseases, gypsies and the senile, was intimately bound up with the Final Solution. It was born of the same callous and evil disrespect for life

in my brain: is this man a German? I turned to books for help in removing my doubts. For the first time in my life, I bought myself some anti-semitic pamphlets for a few pence.

From then on, anti-Semitism and his belief in a worldwide Jewish 'conspiracy' became an obsession with Hitler. Once in power, he began slowly, but later with increasing speed, to put his racist creed into practice. First of all, Nazi storm troopers began to enforce a boycott of Jewish shops. Many Germans complied, but some ignored or resisted the boycott. They included the formidable grandmother of Dietrich Bonhoeffeur, the Protestant theologian who was to hang in 1945 for his opposition to the Nazis. This valiant old lady pushed her way past storm troopers trying to turn customers away from a Jewish-owned establishment on the grounds that she had always shopped there and meant to go on doing so. Not everyone, however, was so courageous. Some were bullied into compliance by Nazi threats. Some, of course, approved of the persecution of Jews.

Hitler's desire to drive the Jews from German national life was placed on the statute book when, in 1935, the Nuremberg Laws were passed banning all Jews from holding German citizenship. From then on, no Jew could be considered a German. Under these Laws, a Jew was classified as someone who had just one Jewish grandparent; in order to qualify for membership of the elite SS, however, it was necessary to prove a 'pure', non-Jewish lineage going back

ABOVE: HERSCHELL GRYNSZPAN, WHO SHOT DEAD THE GERMAN AMBASSADOR IN PARIS IN PROTEST AT THE TREATMENT METED OUT BY GERMANY TO THE JEWS.

ABOVE: NAZI STORMTROOPERS AND PARTY MEMBERS ORGANISING THE BOYCOTT OF JEWISH SHOPS, 1933.

LEFT: A NAZI WARTIME PROPAGANADA POSTER FROM 1942 PROCLAIMS: 'BEHIND THE ENEMY POWERS, THE JEW!' THE NAZIS CONSISTENTLY PORTRAYED THE WAR AS THE OUTCOME OF A SINISTER WORLDWIDE JEWISH CONSPIRACY RATHER THAN AS THE DIRECT RESULT OF HITLER'S DESIRE TO ESTABLISH A 'NEW ORDER' IN EUROPE.

ABOVE: JEWISH WOMEN
PEER OUT OF THE CATTLE
TRUCKS TAKING THEM TO
THE CONCENTRATION CAMPS
AND TO ALMOST CERTAIN
DEATH. CONDITIONS INSIDE
THESE RAILWAY CARRIAGES
WERE FOUL. THERE WAS
STANDING ROOM ONLY,
NO FOOD OR WATER,
NO HEATING AND NO
SANITATION. AS A RESULT
MANY INNOCENT PEOPLE
WERE TO DIE BEFORE THEY
EVEN REACHED THE CAMPS.

ABOVE RIGHT: RECENT
ARRIVALS AT THE
BIRKENAU CONCENTRATION
CAMP, POLAND, 1944.
THEY WOULD SOON BE
SPLIT UP FROM THEIR
FAMILIES AND FRIENDS,
STRIPPED AND TATOOED
WITH A CAMP IDENTITY
NUMBER. DEATH THROUGH
STARVATION, OVERWORK
OR THE GAS CHAMBERS
AWAITED ALMOST ALL WHO
ENTERED HERE.

six generations, or 150 years. Further measures designed to preserve the 'honour' of Germany forbad Jews and Aryans to marry. Those already married would be forced to separate.

At this stage, the Nazis aimed to solve the 'Jewish Question' by making life in Germany so unpleasant that Jews would emigrate rather than remain as an underclass in their own country. The cynicism with which the emigration of German Jews was handled was breathtaking. Jews were unable to take their property out of the country, and were given little or no compensation for their businesses or homes, which they had to 'sell' before leaving. In practice, this meant confiscation for re-sale to 'Aryans' at a vast profit for the state. This 'Aryanisation' of the German economy proceeded at breakneck speed after Ernst von Rath, a member of the German embassy staff in Paris, was gunned down by a 17-year-old Polish Jew named Herschel Grynszpan. The killing gave the Nazis the excuse they wanted to launch their first nationwide, state-sponsored pogrom. As a result, 9 November 1938, the same day von Rath died, became known as *Kristallnacht*, or the Night of Broken Glass.

In a 'spontaneous' demonstration of German feeling organised by the Nazi Party, 7500 Jewish businesses were destroyed, 267 synagogues were set on fire and 91 Jews killed by gangs of thugs who looted shops, destroyed their goods, beat their owners and torched religious shrines. In fact, the Nazis took special care to ensure that as many sacred Jewish artefacts as possible were consumed by the flames. Piles of books and the Torah scrolls, which contained the sacred Jewish scriptures, together with much other precious material, were flung down in the road and burned.

In addition to the destruction of their homes, possessions and livelihoods, German Jews were hit by the further humiliation of having to pay a one-billion Deutschmark fine to the government as compensation for von Rath's death. Jewish shopkeepers were also expected to pay for the damage done to their shops. The decree for the fine was issued by Hermann

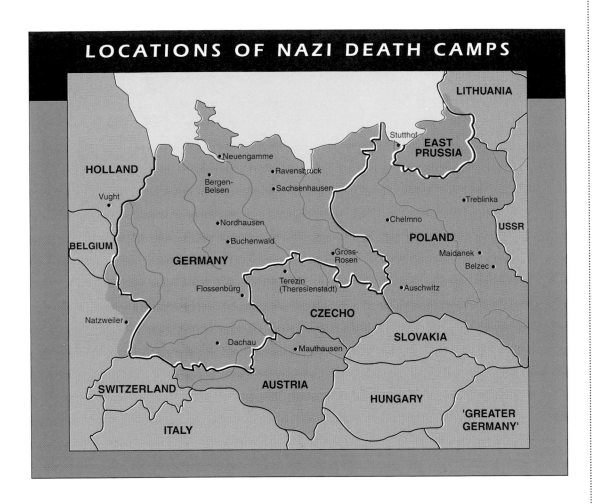

LOCATIONS OF NAZI DEATH CAMPS

The Nazis took special care to ensure that as many sacred Jewish artefacts as possible were consumed by the flames. Piles of books and the Torah scrolls, which contained the sacred Jewish scriptures, together with much other precious material, were flung down in the road and burned

Göring himself. Measures were also taken by the Nazis to ensure that insurance companies paid out compensation – not to the Jews whose property had been destroyed, but to the state, which had organised the orgy of violence.

Kristallnacht stunned many people, both in Germany and abroad, who had formerly persuaded themselves that stories of Nazi persecution of the Jews were exaggerated or

LEFT: THE ENTRANCE TO AUSCHWITZ-BIRKENAU. THESE TWIN CAMPS FORMED ONE OF THE NERVE CENTRES OF THE FINAL SOLUTION, WHERE MASSIVE GAS CHAMBERS AND CREMATORIA (CAPABLE OF BURNING AS MANY AS 2000 BODIES AT A TIME) REDUCED LIVING AND BREATHING HUMAN BEINGS TO ASHES WITH INSANE SPEED.

SOPHIA LITWINSKA: SURVIVOR

The Polish Jewess Sophia Litwinska was taken to the gas chambers in the Auschwitz concentration camp on 25 December 1941. She arrived in the camp from the Polish city of Lublin. Her head had already been shaved and she had been tattooed with a camp identity number before being picked out for the gas chambers while she was in the camp hospital where she was recovering from a broken leg. It was on Christmas Day that Litwinska and dozens of her fellow patients were taken by their SS guards to the gas chambers, where they were to be murdered.

Sophia Litwinska takes up the story in her own words:

We were led into a room which gave me the impression of a shower-bath. There were towels hanging round, and sprays, and even mirrors. I cannot say how many were in the room altogether, because I was so terrified, nor do I know if the doors were closed. People were in tears; people were shouting at each other; people were hitting each other. There were healthy people, strong people, weak people and sick people, and suddenly I saw fumes coming in through a very small window at the top. I had to cough very violently, tears were streaming from my eyes, and I had a sort of feeling in my throat as if I would be asphyxiated. I could not even look at the others because each of us concentrated on what happened to herself.

At that moment I heard my name called. I had not the strength to answer it, but raised my arm. Then I felt someone take me and throw me out from that room.

Litwinska, bemused at her reprieve, put her survival down to the fact that her husband, who was not a Jew, was a Polish officer. Litwinska had been saved at the point of death and had the unique and ghastly experience of knowing what it was like to die in a concentration camp gas chamber and yet survive.

After being taken from the chamber Litwinska spent six weeks in hospital. 'As the result of the gas I had still, quite frequently, headaches and heart trouble, and whenever I went into the fresh air my eyes were filled with tears.' Litwinska's testimony was used in the trial of the camp commandant, Joseph Kramer, after the war.

PATRICK GORDON WALKER: LIBERATOR

On 4 April 1945 British troops liberated the Nazi concentration camp at Belsen. The SS camp guards were well aware that the approach of Allied troops meant they would be forced to pay for the appalling crimes they had committed during the years of war. So, during the last days before liberation, they began attempts to cover up their crimes. Those camp inmates who were still able to work were forced to begin clearing up the mounds of corpses that littered the camp before the British troops arrived. They were allowed no food or water while they worked and some, forced by unbelievable levels of hunger, ate parts of the corpses they were ordered to bury. When the British finally arrived, one inmate, a French school teacher, was eating his first meal in six days; it was grass.

Despite the best attempts of the SS when the British soldiers entered the camp they were greeted by stacks of corpses left in open mass graves. The dead, more than 35,000 in total, outnumbered the living by several thousand.

A British officer, Patrick Gordon-Walker, told listeners in a radio broadcast of the scenes that had been described to him by the officers and men of the Oxfordshire Yeomanry and the horrors he himself had found when he arrived in Belsen shortly after its liberation:

The first night of liberty, many hundreds of people died of joy. Next day some men of the Yeomanry arrived. The people crowded around them kissing their hands and feet – and dying from weakness. Corpses in every state of decay were lying around, piled on top of each other in heaps. There were corpses in the compound in flocks. People were falling dead all around, people who were walking skeletons. One woman came up to a soldier who was guarding the milk store and doling out milk to the children, and begged for milk for her baby. The man took the baby and saw that it had been dead for days, black in the face and shrivelled up. The woman went on begging for milk. So he poured some on the dead lips. The mother then started to croon for joy and carried the baby off in triumph. She stumbled and fell dead in a few yards.

Despite the best effort of British medical teams and the Red Cross, 20,000 of the 30,000 survivors of Belsen died soon after their liberation.

were then gassed and their bodies burned in specially constructed ovens. The evil smell of burning flesh gave the inhabitants of the areas surrounding these camps no doubt as to their purpose. What was happening in the camps was no secret to the Allies, who let it be known that retribution for these unspeakable crimes would be exacted once the War was over. However, the Allies failed to respond to repeated pleas from Jewish organisations and others that the camps and the railway lines that led there from occupied Europe should be bombed.

In the concentration camps Jews toiled, making munitions, and when their usefulness was at an end, they were taken to the extermination camps and gassed. Jews were also brutally murdered in sadistic 'medical experiments'. In Dachau, inmates were deliberately infected with malaria. Others were exposed to extremes of air pressure until they died. Some were submerged in ice-cold water until they became unconscious to test for ways of reviving those suffering from extreme exposure. Those who managed to survive these tests were also killed.

The first extermination camp to be liberated, on 25 July 1944 by the Russians, was Maidanek. It was situated near Lublin in Poland and by the time the Red Army arrived, over 1.5 million people had died there. Despite the attempts of the SS to hide what they had done from the advancing Allies, the shocking truth of the Final Solution was subsequently revealed to a horrified world, which after nearly six years of savage warfare had believed itself unshockable. People were truly appalled by the obscene acts committed in the name of racial supremacy and Nazi ideology.

During the war, the Final Solution claimed the lives of approximately six million Jews. Only around one-twentieth of Europe's pre-War Jewish population survived. Approximately two million gypsies had also been killed in the name of Aryan purity.

ABOVE: CORPSES AWAITING CREMATION IN DACHAU. CREMATORIA CAME INTO USE AFTER EXPERIMENTS WITH MASS BURIALS OFTEN HAD GHASTLY RESULTS. THE DECOMPOSITION OF SO MANY CORPSES IN A SMALL AREA OFTEN LED TO THE BODIES RISING THROUGH THE SOIL TO THE SURFACE ONCE MORE.

FAR LEFT: TWO INMATES GAZE OUT AS THEIR LIBERATORS FINALLY ARRIVE.

LEFT: FREEDOM. THE STARS AND STRIPES RISES OVER DACHAU, GERMANY'S FIRST AND OLDEST CONCENTRATION CAMP, WHICH WAS LIBERATED BY US SOLDIERS IN 1945. IT WAS AT DACHAU THAT SOME OF THE WORST 'MEDICAL EXPERIMENTS' TOOK PLACE.